Development and Review of E-Learning

Edited by Jian-Hong Ye,
Weiguaju Nong, Li Wang and Jun Li

Published in London, United Kingdom

Development and Review of E-Learning
http://dx.doi.org/10.5772/intechopen.1005701
Edited by Jian-Hong Ye, Weiguaju Nong, Li Wang and Jun Li

Contributors
Arturo Amaya Amaya, Badaruddin Anwar, Bo Pei, Daniel Cantú Cervantes, Daniel García Mercado, Daouda Yacouba, Fortunate Tintswalo Silinda, Hendra Jaya, Irina Severin, Jehad Ali Tawfiq Almomani, Jian-Hong Ye, Li Liao, Mihai Caramihai, Nana Aicha Goza, Nicoleta Radu, Rina Febriana, Sapto Haryoko, Sutarsi Suhaeb

First published in London, United Kingdom, 2025 by IntechOpen
IntechOpen is the global imprint of INTECHOPEN LIMITED, registered in England and Wales, registration number: 11086078, 167-169 Great Portland Street, London, W1W 5PF, United Kingdom

For EU product safety concerns: IN TECH d.o.o., Prolaz Marije Krucifikse Kozulić 3, 51000 Rijeka, Croatia, info@intechopen.com or visit our website at intechopen.com.

British Library Cataloguing-in-Publication Data
A catalogue record for this book is available from the British Library

Development and Review of E-Learning
Edited by Jian-Hong Ye, Weiguaju Nong, Li Wang and Jun Li
p. cm.
Print ISBN 978-1-83634-065-2
Online ISBN 978-1-83634-064-5
eBook (PDF) ISBN 978-1-83634-066-9

Meet the editors

Dr. Jian-Hong Ye is a lecturer in the Faculty of Education at Beijing Normal University, a distinguished expert at the National Institute of Vocational Education at Beijing Normal University, and a visiting professor at Ningxia Polytechnic. He graduated from the Department of Industrial Education at National Taiwan Normal University, where he also served as a postdoctoral researcher. Dr. Ye is an honorary member of the Phi Tau Phi Scholastic Honor Society (Taiwan) and an outstanding alumnus of the Department of Fashion Design at Tainan University of Technology. In recent years, Dr. Ye has served as an associate editor for a section of Heliyon and has also worked as a guest editor and peer reviewer for several SSCI, SCI, and Scopus-indexed journals. He enjoys conducting empirical research from a psychological perspective. His research interests include the digitalization of vocational education, curriculum and teaching innovation, student psychological health and well-being, as well as interdisciplinary topics.

Dr. Weiguaju Nong is currently a lecturer in the School of Education at Guangxi University of Foreign Languages. With expertise in innovative teaching and interdisciplinary research of pedagogy and psychology, Nong specializes in experimental and empirical research on education. At present, he has published 16 academic papers in high-level domestic and international journals, among which 10 papers (including two as the first author and two as the corresponding author) are published in SSCI and SCI journals, and two papers are published on CNKI, with a total citation of over 100 times on Google Scholar, demonstrating a solid foundation in interdisciplinary research. Meanwhile, Nong also serves as a peer reviewer for various SSCI and SCI journals, including Scientific Reports, Frontiers in Public Health, Frontiers in Psychology, and Acta Psychologica. Currently, he has successfully led one municipal and one departmental research project, as well as one university-level research project. Furthermore, he has been a key participant in completing two key projects: the National Educational Sciences Planning Project of the Ministry of Education and the Guangxi Higher Education Undergraduate Teaching Reform Project.

Dr. Li Wang is an Associate Professor and serves as the Vice Dean of the School of Education and Music at Hainan Vocational University of Science and Technology. Her main research fields include vocational education teachers' and students' career development, as well as educational informatization. She has been selected as an in-house talent in the "Nanhai New Star" project of Hainan Province. She has published nine academic papers as the first author (including two in the SSCI) and has approved three decision-making consultation reports. She has received a provincial teaching achievement award and has been responsible for one provincial-level project and one school-level project. She has also participated in multiple provincial and ministerial-level projects.

Dr. Jun Li has been listed as a high-level talent in Hainan Province and an education talent of the "South China Sea Rising Star" in Hainan Province. She used to work at Yunnan Normal University and is now the Vice Dean of the School of Design of Hainan Vocational University of Science and Technology. She has been the reviewer of SSCI and SCI English core journals since May 2022. Over the past three years, she has published 27 academic papers, 20 of which have been included in Chinese and English core journals. As the host, she has been approved for one project by the Ministry of Education of China and six provincial projects. She has published five monographs, presided over, and participated in several government-sponsored projects.

Contents

Preface

Since the year 2000, the rapid development of educational technology and internet technology has brought significant attention to e-learning. Many studies have focused on understanding how to enhance learners' experiences and promote deeper engagement with learning content through e-learning to achieve better learning outcomes. Subsequently, from early 2020 over the span of three years, due to the impact of the COVID-19 pandemic, governments across many countries and regions implemented policies such as "Classes Suspended but Learning Continues", by conducting teaching and learning online. This has led to significant attention to e-learning by the academic and educational communities. Consequently, during these years, many studies on e-learning in the context of the pandemic have been published. However, as we enter the post-pandemic era, physical learning spaces are no longer restricted, and people have gained new insights into e-learning based on their experiences during the pandemic. Additionally, in the context of the ongoing digital transformation of education, it is also necessary to further explore e-learning topics in the era of Education 4.0. In summary, this book compiles the latest research findings on e-learning, helping readers to understand the e-learning research outcomes of scholars from different countries and regions.

Drawing on the latest research in e-learning, the book compiles the most recent theoretical developments and practical applications from different regions. It aims to provide educators, learners, and their supporters with practical guidance based on empirical and critical studies. It is hoped that this book will serve as a valuable reference guide for educators and digital learning designers, offering both theoretical depth and practical value. It consists of eight chapters, including reviews, perspectives, and original research. It provides descriptions and reviews of international research experiences and perspectives from scholars in China, the United States of America, Niger, Mexico, Indonesia, Romania, Jordan, and South Africa. This will enable government agencies, social organisations, professionals, scholars, and the general public to gain a better understanding of the current state of e-learning research in countries at different levels of development.

This work was financially supported by the 2025 Guangxi Higher Education Undergraduate Teaching Reform Project, "Artificial Intelligence-Empowered Construction of a Knowledge Graph for Fundamental Courses in Early Childhood Education and Its Application in Teaching Reform Practice" (Grant No.: 2025JGA417).

We are grateful to Miss Li Liao and Mr. Yongjian Wang of the Faculty of Education at Beijing Normal University for their assistance in editing and proofreading this book.

Jian-Hong Ye
Faculty of Education,
National Institute of Vocational Education,
Beijing Normal University,
Beijing, China

Weiguaju Nong
School of Education,
Guangxi University of Foreign Languages,
Nanning, China

Li Wang
School of Education and Music,
Hainan Vocational University of Science and Technology,
Haikou, China

Jun Li
School of Design,
Hainan Vocational University of Science and Technology,
Haikou, China

Chapter 1

Knowledge Base, Hot Topics, and Frontier Evolution of Adult Online Learning Research in the Last Decade: CiteSpace-Based Visual Analytics

Li Liao and Jian-Hong Ye

Abstract

Adult online learning, as an important form of realizing information technology in education, is crucial to achieving the sustainable development goals. In the past decade, with the rapid development of internet technology and the global spread of the COVID-19 epidemic, the number of online open courses has surged, attracting the participation of a large number of adults. Exploring academic research on adult online learning contributes to an in-depth understanding of adult online learning and its impact on global education. Using the information visualization software CiteSpace to analyze 691 Social Sciences Citation Index (SSCI)-indexed research papers on adult online learning in the Web of Science database, the results showed that six scholars from the United States, the United Kingdom, Australasia, and Canada, and seven highly cited articles established the knowledge base in the field of adult online learning, focusing on innovations in technology adoption, health support, and educational policy practices. Research frontiers include "women," "people," and "stress." Evolutionary paths range from the interpretation of adult online learning outcomes to a focus on global education policy implications to emerging technologies. In the future, research will continue to diversify and grow, contributing to the enrichment and renewal of the adult education body of knowledge.

Keywords: adult online learning, adult pedagogy, CiteSpace, visual analytics, distance education

1. Introduction

Adult education plays a crucial role in addressing the challenges of employment, digital transformation, globalization, aging, and the climate crisis, while also contributing to the attainment of the Sustainable Development Goals (SDGs; [1]). Over the past few decades, limited access to learning opportunities and resources has hindered many adults from engaging in essential education and training. However, in recent years, advancements in information and communication technologies (ICT) have begun to change this. Online learning has, in some ways, dramatically eliminated the boundaries of traditional learning styles of education, enabling a growing number of people to receive educational opportunities and resources [2]. Online learning activities are an important part of Internet-based teaching and learning activities and are the sum of interactions between learners and their associated learning communities with the external learning environment using the internet to accomplish specific learning objectives [3]. Flexibility, accessibility, and time and space characteristics that are not physically limited make online learning an important means of learning that connects the formal and informal and facilitates the realization of the learner's vision of lifelong education [4]. Since the outbreak of novel coronavirus pneumonia (COVID-19) in 2019, online learning has become a mainstay in the field of education. OECD survey data show that, as a result of the outbreak, about 92.21% of learners globally utilize existing online resources for self-directed learning, and 93.32% of learners learn interactively through real-time online instruction by instructors [5].

In the field of adult online learning, scholars have analyzed literature reviews. For example, Lu et al. [6] identified and analyzed the influencing factors and related strategies in the field of adult online learning by using the literature visualization software CiteSpace to analyze the empirical studies reported in 124 SSCI publications. The study found that adult online learning requires flexible, structured courses; adult learners need preparatory learning to improve their technical skills, and integrated discussion is more effective than open discussion. Schmid et al. [7] conducted a meta-analysis that found that, compared to traditional instruction, online learning (OL), blended learning (BL), and the flipped classroom (FC) had a moderately positive effect on the academic achievement of both preparatory and in-service teachers, while having moderate positive and nonsignificant effects on attitudes and satisfaction, and a significant increase in self-efficacy, emphasizing the importance of pedagogy over technology per se. Abedini et al. [8] analyzed 37 empirical studies based on self-directed learning theories to explore the characteristics of learning in online communities of practice (OCOPs) for adults and the facilitators and impediments affecting adults' participation in these communities. The results of these studies are summarized in the following tables.

Despite the growing interest in online learning following the COVID-19 pandemic, there is a notable absence of comprehensive bibliometric analyses that systematically map emerging trends and future directions in adult online learning research. This gap is especially significant as countries are increasingly turning to adult online education to enhance the accessibility and quality of lifelong learning. Therefore, this study aimed to fill this gap by conducting a detailed scientometric analysis of the literature on adult online learning research in the Web of Science database in the last decade in the form of a mapping exercise to understand the current state of adult online learning research, grasp the research hotspots and trends in adult online learning, and propose useful lessons for the future development of adult online learning models by examining publications, citations, and scholars.

2. Data sources and research methods

2.1 Data sources and analysis

The study selected the Web of Science database of the Social Sciences Citation Index (SSCI) core collection SSCI database as the data retrieval platform to search for research literature on adult online learning. The search formula was ((TS = ("adult" OR "adults" OR "adult human" OR "adult individuals")) AND TS = ("online learning" OR "e-learning" OR "online study" OR "on-line studying")), type "Article," time span 2014–2024. A total of 691 documents were obtained after an exact-criteria search with de-weighting and cleaning in the CiteSpace software. It should be noted that while the Web of Science provides high-quality, peer-reviewed content, its exclusive use may limit the scope of findings due to database coverage biases, particularly regarding non-English publications and discipline-specific journals not indexed in the SSCI.

From the change in the number of publications, the overall trend of research on adult online learning in the past 10 years is obviously upward, with a high number of publications of above 25 articles for all years except 2014. The increase in the number of publications in 2014–2015 is related to the policies issued by international organizations. *The 2030 Agenda for Sustainable Development* promulgated by the United Nations General Assembly in 2014–2015 and UNESCO's *Recommendation on Adult Learning and Education* both emphasize the importance of lifelong learning, encouraging governments to provide more adult education opportunities, resulting in more scholars shifting their research interests to adult online learning; the competition within the field of online learning research intensified in 2015–2018, and emerging alternative learning modes began to receive more attention from scholars.

The number of articles on the topic then showed a downward trend, with a trough value of 32 articles in 2016. Starting from 2018, the number of articles continued to rise, and although there were fluctuations in 2019, the overall tendency stabilized. The quadrupling of the number of publications in 2022 compared to 2016 is related to the actual situation in countries that had to close schools and workplaces and stop offline teaching due to the impact of COVID-19. In this context, governments have been paying more attention to adult e-learning, and scholars have been actively exploring new modes of adult e-learning and strengthening research on learner engagement, satisfaction, and learning outcomes in the process of adult e-learning, which has contributed to the increase in the number of papers on "adult e-learning" (**Figure 1**).

In terms of country distribution status, 72 countries have published research articles related to adult online learning. Among them, the United States has the highest contribution rate and the largest number of published articles, amounting to 247, accounting for more than 1/3 of the total literature retrieved. It also has the highest centrality score of 0.54, indicating that the United States is among the global leaders in both the quality and quantity of published articles in this field, demonstrating a strong capacity for scientific output. This is closely related to the global leadership of U.S. universities in the discipline of education, with the University of California, Berkeley, occupying the top spot according to the Times Higher Education Rankings 2024, driving the output and international influence of academic results related to adult online learning. It is followed by the United Kingdom, China, Canada, and Australia, which all have more than 50 publications, accounting for more than 7% of the total number of publications. This suggests that the articles published in these countries are of high quality, and the related topics in this research area attract significant attention from international scholars (**Table 1**).

In terms of the distribution of source publications, there are 371 SSCI journals that publish research related to adult online learning. The five journals with the most publications and their publication status are introduced as follows. *Frontiers*

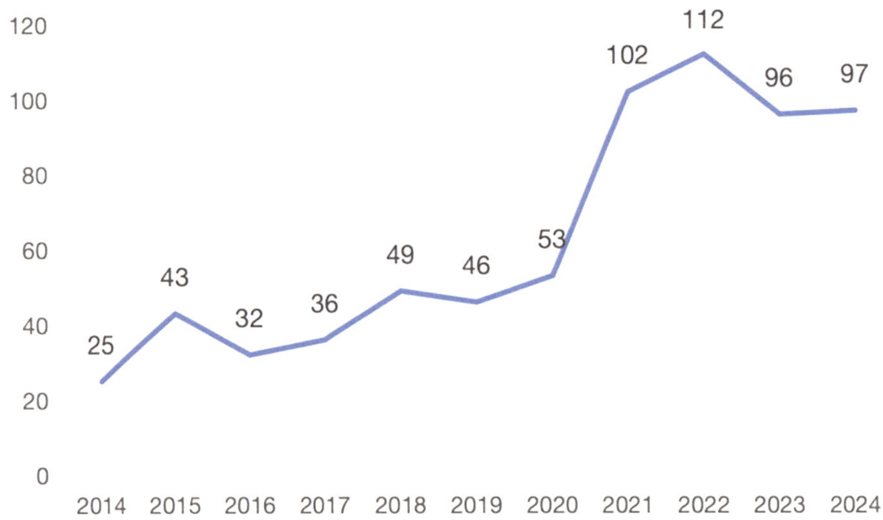

Figure 1.
Temporal distribution of adult online learning research publications (2014–2024).

Ranking	Number	Centrality	Year	Countries
1	247	0.54	2014	USA
2	78	0.33	2014	England
3	67	0.17	2014	PRC
4	66	0.11	2014	Canada
5	66	0.09	2014	Australia
6	55	0.07	2014	Germany
7	24	0.23	2014	Spain
8	23	0.04	2014	Netherlands
9	18	0.00	2015	South Korea
10	14	0.00	2015	Italy

Table 1.
Distribution of the top 10 countries in terms of the number of publications on adult online learning literature.

in Psychology is located in Q2 in the journal citation reports (JCR) partition, with an impact factor of 3.3 in the past 5 years and 27 publications, accounting for 3.9% of the total. *Computers in Education* is located in Q1 in the JCR partition data, and the impact factor of the journal has continued to be at a high level for the past 5 years, at about 11.6, showing its important influence, and the topic of adult online learning has a significant influence; 18 articles were published in this journal on the topic of adult online learning, accounting for 2.6%. The *International Journal of Environmental Research and Public Health* is located in the Q1 area in the JCR partition data, and 14 articles were published, accounting for 2.02% of the total articles. *ETRD Educational Technology Research and Development* is located in Q1 in JCR, with an impact factor of 4.8 in the past 5 years, and has published 12 articles, accounting for 1.74% of the total number of articles. *Education and Information Technologies* is located in Q1 in the JCR partition data, with an impact factor of 4.8 in the past 5 years, publishing 10 articles, accounting for 1.45% of the total number of articles.

In terms of content, *Frontiers in Psychology* focuses on topics such as cognitive science, consciousness, personality development, and social psychology, such as motivation, learning strategies, and the online learning experience in adult online learning environments; *Computers in Education* focuses on topics such as the use of communication technologies in cognition, education, and training; *Education and Information Technologies* focuses on the use of technology in education and empirical research, such as exploring how adult learners can optimize and improve their interactions with online learning environments; *ETRD Educational Technology Research and Development* focuses on the application of technology in education and empirical research, such as exploring how adult learners can optimize and improve their interaction with online learning environments; while the *International Journal of Environmental Research and Public Health* focuses more on the impact of IT-enabled open learning environments on human behavioral health, such as how Open Educational Resources (OERs) and Massive Open Online Courses (MOOCs) for adult online learning affect adult learners' mental health, and how to affect the mental health and behavioral characteristics of adult learners.

2.2 Research tools and methods

In order to visually present the research overview, hot topics, and general research trends of adult online learning, this study selected the bibliometric and analytical tool CiteSpace for visualization and analysis. CiteSpace is a Java-based information visualization tool that leverages co-citation analysis theory and path-finding network algorithms to quantify and analyze data. By generating a variety of visual representations, CiteSpace enables researchers to gain insights into the underlying dynamic mechanisms of discipline evolution and identify emerging trends in the field's development [9].

This tool was selected for this study to visualize and analyze the collected literature data in three ways. First, key authors and key publications in the field were analyzed by analyzing author co-citations and literature co-citations to understand their knowledge base. Second, keywords in the literature were analyzed by co-occurrence and clustering to explore the hotspots of adult online learning research. Finally, based on keyword co-occurrence, we conduct emergent word detection and time zone map analysis, allowing us to understand the research frontiers and evolutionary paths in the field of adult online learning based on the citing literature where the keywords are located. Specific parameter values include the time range of research literature, 2014–2024, and the time slice (year per slice) is 1 year. The node type in the co-citation analysis was set as cited authors and cited literature, and the node type in the co-occurrence analysis was keywords. The node threshold was g-index (k-25) in the co-citation analysis and TopN-50 in the co-occurrence analysis, and the software version was CiteSpace 6.4.R4. The time slice was set to 1 year, and the Pathfinder algorithm was used to analyze the top 10% of the cited documents each year (top N% = 10%) in order to take into account the clarity of the data network and the representativeness and accuracy of the data. The Pathfinder algorithm was used to analyze the top 10% of cited literature each year (top N% = 10%), taking into account the clarity of the data network and the representativeness and accuracy of the data.

3. Results and analysis

3.1 Knowledge base

In the CiteSpace analysis, the author's co-citation data can reflect the key scholars with high influence in the field, that is, the scholars whose research plays an important role in the knowledge evolution of the field. In contrast, the literature co-citation data can present the highly cited literature in the field, which constitutes the knowledge base of the field.

3.1.1 Author co-citation analysis

An analysis of the authors' total citation frequency shows that there are six scholars with a frequency of more than 25 citations. Jonathan Cohen is a professor at Columbia University with a primary focus on educational sciences, adult learning in educational leadership, and research on instructional behaviors, with a total of 48 citations. His work is exemplified by the article *Recognizing Community Voice and a Youth-Led School-Community Partnership in the School Climate Improvement Process* [10].

Andrew F. Hayes is a professor at the University of Calgary. His research areas include organizational behavior and quantitative research methods in human resources, with research interests in linear models, structural equation modeling, and statistical methods analysis, and his articles have been cited a total of 36 times. His representative treatises include *Introduction to Mediation, Moderation, and Conditional Process Analysis* [11] and *Regression Analysis and Linear Models* [12], among others. Professor Hayes emphasizes the importance of using statistical tools for data analysis in online learning environments to enhance learner effectiveness and satisfaction.

D. Randy Garrison is a professor emeritus at the University of Calgary, with a longstanding commitment to online learning research in adult education, higher education, and distance education. His articles have a total citation frequency of 27. A representative work is *Toward the development of a metacognition construct for communities of inquiry* [13]. Virginia Braun is a professor at the University of Auckland, focusing on social issues such as public health policy and adult practice, with 27 total citations, represented by *The online survey as a qualitative research tool* [14]. Richard M. Ryan is a professor at the Institute of Education at the Australian Catholic University, focusing on various theories in psychology, such as self-determination theory, as well as adult motivation and autonomy, with 26 citations, including his book, *Self-Determination Theory and the Facilitation of Intrinsic Motivation, Social Development, and Well-Being* [15]. John W. Creswell is a professor at the University of Michigan who has authored numerous articles and books on research design, qualitative research, and mixed-methods research, represented by *Qualitative Inquiry & Research Design* [16].

To summarize, the above scholars mainly come from the United States, Australasia, and Canada, and all of them have long been engaged in research on education-related research methods, adult cognitive neuroscience, and adult education theories. Research topics in adult online learning demonstrate considerable diversity.

3.1.2 Literature co-citation analysis

If two articles are cited in a third article, then these two articles constitute a co-citation relationship. Literature co-citation analysis can be used to understand the important literature in a particular field. There are seven articles in this study

Citation frequency	Author	Title
8	Wenjun Cao	The psychological impact of the COVID-19 epidemic on college students in China
7	Changwon Son	Effects of COVID-19 on college students' mental health in the united states: Interview survey study
7	Cuiyan Wang	Immediate psychological responses and associated factors during the initial stage of the 2019 coronavirus disease (COVID-19) epidemic among the general population in China
6	Jonathan Peircel	PsychoPy2: Experiments in behavior made easy
6	Yeen Huang	Generalized anxiety disorder, depressive symptoms and sleep quality during COVID-19 outbreak in China: A web-based cross-sectional survey
6	Alexander L. Anwyl-Irvine	Gorilla in our midst: An online behavioral experiment builder
6	Mehmet Kara	Challenges faced by adult learners in online distance education: A literature review

Table 2.
Co-cited high-frequency literature on adult online learning research (2014–2024).

that have been co-cited no less than five times (**Table 2**). These articles constitute the knowledge base of adult online learning research in two ways.

First, the psychological and behavioral characteristics of adult learners are explored by considering online learning as a new educational model. Online learning is a distance learning mode that takes advantage of student heterogeneity and quantity, and the scale of students involved in it far exceeds that of traditional forms of learning. As a result, scholars have studied online learner characteristics, mainly including motivation, experience of learning, and self-regulation. Kara et al. [17], in their study titled *Challenges Faced by Adult Learners in Online Distance Education: A Literature Review,* revealed three major internal, external, and programmatic challenges faced by adult learners in online education. These include internal challenges such as unbalanced time management, lack of motivation, and lack of technical skills; external challenges such as work overload and lack of family support; and curricular challenges such as mismatch of resources and lack of student-faculty interaction. These challenges reflect the unique characteristics of adult learners in online learning environments and emphasize the need to consider their individual backgrounds, experiences, and motivations when designing adult online learning programs. Son et al. [18], in their study, *Effects of COVID-19 on College Students' Mental Health in the United States: Interview Survey Study,* concluded that 71% of students experienced a dramatic increase in stress and anxiety as a result of the COVID-19 outbreak, arguing that adult learners adopt either positive or negative coping mechanisms in the face of stressors such as concerns about their health and academic performance and that therefore, the psychological state and behavioral characteristics of adult learners require special attention and consideration, and behavioral characteristics need to receive special attention and self-regulation. Similarly, Huang and Zhao [19] analyzed 723 adult learners' psychological status and behavioral characteristics. Their sectional survey analyzed data from 7236 volunteers and found that anxiety disorders, depressive symptoms, and sleep quality were prevalent among the public during the COVID-19 outbreak, arguing that mental health problems directly affect adult learners' learning efficiency and quality of life and emphasizing the importance of improving learners' mental health in online learning experiences.

Research on the practical application of online learning platforms and models for adult online learning was analyzed by considering online learning as a lifelong learning process. The realization of online learning is based on technology and media support. Thus, research on the design, construction, and development of online learning platforms and models has become a common focus of scholars. Anwyl-Irvine et al. [20], in *Gorilla in Our Midst: An Online Behavioral Experiment Builder,* described the openness and application of online experimentation tools, noting that the Gorilla Experiment Builder provides a platform that allows researchers to conduct online learning experiments for adults across different devices and network conditions. Peirce et al. [21], in *PsychoPy2: Experiments in behavior made easy,* detailed the development and operational process of PsychoPy2, an application platform for creating behavioral science experiments, arguing that it provides precise spatial and temporal control, making it easy for researchers to use the technology to support adult online learning research.

From the results of author co-citation and literature co-citation, Jonathan Cohen, Andrew F. Hayes, and D. Randy Garrison are the authors with higher co-citations, while the research results of Wenjun Cao and Changwon Son also have high co-citations. This suggests that the knowledge production in the field of adult online learning research is more concentrated, with its knowledge base laid down mainly by relevant research by European, American, and Chinese scholars.

3.2 Research hotspots

Analyzing the frequently occurring keywords in the literature can reveal the research trends and hotspots in specific academic fields. In this study, the keywords in the collected literature were analyzed for co-occurrence (the synonymous keywords with singular and plural, lexical properties, abbreviations, and other forms of differences were merged), and keyword clustering was carried out on the basis of the keyword co-occurrence. After keyword clustering, 14 clusters were generated, including 328 keyword nodes and 1730 node links. The first eight clusters were selected, and the specific research content contained in different clusters was read in depth, combined with the high-frequency keywords to further integrate and explore the hot topics of adult e-learning research, which resulted in "adult online learning and technological innovation," "adult online learning and health support," and "adult online learning and education policy practice" being identified (**Table 3**).

3.2.1 Adult online learning and technological innovation

This hot topic examines technology integration through three subthemes: learning platform efficacy, engagement mechanisms, and employability impacts.

Kuo and Belland [22] demonstrated that learner-content/instructor interactions predict satisfaction in Blackboard-based courses ($N = 167$), particularly in environments lacking group activities. Their findings established internet self-efficacy as a cross-cutting success factor.

Goh and Yang [23] conducted a study on the continued use of an adult learning management system (Moodle LMS) in a blended learning environment, examining

Topic	Cluster	Name	Silhouette	Size	Top terms
Adult online learning and technological innovation	0	Adult learning	0.672	72	Online learning; lifelong learning; distance education; cooperative/collaborative learning
	3	Higher education	0.818	35	Online education; adult education; internet self-efficacy; active learning
	6	Online study	0.811	24	Photovoice; multiple sclerosis; positive psychology; behavior change
Adult online learning and health support	1	Coping	0.633	68	Depression; COVID-19 pandemic; autism; e-learning
	2	Dementia	0.63	46	Older adults; intervention; behavior; adult learning
Adult online learning and education policy practice	4	Young adults	0.647	31	Ecological momentary assessment; emerging adulthood; college students; chronic illness
	5	Impact	0.777	26	Evidence-based practice; policy; adult smokers; women
	7	Parenting	0.866	18	Outcome; adults; child maltreatment; knowledge

Table 3.
Adult online learning research clustering and hot topics (2014–2024).

the relationship between online learning engagement, mindstream experience, and LMS continuity through mediated moderated interaction modeling. Partial least squares structural equation modeling (PLS-SEM) analyses were conducted on a sample of 92 learners after controlling for age and gender. The results indicated that the mindstream experience mediated the relationship between e-learning engagement and perceived ease of use and had a significant positive effect on e-learning system continuity.

Martínez-Cerdá et al. [24] quantified STS-ICT's positive impacts on employability through PLS-PM modeling, reinforcing the macro-level connection between technological infrastructure and socioeconomic outcomes first observed in [22] satisfaction-performance correlation.

3.2.2 Adult online learning and health support

This theme includes two clusters that explore the impact of online learning environments on the mental and physical health of adult learners, primarily from cognitive assessment to behavioral analysis to professional development.

Ng et al. [25] compared the overall effects of using computerized cognitive training for older and younger adults in terms of three key dimensions: study design, data analysis, and practical application, and concluded that computerized cognitive training (CCT) had a significant positive impact on cognitive functioning in older and younger adults and that no significant differences in effects were found between the two age groups. Thus, at the practical application level, the study points to the significant advantages of CCT delivered *via* the internet for improving accessibility and reducing the costs of cognitive training for adult health as the global population ages.

Gijselaers et al. [26] revealed that while prolonged screen time enhances learning progress, it necessitates activity-integrated interventions (e.g., micro-exercises, flexible scheduling) to mitigate physical risks.

Diabetes distress is associated with worsening self-management of diabetes and reduced quality of life in adults, yet in practice, only half of diabetes healthcare professionals provide specialist support. Halliday et al. [27] therefore developed an e-learning program designed for diabetes educators to meet their needs for professional support training in clinical diabetes care by using intervention mapping, bridging the gap between technological accessibility and specialized care demands.

3.2.3 Adult online learning and education policy practice

With the popularity of online learning platforms and the abundance of digital teaching resources, adult online learning is no longer confined to the traditional education system but has expanded into a variety of areas such as workplace training, community education, and personal self-improvement. Therefore, this theme involves three clusters, namely the impact of adult online learning on education policy formulation, implementation, and evaluation, and how to achieve equity and quality improvement in education in different socioeconomic contexts.

Radovanović et al. [28] explored the impact of information technology on higher education in the countries of South-Eastern Europe. Applying Weber's theory of stratification, the study analyzed the impact of the digital divide on adult education through an empirical case study and discussed stratification issues that arise when integrating new technologies and technology-oriented pedagogical practices, where the rapid development of information technology not only profoundly changes the education system but also exacerbates inequalities in digital skills. Thus, the study highlights the need for researchers and users to remain rational and attentive to the more complex issue of social and technological stratification when it comes to adult digital literacy and e-learning tools, recognizing that they may be affected by underlying inequalities.

Yu and Liu [29] extended this through Chinese socioeconomic metrics, revealing a paradox of participation: while middle-income groups dominate online time, high-SES individuals retain productive usage monopolies. The authors focused on differences in online usage behaviors and digital inclusiveness among Chinese adults by analyzing data from the China Family Tracking Study (CFPS) from 2010 and 2018 to reveal differences in online usage behaviors (frequency and diversity) in China in terms of educational background and socioeconomic status. They argued that using educational background and socioeconomic status to gauge differences in online usage behaviors in China serves as a way to assess individuals' digital inclusiveness. However, for policymakers, this approach not only highlights the evolution of the digital divide but also has unjust implications for the long-term distribution of digital resources and the social structure.

A study of adult online learning environments [30] revealed that the central challenge in introducing adaptive support strategies into online education programs is to determine which types of learning subjects can benefit from them. The study suggested that if the use of adaptive support strategies is not based on the actual needs of learners but rather on the specific goals or preferences of educational policies, the implementation of the strategies can inadvertently exacerbate educational inequalities. For example, for adult learners who already have a high level of self-regulated learning, too much adaptive support may be seen as redundant and may even interfere with their learning process. On the contrary, for those learners who are less self-regulated, appropriate support may be the key to improving their learning outcomes. Therefore, educational policymakers and practitioners should be wary of the potential inequalities that come with adult adaptive support strategies and ensure that strategies are designed and implemented to truly meet the diverse needs of learners so that they have access to the necessary resources and support on an equal basis.

3.3 Research frontier evolution

In CiteSpace, the emergent terms can reflect the frontiers of the adult e-learning research field, in which the emergence rate represents its contribution to the frontiers of the field, and the year of the end of the emergence indicates its latest progress in the field. The closer the year, the latest the research direction. The timezone view of the keyword co-occurrence network shows the evolution trajectory of the research field in different time stages by accumulating the year of the first appearance of the keywords and the frequency of their subsequent appearances. Therefore, combining the two analyses can better explore the evolution of the frontiers of adult e-learning research.

3.3.1 Research frontier

The high-frequency emergent keywords for adult online learning research from 2014 to 2024 were women, people, primary care, stress, information, and quality (**Table 4**).

"Women" appeared 11 times in 2014–2024, including three times in 2016, two times in 2017, and six times in 2018–2019. At the present stage, the focus on the impact of adult online learning on women's health perceptions and behaviors, as well as their mental attitudes, has triggered a profound reflection on how online learning can contribute to women's health behavior change, cultural sensitivity, and gender equality, among other aspects.

Nahm et al. [31] divided 866 learners aged 60 years or older into a bone-powered group and a control group by designing an 8-week online learning program, and the results of the experiment showed that the bone-powered group showed significantly greater improvements in osteoporosis knowledge, calcium intake, and self-efficacy/

Keywords	Strength	Begin year	End year
Women	5.13	2016	2019
People	5.1	2015	2019
Stress	3.58	2019	2021
Primary care	3.53	2022	2024
Information	3.49	2018	2021
Quality	3.17	2018	2019

Table 4.
Adult online learning research high burst rate keywords (2014–2024).

behavioral expectancies of exercise than did the control group, pointing out that the online health education program significantly improved older women's osteoporosis knowledge, exercise self-efficacy, and health behaviors. Hauck et al. [32] revealed key factors influencing adult birth preferences, including the experiences of family members and friends and the impact of online media, through an online cross-sectional survey of attitudes toward childbirth among the next generation of Australian parents. The study found that only 23.4% of respondents felt confident in their knowledge of childbirth, suggesting that a lack of knowledge is an important factor when making decisions about childbirth. The study emphasized that in order to ensure that adult women's childbirth choices are informed decisions based on sufficient information rather than being subject to a lack of knowledge or fear, it is important to provide educational resources through online platforms to enable adult women to access detailed information about normal births and cesarean sections to alleviate the fear and stress associated with childbirth. Fiery et al. [33] focused on the impact of online learning on ethnically diverse women's body image conversations. The study showed differences in unfavorable body talk and positive self-acceptance body talk among women of different races, revealing that online learning cultural exchange platforms have a significant positive impact on women's body image attitudes.

"People" appeared 21 times in 2014–2024, including 10 times in 2015–2017, six times in 2018–2019, and five times in 2020–2022. At the present stage, it mainly involves themes such as health and society to explain the needs and applications of online learning for different adult learning subjects.

In terms of learners, Roldan & Reina [34] assessed the impact of online instruction induced by COVID-19 on the self-efficacy of college students majoring in sport science in physical activity, comparing the gain in student self-efficacy before and after the pandemic and exploring the impact of three demographic variables. Findings indicated that rather than decreasing students' self-efficacy, online instruction increased their self-efficacy by encouraging students to engage in and reflect on their learning. In terms of knowledge transmitters, one study conducted a randomized controlled trial of a behavioral intervention based on social cognitive theory and showed that physical activity was increased, and there were improvements in mobility, cognition, symptoms, and quality of life for people with multiple sclerosis through the internet and e-learning methods [35]. Moody et al. [36] analyzed the impact of online learning through web-based self-management resources to meet the self-management and support needs of adult cancer survivors and found that an online self-management system provided young cancer survivors with a platform for information and support that complemented the direct interactions of clinical staff and had a significant positive impact on posttreatment recovery and self-management. In terms of social supporters, Su et al. [37] assessed the impact of a 12-week dementia care training program, which included mobile e-learning, social networking, and mentor-supported group meetings, on home care workers. The results showed that through online learning, home care workers were able to improve their caregiving knowledge, attitudes, and competencies, which played a key role in improving the quality of home care for people with dementia. McGlade et al. [38] analyzed the difficulties and challenges of implementing a Let Me Decide program in a long-term care population, and the results of the study demonstrated that online learning can be used to improve the quality of home care for people with dementia. McGlade et al. [38] found that online learning platforms make training more accessible to long-term care staff, improve caregiver education, and positively promote resident and family engagement in caregiving programs.

"Stress" occurred 22 times in 2020–2024, with seven occurrences in 2020–2021, seven in 2022, and eight in 2023–2024. At this stage of the epidemic, it was mainly concerned with the use of online learning to explain and cope with three different types of stress and their influencing factors in the adult population.

First, in terms of psychological stress during the epidemic, the study focused on the psychological stress experienced by adults during COVID-19, including stress caused by factors such as isolation and economic uncertainty, and how online learning could help cope with the stress. Weber et al. [39] conducted an online assessment of symptom levels and changes in anxiety, depression, and loneliness in 636 adults. The study found that although these symptoms declined over time, they increased during two national lockdowns, emphasizing that online learning platforms should provide timely mental health support and interventions. Álvarez & Pinto [40] analyzed predictors of resilience among Spanish adults during the COVID-19 pandemic. Findings showed that individuals who learned online to receive knowledge about mask use, vaccinations, and lockdown measures demonstrated higher resilience, emphasizing the importance of online learning in providing adaptive beliefs and promoting prosocial behavior. Second, in the area of discrimination and identity-related stress, a study by Bravo et al. [41] compared thoughts about dropping out of school, burnout, mental health, and coping styles between students with and without autism during the pandemic. The study found that students with autism were more likely to experience burnout and mental health symptoms and consider dropping out. The role of online learning in providing targeted support and resources to help students with autism cope with stress related to discrimination and identity was emphasized. Third, in the area of educational and professional stress management, Hidalgo-Andrade et al. [42] assessed teachers' psychological distress, life satisfaction, and perceived stress during COVID-19 and reported their coping strategies for maintaining mental health and well-being. The study gave recommendations for disseminating and implementing useful information that can help promote teachers' well-being and initiatives through online learning platforms. Fodor et al. [43] used an online research program to test the relationship between vigorous-intensity aerobic exercise (VPA) and moderate-intensity aerobic exercise (MPA) and work stress management in adults. The results showed that VPA helped to cope with high work stress and that online physical activity and online wellness programs had a significant positive impact on adults' management of work stress.

3.3.2 Evolutionary path

The time zone map presents the evolution of knowledge in the field from a temporal dimension, which helps to understand the themes and trends of adult online learning research in different time periods. **Figure 2** presents a time zone map of keywords in adult online learning research.

In 2014–2016, the keywords "behavior," "performance," "impact," "technology," and "education" began to come to the fore. Analysis of the citation literature where the keywords were located showed that the research in this period focused on the interaction between behavior, technology application, and educational practice in the field of adult online learning and explored adult online learning outcomes and their influencing factors and mechanisms. In 2017–2019, "knowledge," "depression," "motivation," "quality," "lifelong learning," and "skills" began to come to the forefront, and this period began to focus on the impact of online learning on enhancing adult learners' knowledge and skills, deep motivation, and social development. From 2020 to the present,

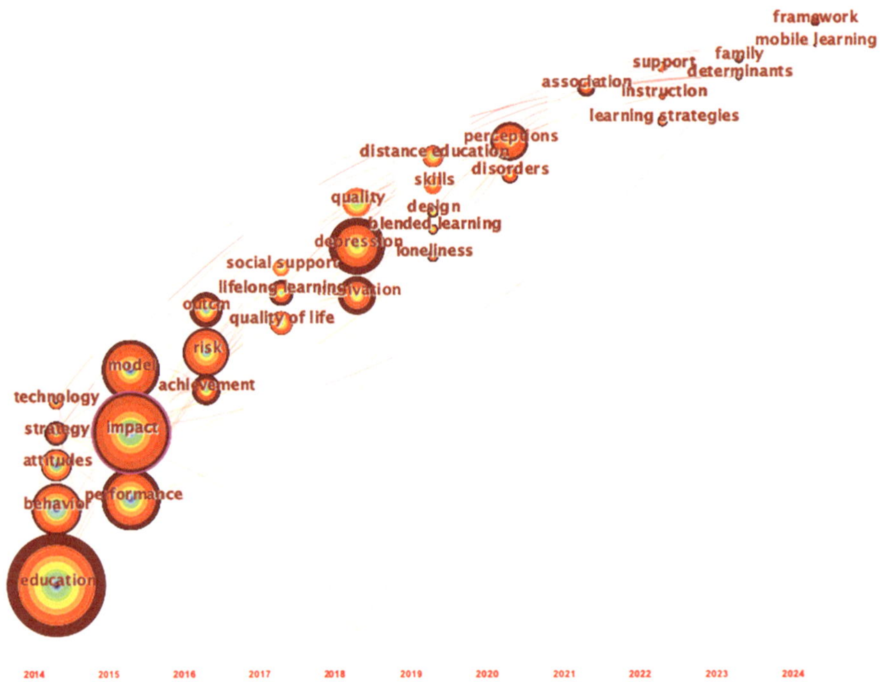

Figure 2.
Map of keyword time zones for adult online learning research (2014–2024).

"perceptions," "learning strategies," "family," "framework," and "mobile learning" have begun to emerge as new research points. This reflects that adult online learning research has shifted from a single assessment of learning outcomes in the early days to a multidimensional impact on national and educational policies, and in recent years, more diversified research directions have emerged on the basis of the deepening of the existing research, including focusing on the mathematical and physical logic of the development of adult online learning platforms, the impact of online learning on family education, as well as the impact of adult online learning and the emerging perspective modes.

4. Conclusions and insights

Using CiteSpace to visualize and analyze the adult online research literature from 2014 to 2024, it can be seen that the international academic research on adult online learning presents an inherent developmental logic and evolutionary pathways. Analysis of its developmental logic and evolutionary pathways can deepen understanding of adult online learning and its research and provide an important reference for future participation and interpretation of adult online learning.

First, at the macro level, research on adult online learning focuses on changes in social patterns and national education strategies caused by technological change. Among the hot topics of research, the category of "Adult Learning and Technological Innovation and Application" mainly emphasizes the emerging development of online learning in the context of digitization and intelligence through technological

DOI: http://dx.doi.org/10.5772/intechopen.1011147

innovation, as well as the application of artificial intelligence (AI) technology in lifelong education, such as real-time online automated assessment, mobile self-directed learning, and real-time online personalized learning. It is worth noting that several key scholars from Europe and the United States have laid the knowledge foundation of adult online learning research, showing a "center-edge" knowledge production structure. From the point of view of co-cited high-frequency authors, scholars such as Jonathan Cohen from the United States, Andrew F. Hayes from Canada, and Richard M. Ryan from Australia have laid down the knowledge foundation of this field and, in a sense, monopolized the knowledge production in this field. Therefore, future research on adult online learning should focus on international comparative research, carrying out comparative research between countries, and research on the current situation of online learning in certain countries and policies around online learning so that the exploration of the field of online learning can move forward in the direction of cross-cultural and globalized research. At the same time, scholars from various countries should actively exchange experiences and engage in discussions, learn from the useful experiences of other countries in practice and theoretical research, and strengthen ties through study visits and cooperation in publishing articles so as to gradually establish high-level research institutions and high-quality scholars in the field of adult e-learning and ultimately form the e-learning mode of pluralistic fusion and synergistic promotion. Eventually, an online learning model of diversified integration and synergistic promotion can be formed, which would contribute to the development of adult online learning in all countries in the world.

Second, at the meso-level, critical analysis of the implementation of educational policies on adult e-learning has become a hot research topic. Both the hot topics presented and the keywords of the research frontiers focus on the disenchantment of adult online learning; that is, they no longer regard adult online learning as a single beneficial way and objective fact of technology-enhanced learning but rather are testing its legitimacy and validity from the underlying logic or statistical technology of online learning and regard it as a new open learning mode to explore the extreme impact on the educational policies of various countries and other harms that may be caused by the excessive commodification. On the one hand, among the hot topics of research, the category of "adult online learning and educational policy practice" focuses on the powerful call for online education reform brought about by the wave of digital intelligence. However, the educational governance policies that are in line with the rapid development of the digital intelligence of adult online learning are lagging behind, failing to avoid the risks brought about by the technology, and making it difficult to safeguard educational equity, educational ethics and norms, and educational nurturing. It is difficult to guarantee educational fairness and ethical norms of education and to maximize the function of education in nurturing people, which hinders the healthy, orderly, and efficient formation of adult online learning. In particular, the digital divide is polarized, and educational equity is not guaranteed. Digital intellectual transformation by economic, political, cultural, and other influences: the digital development of adult online learning in different countries, regions, and schools is not the same, and there is even a serious imbalance, with the digital divide continuing to widen, and the majority of people's right to education, willingness, and interests cannot be met. On the other hand, regarding the keyword "stress" in the research frontier, the core viewpoints of the cited literature mainly focus on the stress and confusion of adult online learning. Online learning expands the spatial and temporal boundaries of adult education, brings people closer together, and enriches their social networks, but at the same time, overindulgence in the virtual world of online learning, constituted by technology and neglect of vivid real-life experiences, may weaken the social attributes of adult learners. The most notable of these is that digital substitution dilutes emotional interactions, and digital symbols replace face-to-face teaching interactions, which can lead to insufficient attention to the emotional needs, personality differences, and developmental aspirations of adult learners and can reduce the cultivation of human socioemotional attributes in the educational process. From the perspective of the law of research development, critical reflection on adult online learning is its inevitable stage, which will inevitably usher in a more rational and cautious research attitude after experiencing the pursuit and shock of adult online learning. This will also be an ongoing concern in the future.

Third, from the micro level, adult online learning focuses on the specific process of interaction between individual learners and technology. First of all, in terms of research topics, the research on adult online learning selects more microscopic topics, focuses on the combination of theory and practice, and is highly specialized and targeted, such as exploring the characteristics of adult online learning under different types of self-regulation on the basis of the application of the self-regulated learning (SRL) model. Its research process mostly adopts quantitative research methods, such as controlling variables, setting experimental and control groups, and comparing the learning effectiveness of online learning and blended learning. Second, in terms of the selected research objects, the keyword "people" in the research frontiers of adult online learning research shows a relatively systematic and comprehensive coverage of learners, knowledge transmitters, and social supporters (including family members, peers, colleagues, leaders, communities, etc.). However, there are fewer studies on the target of teachers, and the content is shallow; that is, there are few studies exploring adult career development planning, adult online learning environments, and adult education methods and approaches from the perspective of teachers. Therefore, in the future, the research on adult online learning should expand the scope of the research object, starting from multiple subjects such as educators and supporters; that is, it is recommended to conduct detailed research on individual subjects from the perspective of students and also to pay attention to the close connection and interaction between different subjects. Teachers play an important role in transferring knowledge and guiding learners' behaviors, and researchers should explore their role positioning, educational motivation, self-reflection, and learning and communication in order to clarify the development path of teachers in adult e-learning and to promote the process of teacher professionalization.

This analysis highlights critical directions for future research and policies. Academically, cross-cultural studies should examine the "center-edge" knowledge dynamic in underrepresented regions, while interdisciplinary teams must address the emotional impacts of AI on learning. Policymakers require adaptive governance integrating technological advancement with equity safeguards, including digital inclusion metrics and ethical AI certification. The teacher-research gap necessitates professional ecosystems that develop educators' hybrid competencies in data literacy and socioemotional support. These coordinated efforts could transform adult online learning into a proactive framework for sustainable human development amid digital transformation.

Funding

This work was supported by the First-Class Education Discipline Development of Beijing Normal University (Grant Numbers: YLXKPY-XSDW202408, YLXKPY-ZYSB202201).

Author details

Li Liao and Jian-Hong Ye*
Faculty of Education, Beijing Normal University, Beijing, China

*Address all correspondence to: jianhong.ye@bnu.edu.cn

References

[1] UNESCO. Embracing a culture of lifelong learning: Contribution to the futures of education initiative; report; a transdisciplinary expert consultation. 2021. Available from: https://unesdoc.unesco.org/ark:/48223/pf0000374112

[2] Sarilita E, Rafisa A, Desai P, Mossey PA. Utilising massive open online courses to enhance global learning dissemination in cleft lip and palate: A case report of penta helix collaboration. BMC Medical Education. 2024;**24**(1):301-314. DOI: 10.1186/s12909-024-05225-4

[3] Wang N, Qiao A. On the nature and underlying theories of online learning activities. Chinese Journal of Distance Education. 2009;**8**(1):36-40. DOI: 10.13541/j.cnki.chinade.2009.01.016

[4] Liang JZ, Ng DKW, Raveendran V, Teo MYK, Quah ELY, Krishna LKR. The impact of online education during the COVID-19 pandemic on the professional identity formation of medical students: A systematic scoping review. PLoS One. 2024;**19**(1):e0296367. DOI: 10.1371/journal.pone.0296367

[5] OECD. Schooling disrupted, schooling rethought: How the COVID-19 pandemic is changing education. 2020. Available from: https://www.oecd-ilibrary.org/education/schooling-disrupted-schooling-rethought-how-the-covid-19-pandemic-is-changing-education_68bllfaf-en

[6] Lu Y, Hong X, Xiao L. Toward high-quality adult online learning: A systematic review of empirical studies. Sustainability. 2022;**14**(4):2257-2261. DOI: 10.3390/su14042257

[7] Schmid RF, Borokhovski E, Bernard RM, Pickup DI, Abrami PC. A meta-analysis of online learning, blended learning, the flipped classroom and classroom instruction for pre-service and in-service teachers. Computers and Education Open. 2023;**5**:100142. DOI: 10.1016/j.caeo.2023.100142

[8] Abedini A, Abedin B, Zowghi D. Adult learning in online communities of practice: A systematic review. British Journal of Educational Technology. 2021;**52**(4):1663-1694. DOI: 10.1111/bjet.13120

[9] Chen Y. Principles and Applications of Citation Space Analysis: A Practical Guide to CiteSpace. 1st ed. Beijing: Science Press; 2014. pp. 23-24

[10] Cohen J, Ice M, Thapa A. Recognizing community voice and a youth-led school-community partnership in the school climate improvement process. School Community Journal. 2015;**25**(1):9-28

[11] Hayes AF. Introduction to Mediation, Moderation, and Conditional Process Analysis: A Regression-Based Approach. New York: Guilford Press; 2013

[12] Darlington RB, Hayes AF. Regression Analysis and Linear Models: Concepts, Applications, and Implementation. New York: Guilford Publications; 2016

[13] Garrison DR, Akyol Z. Corrigendum to 'toward the development of a metacognition construct for communities of inquiry. The Internet and Higher Education. 2015;**26**:56-66. DOI: 10.1016/j.iheduc.2014.10.001

[14] Braun V, Clarke V, Boulton E, Davey L, McEvoy C. The online survey as a qualitative research tool. International Journal of Social Research

Methodology. 2020;**24**(6):641-654. DOI: 10.1080/13645579.2020.1805550

[15] Ryan RM, Deci EL. Self-determination theory and the facilitation of intrinsic motivation, social development, and well-being. American Psychologist. 2000;**55**(1):68-78. DOI: 10.1037/0003-066X.55.1.68

[16] Creswell JW, Poth CN. Qualitative Inquiry and Research Design: Choosing among Five Approaches. Thousand Oaks, CA: Sage Publications; 2016

[17] Kara M, Erdogdu F, Kokoc M, Cagiltay K. Challenges faced by adult learners in online distance education: A literature review. Open Praxis. 2019;**11**(1):5-22. DOI: 10.3316/informit.234110355704611

[18] Son C, Hegde S, Smith A, Wang X, Sasangohar F. Effects of COVID-19 on college students' mental health in the United States: Interview survey study. Journal of Medical Internet Research. 2020;**22**(9):e21279. DOI: 10.2196/21279

[19] Huang Y, Zhao N. Generalized anxiety disorder, depressive symptoms and sleep quality during COVID-19 outbreak in China: A web-based cross-sectional survey. Psychiatry Research. 2020;**288**:112954. DOI: 10.1016/j.psychres.2020.112954

[20] Anwyl-Irvine AL, Massonnié J, Flitton A, Kirkham N, Evershed JK. Gorilla in our midst: An online behavioral experiment builder. Behavior Research Methods. 2020;**52**:388-407. DOI: 10.3758/s13428-019-01237-x

[21] Peirce J, Gray JR, Simpson S, MacAskill M, Höchenberger R, Sogo H, et al. PsychoPy2: Experiments in behavior made easy. Behavior Research Methods. 2019;**51**:195-203. DOI: 10.3758/s13428-018-01193-y

[22] Kuo YC, Belland BR. An exploratory study of adult learners' perceptions of online learning: Minority students in continuing education. Educational Technology Research and Development. 2016;**64**:661-680. DOI: 10.1007/s11423-016-9442-9

[23] Goh TT, Yang B. The role of e-engagement and flow on the continuance with a learning management system in a blended learning environment. International Journal of Educational Technology in Higher Education. 2021;**18**(1):49-58. DOI: 10.1186/s41239-021-00285-8

[24] Martínez-Cerdá JF, Torrent-Sellens J, González-González I. Socio-technical e-learning innovation and ways of learning in the ICT-space-time continuum to improve the employability skills of adults. Computers in Human Behavior. 2020;**107**:105753. DOI: 10.1016/j.chb.2018.10.019

[25] Ng NF, Osman AM, Kerlan KR, Doraiswamy PM, Schafer RJ. Computerized cognitive training by healthy older and younger adults: Age comparisons of overall efficacy and selective effects on cognition. Frontiers in Neurology. 2021;**11**:564317. DOI: 10.3389/fneur.2020.564317

[26] Gijselaers HJ, Kirschner PA, Verboon P, de Groot RH. Sedentary behavior and not physical activity predicts study progress in distance education. Learning and Individual Differences. 2016;**49**:224-229. DOI: 10.1016/j.lindif.2016.06.021

[27] Halliday JA, Speight J, Russell-Green S, Eric O, Hagger V, Morris A, et al. Developing a novel diabetes distress e-learning program for diabetes educators: An intervention mapping approach. Translational Behavioral Medicine. 2021;**11**(6):1264-1273. DOI: 10.1093/tbm/ibaa144

[28] Radovanović D, Hogan B, Lalić D. Overcoming digital divides in higher education: Digital literacy beyond Facebook. New Media & Society. 2015;**17**(10):1733-1749. DOI: 10.1177/1461444815588323

[29] Yu X, Liu S. Disparities in online use behaviours and Chinese digital inclusion: A 10-year comparison. International Journal of Environmental Research and Public Health. 2022;**19**(19):11937-11948. DOI: 10.3390/ijerph191911937

[30] Teich K, Loock VS, Rummel N. Meeting the challenges of continuing education online courses: Can we promote self-regulated learning strategies with adaptive support? British Journal of Educational Technology. 2024;**55**(4):1437-1455. DOI: 10.1111/bjet.13453

[31] Nahm E-S, Resnick B, Brown C, Zhu S, Magaziner J, Bellantoni M, et al. The effects of an online theory-based bone health program for older adults. Journal of Applied Gerontology. 2017;**36**(9):1117-1144. DOI: 10.1177/0733464815617284

[32] Hauck YL, Stoll KH, Hall WA, Downie J. Association between childbirth attitudes and fear on birth preferences of a future generation of Australian parents. Women and Birth: Journal of the Australian College of Midwives. 2016;**29**(6):511-517. DOI: 10.1016/j.wombi.2016.05.001

[33] Fiery MF, Martz DM, Webb RM, Curtin L. A preliminary investigation of racial differences in body talk in age-diverse US adults. Eating Behaviors. 2016;**21**:232-235. DOI: 10.1016/j.eatbeh.2016.03.004

[34] Roldan A, Reina R. Are self-efficacy gains of university students in adapted physical activity influenced by online teaching derived from the COVID-19 pandemic? Frontiers in Psychology. 2021;**12**:654157. DOI: 10.3389/fpsyg.2021.654157

[35] Motl RW, Sandroff BM, Wingo BC, McCroskey J, Pilutti LA, Cutter GR, et al. Phase-III, randomized controlled trial of the behavioral intervention for increasing physical activity in multiple sclerosis: Project BIPAMS. Contemporary Clinical Trials. 2018;**71**:154-161. DOI: 10.1016/j.cct.2018.06.017

[36] Moody L, Turner A, Osmond J, Hooker L, Kosmala-Anderson J, Batehup L. Web-based self-management for young cancer survivors: Consideration of user requirements and barriers to implementation. Journal of Cancer Survivorship. 2015;**9**:188-200. DOI: 10.1007/s11764-014-0400-4

[37] Su HF, Koo M, Lee WL, Sung HC, Lee RP, Liu WI. A dementia care training using mobile e-learning with mentoring support for home care workers: A controlled study. BMC Geriatrics. 2021;**21**:1-10. DOI: 10.1186/s12877-021-02075-3

[38] McGlade C, Daly E, McCarthy J, Cornally N, Weathers E, O'Caoimh R, et al. Challenges in implementing an advance care planning programme in long-term care. Nursing Ethics. 2017;**24**(1):87-99. DOI: 10.1177/0969733016664969

[39] Weber M, Burchert S, Sijbrandij M, Patanè M, Pinucci I, Renneberg B, et al. Mental health across two years of the COVID-19 pandemic: A 5-wave longitudinal study in Germany. Frontiers in Psychiatry. 2023;**14**:1229700. DOI: 10.3389/fpsyt.2023.1229700

[40] Álvarez MA, Pinto NS. Experiential COVID-19 factors predicting resilience among Spanish adults. BMC Psychology.

2023;**11**(1):118-129. DOI: 10.1186/s40359-023-01131-4

[41] Bravo AJ, Wedell E, Villarosa-Hurlocker MC, Looby A, Dickter CL, Schepis TS, et al. Perceived racial/ethnic discrimination among young adult college students: Prevalence rates and associations with mental health. Journal of American College Health. 2023;**71**(7):2062-2073. DOI: 10.1080/07448481.2021.1954012

[42] Hidalgo-Andrade P, Hermosa-Bosano C, Paz C. Teachers' mental health and self-reported coping strategies during the COVID-19 pandemic in Ecuador: A mixed-methods study. Psychology Research and Behavior Management. 2021;**14**:933-944. DOI: 10.2147/PRBM.S314844

[43] Fodor DP, Pohrt A, Gekeler BS, Knoll N, Heuse S. Intensity matters: The role of physical activity in the job demands-resources model. Journal of Work and Organizational Psychology. 2020;**36**(3):223-229. DOI: 10.5093/jwop2020a21

Chapter 2

Understanding Students' Learning Motivations in Online Learning Settings: From a Quantitative Perspective

Bo Pei

Abstract

This study investigates the role of learning motivation as a significant predictor of learning performance in online learning environments. Grounded in the Self-Determination Theory (SDT), we explored approaches to conceptualize, construct, and validate quantifiable indicators of student learning motivations in online learning settings. Traditional approaches, like surveys and questionnaires, rely heavily on self-reported data, making it challenging to characterize students' learning motivations objectively and detect the corresponding dynamics over time. This study explores an approach to quantify students' learning motivations based on online learning activities with the aim to profile students' learning motivations objectively and dynamically. We employed clustering approaches to group students into different motivation groups based on those extracted learning activities. Multiple statistical approaches and machine learning approaches were adopted to validate the effectiveness of the proposed motivation quantifying metrics. The analytical results indicate that students' learning motivation can be effectively modeled through students' online learning activities, even at an early stage in the learning process. This study contributes to the field by providing insights for quantifying students' learning motivations and detecting their dynamics in learning in virtual learning environments. Practical recommendations include optimizing instructional strategies that focus on activities that impact motivation and offering targeted support according to motivation categories. Future research will focus on validating the proposed metrics across various learning settings and further investigate fine-grained factors that influence students' learning motivations.

Keywords: online learning, self-determination theory (SDT), machine learning, clustering approaches, student engagement

1. Introduction

Learning motivation has been considered as a pivotal driver of consistent learning practices, which significantly influence students' academic accomplishments [1, 2].

IntechOpen

Research on MOOCs has suggested that students' enrollment in courses is driven by a multitude of motivations, which further leads to significant differences in their learning patterns, preferences, and performance [3]. Generally, the willingness of students' registration for a course related to motivations such as curiosity about the subjects, interests in social interactions on the Internet, and requirements of career development [4]. Further studies also indicated that learners who were highly motivated tend to engage in challenging tasks, adopt deep learning approaches, and demonstrate improved performance and persistence [5]. A clear understanding of the associations among student learning motivations and activities has the potential to help instructors design more targeted learning materials and teaching strategies to better support students' learning.

Recently, an increasing number of studies have been focused on investigating relationships between student learning motivation and success in online environments [6–8]. Most of these studies evaluate students' motivation through quizzes and surveys administered conducted prior classes begin. Basically, motivation, in these studies, is considered as a personal trait, which complicates the interpretation of such studies [9]. However, evidence suggests that student motivation is not a static characteristic, which changes with various factors as the course progresses, including emotional states, economic conditions, personal issues, and course content. However, in online learning settings where face-to-face interactions are limited, it could be challenging for instructors to detect how students' personal status impact their learning motivations in a timely manner. In addition, studies have shown that factors such as students' age, gender, cultural background, and socioeconomic status may have a significant impact on their motivation to learn [10–12]. For example, students from different cultural backgrounds may demonstrate various types of motivation in the learning process, which may be related to their expectations of education, values, and personal life experiences [11]. Particularly, students from lower socioeconomic status may face more learning challenges, which may affect their motivation and learning strategies [12]. Therefore, understanding the impact of these factors on motivation to learn is critical to designing more individualized and targeted instructional interventions. Through in-depth analysis of students' demographic backgrounds, educators are able to identify key factors that may affect motivation to learn, allowing for more customized support for students from diverse backgrounds.

Given the capacity of machine learning techniques in processing large datasets and the availability of student learning data in online settings, there has been a growing amount of research focusing on exploring machine learning approaches to facilitate timely and targeted learning support for students [13–15]. However, little research was conducted to assess student academic motivation and the corresponding factors over time based on learning data. This lack of research precludes providing timely and targeted instructions for students during their learning process. Especially considering that motivation has been identified as the most critical factor that determines students' choices regarding what to learn, how to learn and when to learn [5]. For example, Elshareif and Mohamed analyzed student learning data during COVID-19 to investigate the associations between the key aspects of e-learning and motivation to learn [16]. The authors employed two surveys to investigate students' overall perceptions regarding both the e-learning experience and the corresponding factors influencing the experience. The study identified key aspects of e-learning (i.e., e-teaching materials, e-assessments, e-discussions, etc.) in relation to students' learning motivation. However, this association was identified based on the data at the end of the course, which in part shows that authors considered student learning motivation as a static trait. Moreover, the analytical data in this study mainly relied on student self-reported data without examining student-by-student interaction data that incorporated more detailed information about learning motivation. Similarly, Alioon and Delialioğlu collected quantitative data through the utilization of a student engagement survey and a motivation questionnaire [17]. The analytical results highlighted the importance of authentic, collaborative m-learning activities in the domain of "communication" and "collaboration", without considering the interactive data.

Given the limited research on investigating learning motivation from a quantitative perspective, it is essential to explore methods for characterizing learning motivations and identifying the underlying factors that influence them in online learning settings. Specifically, in this study, we derived a set of metrics informed by Self-Determination Theory (SDT) to characterize student learning motivation using learning behaviors and demographic information. We then employed machine learning techniques to validate the proposed metrics. This study aims to address the following research questions:

RQ 1: How can we quantify students' learning motivation based on learning activities in online settings?

RQ 1.1: Whether there are associations between students' motivation and their demographic backgrounds?

RQ 2: To what extent are the SDT-based metrics effective in quantifying students' learning motivations?

2. Literature review

2.1 Learning motivation in online learning settings

Motivation is generally considered the major factor that determines "why people choose to do something, what kinds of efforts they will put into doing such a thing, and how long they will maintain the activity" [18]. Particularly, in online learning settings where there is great flexibility regarding both learning format and learning schedule, motivation has also been considered to be of paramount importance in sustaining student learning activities and performance. Findings from several studies suggest that individuals who partake in online learning are more likely to exhibit intrinsic motivation than those who engage in traditional face-to-face learning [7, 19–21]. This is primarily due to the fact that learners who enroll in online courses are often driven by their internal desire for knowledge and curiosity. Moreover, online learning environments tend to provide students with access to innovative and imaginative technologies, which can further stimulate their intrinsic motivation [5].

However, student learning motivation does not stay at the same level both in the short and long term. For example, student motivation will wane with the increase in the difficulty level of learning content as the course progresses. Additionally, students' curiosities about online learning will also wear off as they become more familiar with the related technologies, which can also lead to a decrease in learning motivation. Motivation should be considered as a dynamic factor that drives students to conduct purposeful actions at every learning stage rather than a static personal trait. Current studies commonly associate learning motivation with students' mental activities such as cognitive and affective status, interactions with learning environments and learning contents and so on [22]. Moreover, in online learning settings, learning motivation is also greatly associated with the learning behaviors and patterns for pursuing the intended learning goals conducted by learners. As has been suggested by researchers and practitioners in learning analytics and educational data mining communities, learning motivation can be inferred from factors such as students' choices of learning tasks, persistence and efforts in learning, learning achievements, and so on [23].

2.2 Measuring learning motivation in online learning settings

Previous studies have primarily analyzed student learning motivation by leveraging theories of achievement goals and expectancy-value, most of the researchers employed these theories to develop surveys or questionnaires that could be used to measure and categorize motivation [24]. As indicated by Xu, the achievement goal theory characterizes student learning as mastery-oriented and performance-oriented, either of them has specific learning patterns associated [24]. On the other hand, the expectancy-value theory focuses on learners' perceptions about the task attributing student learning efforts, self-regulation, task performance and so on to their expectations and values regarding the task. Although focusing on different aspects, these theories identified similar constructs in learning that correlated to learning motivation. For instance, in Xu's study, the author identified behaviors such as managing distractions, arranging the learning environment, time management, emotional engagement, monitoring motivation, and cognitive reappraisal [24]. These behaviors were linked to four distinct categories of motivation: High Motivation, Moderate Motivation, Low Goal Orientation/Moderate Expectancy-Value, and Very High Goal Orientation/Very Low Expectancy-Value. In the study of Hsieh, the author adopted motivated strategies for learning questionnaires to evaluate associations among learning motivation, engagement behaviors, and learning outcomes [25]. Analytical results suggested that factors such as Cognitive effort (i.e., time spent on assignments), Active participation (i.e., asking questions, contributing to forum discussions, working collaboratively) and Instructor interaction (i.e., discussing grades/assignments, careers, etc.) were highly correlated to learning motivation.

2.3 Machine learning approaches in patterning learning behaviors

Recently, a significant body of research has focused on employing machine learning techniques to pattern student learning behaviors and identify the effects of these patterns on learning outcomes [16, 17]. Ramesh, Goldwasser, Huang, Daumé and Getoor, proposed Probabilistic Soft Logic (PSL) to separate student engagement into two groups (passive and active) based on behavioral activities, linguistic features of posts in the course forum and the structure features from forums in MOOCs [18]. The results revealed that there was a significant correlation between student engagement and final performance. Liang et al. established student profiles based on learners' attitudes and the duration of their learning behaviors, grouping them using the Jaccard coefficient algorithm applied to their learning activities [19]. The results showed that student profiles help understand their learning situation, finding their problems, and improving the completion rate of online learning in the end. Qiu et al. observed a significant heterogeneity in students' course selection and learning patterns by analyzing the key factors influencing student engagement in MOOCs [20]. They proposed Latent Dynamic Factor Graph model (LadFG) that incorporates students' demographics, forum activities, and learning activities to predict student final performance. It indicated that the proposed model outperformed the counterpart machine learning models in predicting students' performance on assignments and course certifications.

Most previous studies relied on subjective methods, such as students' responses to questionnaires and interviews, to identify and measure learning motivation. These methods are inherently subjective and fail to capture the factors influencing learning motivation in an objective manner. Additionally, given that motivation is a dynamic construct that evolves over the course, it should be objectively modeled with time-varying features. To address this gap, our study adopts SDT as a guideline to model students' learning motivation through specific learning behaviors that reflect time-varying features and assess its applicability in an online learning setting.

3. Theoretical background

3.1 Understanding online learning motivation from self-determination theory (SDT)

Self-determination theory (SDT) is a contemporary framework for understanding human motivation that addresses the dynamic interrelationships between human needs and psychological well-being within the immediate social context [20, 22]. The conceptualized 3 aspects of human needs: autonomy (a sense of self-determining), competency (a feeling of competency of tasks), and relatedness (a sense of connection with others or the environment), makes the SDT to be one of the most appropriate frameworks for examining student online learning motivation [23]. In this paper, we adapted the general human motivation categories within SDT to the context of student online learning, which includes intrinsic learning motivation, extrinsic learning motivation, and amotivation. Intrinsic motivation in learning is characterized by students who find pleasure in the learning process itself. Extrinsic motivation involves students participating in learning activities to obtain external rewards. Amotivation is observed in students who feel that their efforts do not influence their learning outcomes.

Specifically, intrinsically motivated students engage in learning behaviors for their own sake, deriving pleasure, satisfaction, and other intrinsic rewards from participation. In such cases, extrinsic incentives become unnecessary as the rewards are inherent to the activities. Conversely, extrinsically motivated students pursue learning activities to achieve higher scores, demonstrate competence, avoid negative feedback, and achieve similar goals [22]. Amotivated students fail to see a connection between their learning behaviors and learning achievements, often feeling incompetent and lacking control over their actions [21].

Figure 1 presents the SDT framework adapted from Ryan and Deci to support the primary research objective of this paper: modeling students' learning motivation based on their learning activities. This framework elaborates on the different levels of motivation in relation to the rationale behind learning behaviors in online learning settings [21].

Given the complex and sometimes frustrating nature of learning, especially in online environments where additional critical skills (e.g., self-regulated learning abilities, handling technical challenges) are required, traditional intrinsic motivation alone may not adequately describe students' learning processes. Therefore, this paper expands the concept of intrinsic motivation by incorporating sub-categories from

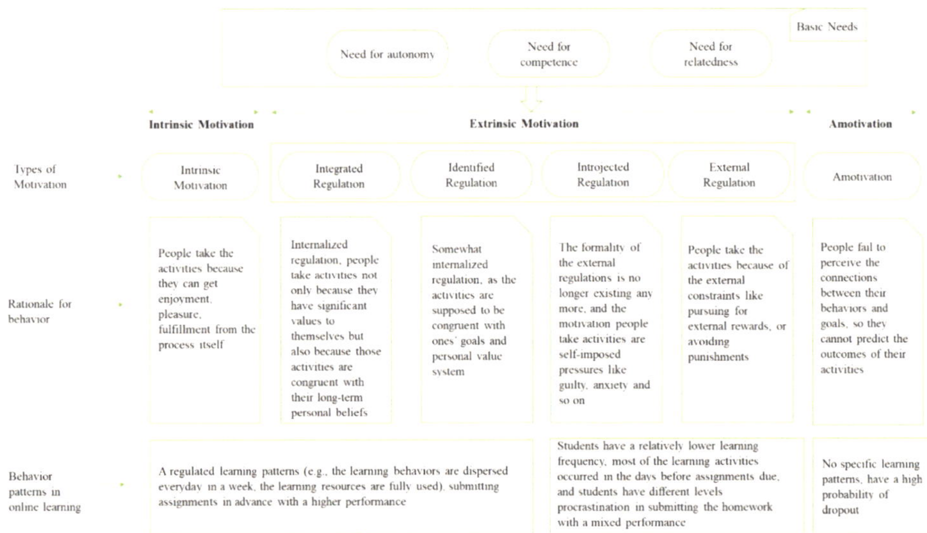

Figure 1.
Different types of motivations under the SDT framework in online learning settings.

the extrinsic motivation category with higher levels of internalized regulation, such as Integrated Regulation and Identified Regulation. This approach aims to describe learning driven by a higher level of motivation.

Students exhibiting higher levels of internalized regulation are more likely to engage in regulated learning (i.e., distributing learning activities evenly across the week), participate in learning activities more frequently, and submit assignments on time or ahead of deadlines. Conversely, extrinsic motivation is characterized by engaging in learning activities driven by external factors (e.g., avoiding punishment, feeling guilty). Learners in this category tend to have lower learning frequency, uneven distribution of learning activities (i.e., concentrating efforts primarily before assignment deadlines), and procrastination in submitting assignments.

Finally, in the amotivation category, learners typically lack a clear perception of how their learning activities relate to learning goals. They have a limited understanding of the potential learning outcomes, and this will increase the likelihood of undesirable academic performances or dropping out of the course.

4. Methodology

4.1 Data collection

4.1.1 Dataset description

The dataset used in this study was collected and organized by researchers at the Open University (OU), one of the largest universities worldwide offering online courses. In this university, course content and materials are delivered via a Virtual Learning Environment (VLE) [21]. Both demographic information of students and aggregated clickstream data from the VLE were collected, enabling researchers to gain an in-depth understanding of the effects of demographic information and learning behaviors on student performance. All data that could identify specific students were anonymized to ensure privacy, preventing any student from being linked to the provided information. We selected two social science courses at the college level, each lasting approximately 38 weeks. All learning resources for the courses were released several days before the courses began in the VLE. Student learning behaviors in these courses were recorded by the VLE. Approximately 350,000 entries for nine different learning activities were analyzed in this study. The recorded log files represented student clickstreams for various activities within the system. Each entry in the log files corresponds to a specific learning activity undertaken by a student.

4.1.2 Metrics construction

In attempts to identify the student motivation levels based on VLE interaction data, in combination with student demographic backgrounds, as early as possible, we also incorporated student interaction data before the course starts. These learning activities have been identified as significant predictors for students' learning performance in the subsequent learning stages [26]. Particularly, in this study, the learning activities before the course starts can also be critical indicators for students' initial learning motivations regarding the course.

In **Table 1**, we calculated the distributions of the final performance of those students who did not submit the first assignment for each of the two courses. According to the table, if a student did not submit the first assignment, the probability of failing the course is over 90% (considering withdrawal as a kind of failure), which makes the first assignment a significant predictor for final performance. However, submission of the first homework alone cannot provide an adequate insight into the different behavior patterns of the student. For this reason, we incorporated and analyzed the behavioral data (such as the clickstreams of dataplus, forum, glossary, collaboration, content, resources, subpage, homepage, URL and so on.) recorded by the VLE before the first assignment was submitted. In addition, we examined students' procrastination tendencies by calculating the average number of days they delayed submitting their homework throughout the course.

Table 2 shows the metrics that we considered for identifying students' learning motivation, which encompasses demographic information and online learning behavior data. The demographic information includes gender (M: 0, F: 1), age (numeric values), highest educational level (HE), and the regions where students reside. In this study, we focused on the college students' online learning behaviors, excluding those older than 55. The highest educational level of the students involved is categorized into four levels: "Lower than A level," "A level or Equivalent," "HE Qualification," and "Post Graduate Qualification," encoded numerically from 1 to 4. The students' geographical areas are divided into 13 regions of England (e.g., "East Anglian Region,"

Course Presentation	Withdrawn	Fail	Pass	Prob. Of Fail
Course A	16	6	2	0.92
Course B	18	9	1	0.96

Table 1.
Final performance distribution for students without the first assignment submission.

Data Types		Features	Description
Demographic Data		Gender	Learner gender
		Age	Learner age
		HE	Learner highest education
		Region	The living areas of a learner when taking the course
Online Learning Behavior Data	Clickstreams Recorded in VLE System	Dataplus clicks	Number of times learner visits his/her records in VLE
		Forum clicks	Number of times learner visits forums
		Glossary clicks	Number of times learner visit higher education acronyms
		Collaborate clicks	Number of times learners visit the online video discussions
		Content clicks	Number of times learners visit the description of assignments
		Resource clicks	Number of times learner visits lecture notes and slides
		Homepage clicks	Number of times learner visits the first page of a lesson
		URL clicks	Number of times learners click the links to audio/video contents
		AvgClicks	Average number of times learner visits different resources
	Assignment Submission Style	AvgDelayed Days	Average number of days delayed in submitting assignments
	Performance	First assignment scores	Score of the first assignment
		Final performance	Learner final performance

Table 2.
Metrics for characterizing students' learning motivation.

"London Region," "Scotland"). These regions are non-ordinal and were encoded using the one-hot encoding approach [22].

The behavioral data includes clickstreams related to each resource provided by instructors via the Virtual Learning Environment (VLE). The system records the aggregated number of times a specific resource is visited by a student per day, which can indicate the students' motivation to participate in the course. Additionally, we constructed the "avgClicks", calculated by dividing the total clicks per day by the number of different resources visited per day. This metric indicates the diversity of resources a student refers to during a particular time span. The feature of assignment submission styles is represented by the average number of days a student delayed in submitting assignments across the course. A negative number indicates how many days on average the student submitted assignments before the due date, while a positive number indicates the number of delayed days. The final performance of the students in the dataset can be categorized into 4 classes: Distinction, Success, Fail, and Withdrawn.

DOI: http://dx.doi.org/10.5772/intechopen.1009790

4.1.3 Quantifying learning motivation with the proposed metrics

Students' final performance was calculated based on their assignment and exam scores. Generally, final performance can be a good indicator of students' learning motivations in the course. However, drawing on the Self-Determination Theory (SDT), for those registrants who fail or withdrew from the course, we cannot conclude their motivations solely from their final performances. It is possible for a student to have strong intrinsic motivation to learn but still fail in the end. Therefore, we considered students who exhibit features of intrinsically motivated learners even if they failed in the final performance. We categorized students based on the proposed motivation metrics into four groups: Intrinsically Motivated Pass Students (IMPS), Intrinsically Motivated Failure Students (IMFS), Extrinsically Motivated Students (EMS), and Amotivated Students (AS). The metrics used to categorize students into these motivation groups include first assignment scores, delayed days for submitting homework, clickstream data of the VLE learning activities, and final performance. The notations of the features that will be used in the study are as follows:

Let S represent the student entries, where $|S| = N$.

g_i (i = 1,2..., N) is the first assignment score for student i;

$a_{i,j}$ (i = 1, 2..., N; j = 1, 2...,9) is the clickstream of the jth activity in the VLE for student i;

d_{ij} (i = 1,2..., N; j = 1,2,3) is the number of delayed days of the jth assignment for student i;

varClicks is the variance of the clickstreams of a specific student during a specific time span. In other words, it represents the frequency of the online behavior changes across different learning resources, shown as Eq. (1).

$$varClicks(i) = \frac{\sum_{i,j=1}^{9} a_{i,j}}{\sum_{i,j=1}^{9} \left(t = 1\ if\ a_{i,j} \neq 0\right)} \quad (1)$$

avgDelay is a measurement of how many days the student delayed in submitting the 3 assignments on average, shown as Eq. (2).

$$avgDelay = \frac{\sum_{i,j=1}^{3} d_{i,j}}{3} \quad (2)$$

The following describes the criteria and procedure to categorize the students based on their different levels of motivation. The criteria we set for the metrics to quantify the three main motivation groups are as follows:

Intrinsically Motivated Students are defined as individuals who are genuinely interested in the course content and complete the course. The primary objective of these students is not necessarily to achieve a passing grade but to focus on the learning process and the knowledge acquired. Consequently, this category encompasses both students who pass the course (IMP) and those who do not (IMF).

Extrinsically Motivated Students are those who enroll in courses with a strong intention to master the material due to external factors such as research or job requirements. The majority of students in this group aim to achieve a distinction at the end of the course to demonstrate their learning achievements.

Amotivated Students are those who withdraw from the course.

4.2 Data analysis

We first preprocessed the data to prepare the appropriate data for subsequent data processing, and the procedure can be divided into data cleaning and data transformation. Data cleaning includes the removal of unrelated features, filling in missing values and so on. Data transformation mainly concerns transforming features in order to equalize the weights of different features to the target values. We used the stand scaler method [22] to transform the values of the numeric features into a normal distribution to avoid particular feature domains and other features that influence the target variables in this study.

To address research question 1, the data were analyzed through multiple stages. Firstly, k-means clustering was employed to categorize students into four groups, corresponding to the four motivation categories. Subsequently, we analyzed the percentages of students' final performances within each respective motivation group to assess the reliability of the proposed criteria. Descriptive statistical analyses, including Poisson Regression, ANOVA, and Chi-squared Test, were then applied to determine whether the scales of the variables used to cluster learners' motivation be consistent across groups.

To answer research question 2, several machine learning algorithms including SVMs, Logistic Regression, Decision Tree, and Random Forest were built to predict the learner's learning motivations at an early stage of the course, using their demographic information and online learning behaviors. The multiclass classification method was employed, whereby students were classified into corresponding categories based on the extracted features. Particularly, the target variables are the learning motivations (intrinsic, extrinsic, amotivation) represented by $T_j,\{j=1,,2,,3\}$, where j is the class to which the observations belong. The features, including both demographic information and learning behaviors, are represented by $F_i \in R^i$, where i is the ith observation.

5-folded cross-validation was employed during the modeling process. In order to build a reliable prediction model, the cross-validation process was run on 80% of the original dataset and left 20% as a testing dataset. The evaluation metrics like AUC (area under the curve) [23], accuracy, precision, recall, and the F1-measure [24] were applied in this paper to evaluate the performances of the models since these metrics are commonly used to measure the performances of machine learning models.

5. Results

5.1 RQ1: How can we quantify students' learning motivation based on learning activities in online settings?

In this study, students were first clustered into three groups based on the proposed motivation grouping criteria using the recorded learning activities before the first assignment. **Figure 2** displays the distributions of students' final performances across different motivation groups, with the Intrinsically Motivated group further divided into Intrinsically Motivated Pass Students (IMPS) and Intrinsically Motivated Failure Students (IMFS). The x-axis represents the clustering criteria, while the y-axis indicates the percentage of students from a detected category that belongs to the actual specific performance category. For example, in the IMPS category, the first bar in the figure represents that approximately 90% of students who passed the course were classified by the IMPS criteria, and the second bar indicates that around 60% of students who failed the course were also classified by the IMPS criteria.

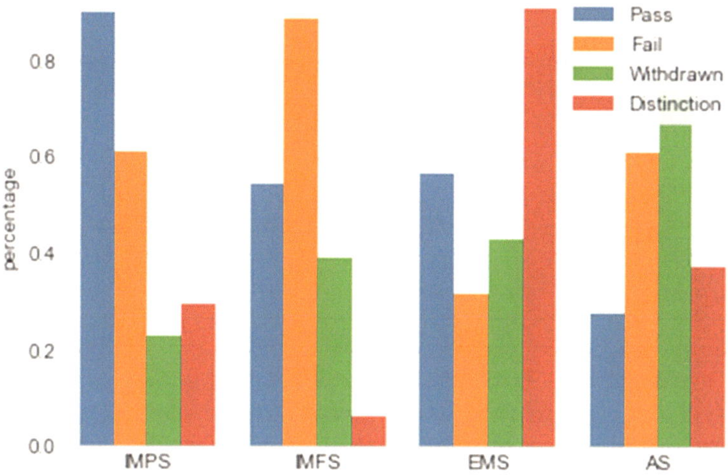

Figure 2.
Final performances across the different motivation groups.

By comparing the distributions of student performances across different motivation groups, it is evident that there is performance categories detected beyond the major performance category in the corresponding motivation group. For example, in the EMS group, while the primary performance category is Distinction, approximately 57% of students who passed the course were also classified under the same criteria. This phenomenon often occurs among students who are initially highly motivated by external rewards (extrinsically motivated) but whose ambition diminishes over time. Therefore, it is reasonable to observe that students who passed and failed the course primarily constituted the Intrinsically Motivated group, those who passed and achieved distinctions primarily fell into the Extrinsically Motivated group, and those who withdrew and failed the course primarily accounted for the Amotivated group.

After investigating the distribution of student performances among the four motivation groups, we proceeded with statistical tests aimed at verifying whether there were significant differences among the average clicks, average delay, and first homework grades. The descriptive statistics for different motivation groups are presented in **Table 3**.

According to **Table 3**, there is a significant difference among the EMS ($\mu = 89.76$), IMS (IMPS ($\mu = 50.33$), and IMFS ($\mu = 25.65$)) groups with respect to the avgClicks. However, the avgClicks and std. in the group of AM ($\mu = 86.75, std = 60.57$) are similar to those of the EMS group ($\mu = 89.76, std = 66.27$). The large avgClicks value and std. value indicated that there may be great struggle experienced by the students in AM group to learn the related materials released before the first assignment.

The average delay (avgDelay), indicating the procrastination levels of students in different motivation groups, reveals that students from the IMFS (students who failed the course) and AS (students who withdrew from the course) groups are more likely to delay in submitting assignments, with averages of 3.34 and 8.77 days, respectively. The larger standard deviation values (std = 12.11, std. = 10.30) in these two groups suggest that students in these groups have less competent time management skills. Conversely, students in the IMPS and EMS groups have similar standard deviation

	Mean				Std			
	IMS		EMS	AM	IMS		EMS	AM
	IMPS	IMFS			IMPS	IMFS		
avgClicks	50.33	25.65	89.76	86.75	45.79	19.86	66.27	60.57
avgDelay	0.35	3.34	2.55	8.77	8.91	12.11	8.23	10.30
g	70.31	66.33	80.41	72.05	8.89	12.63	7.62	10.95

Table 3.
Descriptive statistics for different motivation groups.

values (std = 8.91, std. = 8.23), indicating that students in these groups tend to submit assignments at consistent times and follow a more regular learning pace.

Regarding the scores of the first assignment, the mean scores are reported as follows: 70.31 for students in the IMPS group, 66.33 for those in the IMFS group, 80.41 for those in the EMS group, and 72.05 for those in the AM group. Interestingly, students in the AM group have a higher average score than those in the IMFS group. This suggests that students from the AM group worked harder than those from the IMFS group, as indicated by their higher average number of clicks (avgClicks) and higher assignment scores. However, these students are also more likely to delay submitting assignments, and their learning interests may decline as the course content becomes increasingly complex. In contrast, students in the EMS group achieved the highest average score for the first assignment and maintained a relatively consistent learning pace throughout the period.

To demonstrate the validity of the proposed motivation clustering criteria, follow-up analyses using Poisson Regression and ANOVA were conducted to examine the associations of the related variables with each group. The results for Poisson regression are presented in **Table 4**. The coefficient for IMFS is −.68 (SE = .10, $p < .001$), meaning that the expected number of clicks for the IMFS group is exp. (−.68) = 0.51 times the expected number of clicks for students in the IMPS group. The coefficient for AM is .60 (SE = .15, $p < .001$), which means the expected number of clicks for the AM group is exp. (.60) = 1.82 times the expected number of clicks for students in the IMPS group. However, the expected number of clicks for the EMS group was not statistically significantly different from the IMPS group ($p = .78$).

The results of ANOVA indicate that both students' average delay ($F(3, 698) = 73.86$, $p < .001$) and students' first homework grade ($F(3, 698) = 42.67$, $p < .001$) were significantly different among the groups. The pairwise group comparisons using Tukey's HSD test are presented in **Tables 5** and **6**. As shown in **Table 5**, apart from the difference between the EMS and IMFS groups ($p = .998$), all other pairwise

	Estimate	Robust SE	p	LL	UL
Intercept	3.92	.04	<.001	3.84	4.00
IMFS	−.68	.10	<.001	−0.87	−0.48
EMS	.03	.11	.78	−0.18	0.25
AM	.60	.15	<.001	0.32	0.88

Table 4.
The results of poisson regression.

	Diff	LL	UL	Adjusted p
IMFS-IMPS	8.295	5.358	11.232	0.000
EMS-IMPS	14.610	11.870	17.350	0.000
AM-IMPS	−0.277	−4.088	3.535	0.998
EMS-IMFS	6.315	2.611	10.019	0.000
AM-IMFS	−8.572	−13.125	−4.018	0.000
AM-EMS	−14.887	−19.316	−10.457	0.000

Table 5.
Tukey multiple comparisons of means for average delay.

	Diff	LL	UL	Adjusted p
IMFS-IMPS	−10.015	−13.608	−6.423	0.000
EMS-IMPS	−3.831	−7.119	−0.542	0.015
AM-IMPS	13.149	8.617	17.681	0.000
EMS-IMFS	6.185	1.679	10.690	0.002
AM-IMFS	23.164	17.685	28.643	0.000
AM-EMS	16.979	11.694	22.264	0.000

Table 6.
Tukey multiple comparisons of means for 1st homework grade.

comparisons were significantly different at the $\alpha = .05$ level. For the first homework grade, however, all pairwise comparisons exhibited a significant difference at the $\alpha = .05$ level.

5.2 RQ1.1: Whether there are associations between students' motivation and their demographic backgrounds?

In this section, the associations between the different educational levels and the learning motivations were analyzed in courses 2013 and 2014 J respectively. In this dataset, the educational levels of the participants were divided into 4 categories: "A Level or Equivalent"," HE Qualification", "Lower Than A Level" and "Post Graduate Qualification". **Figure 3** shows the distributions of the students with different educational levels with respect to the different motivation groups. It was observed that students with different educational levels were distributed across each motivation group. Approximately 60% of students with "A Level or Equivalent" and "Lower Than A Level" educational certifications fell into the Intrinsically Motivated group in both courses 2013 and 2014 J. Around 50% of students with "HE Qualification" and "Post Graduate Qualification" fell into the Intrinsically Motivated group in course 2013 J. In course 2014 J, about 40% of students with "HE Qualification" fell into the Intrinsically Motivated group, and no students received the "Post Graduate Qualification."

Table 7 presents the Chi-squared Test results for different educational levels with respect to various motivation groups. The test examines how the expected distributions of different educational levels across the motivation groups differ from the observed distributions. Using this, we calculate the P-value. A P-value ($p < 0.05$)

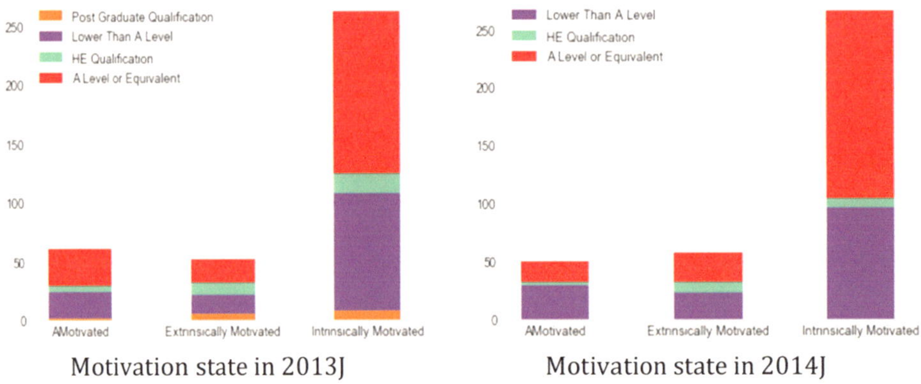

Figure 3.
The distribution of different education levels in different motivation groups.

Course	χ^2 statistic	df	P-value
Course A	6.553	6	0.364
Course B	6.553	4	0.162

Table 7.
Chi-squared Test for comparing different educational levels with different motivation groups in courses 2013 and 2014 J.

would indicate rejection of the null hypothesis and suggest a significant relationship between educational background and learning motivations. The parameter "df" refers to the degrees of freedom, indicating the number of independent values that can vary in the calculation. As there are only three different educational levels in course 2014 J compared to four in course 2013 J, the degrees of freedom are different, 4 and 6, respectively. The P-values in both courses are greater than 0.05, leading to the acceptance of the null hypothesis, indicating no significant relationship between educational levels and motivations in this study.

5.3 RQ2: To what extent are the SDT-based metrics effective in quantifying students learning motivations?

5.3.1 Machine learning models to categorize student motivations based on demographic information and learning activities

In this section, several machine learning algorithms were applied to identify student motivations at an early stage, providing implications for instructors to develop personalized interventions that can benefit students as early as possible. Machine learning algorithms can discover specific patterns in large learning datasets, classifying students into different groups with similar learning motivations. We examined the performance of four machine learning algorithms (Support Vector Machines, Logistic Regression, Decision Tree, and Random Forest) on the dataset, where SVMs include different variants such as Linear SVM, Weighted-Linear SVM, and Weighted-RBF based SVM.

In machine learning, the number of samples in different classes significantly affects the final performance and generalizability of the models. To ensure that models can learn the patterns in different classes without being influenced by dominant classes in the dataset, it is important to balance the dataset, suggesting that the number of students in different motivation categories should be as similar as possible. **Figure 4** shows the distribution of students with respect to different motivation groups. From the figure, it is evident that there is a significant imbalance in the dataset, with the number of students in the Extrinsically Motivated and Amotivated groups each accounting for only about 25% of the students in the Intrinsically Motivated group.

5.3.2 Balance the dataset

To balance the dataset and ensure that the machine learning models perform well across the entire dataset rather than being biased toward the majority class, we applied the Synthetic Minority Over-Sampling Technique (SMOTE) to generate synthetic samples based on the distributions of the minority classes. This process balances the different classes in the original dataset, resulting in an equal number of samples in each class. Consequently, the machine learning models can effectively capture the patterns implied by the minority classes. **Figure 5** compares the differences in the discriminant hyperplanes built by SVM for the original imbalanced dataset and the balanced dataset created using SMOTE.

From **Figure 5 (1)**, it is evident that the built SVM model can detect students from the Intrinsically Motivated group with high accuracy due to the large number of samples in this group. However, for the Extrinsically Motivated and Amotivated groups, the model detects motivation patterns to some extent, but the accuracies are low due to the small sample sizes. In contrast, **Figure 5 (2)** shows that, after balancing the dataset using SMOTE, more samples fall into the corresponding regions, and the generated samples align perfectly with the distribution of the corresponding class. There are sufficient samples in each region defined by the SVM hyperplane, allowing the SVM model to accurately track the underlying patterns in the data.

5.3.3 Model performance evaluation

Table 8 shows the performance of each classification model applied to the balanced dataset in classifying students based on motivation levels. The performance metrics include Accuracy, Precision, Recall, and F1-measure. It can be observed that the accuracies of the classifiers range from around 0.64 to 0.78, and the average performances in terms of Precision, Recall, and F1-measure vary accordingly.

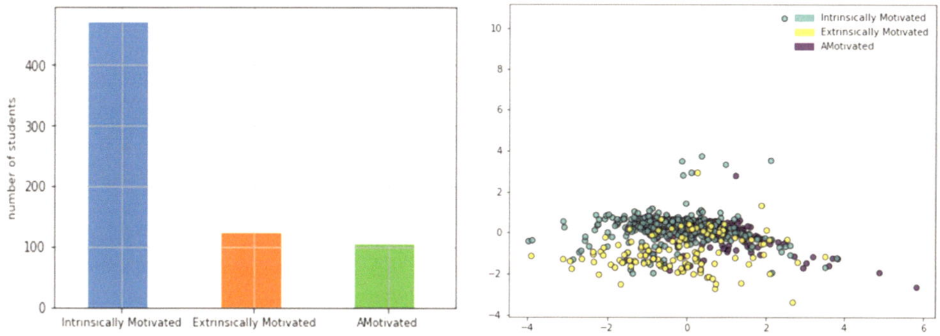

Figure 4.
The distribution of students in different motivation groups.

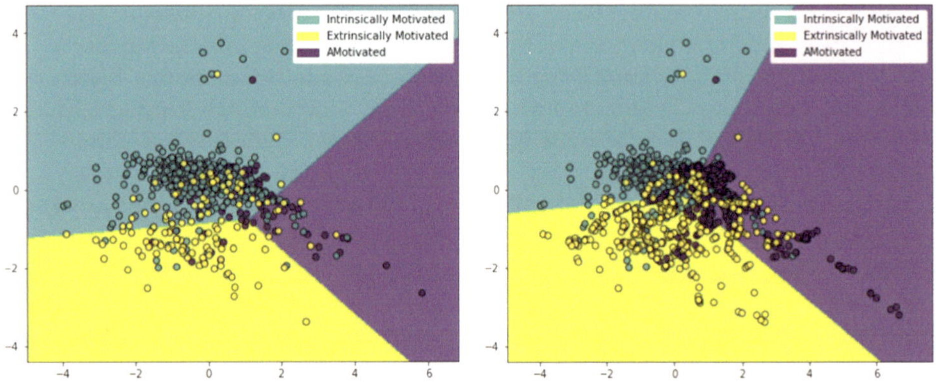

(1) Discriminating hyperplanes on imbalanced dataset

(2) Discriminating hyperplanes on balanced dataset based on SMOTE

Figure 5.
The comparison of the discriminating hyperplane on the imbalanced and balanced dataset.

Model	Accuracy	Precision	Recall	F1-measure
SVM_L	0.68	0.75	0.80	0.77
SVM_L_W	0.72	0.83	0.87	0.85
SVM_R_W	0.66	0.52	0.55	0.53
LR	0.70	0.81	0.85	0.83
DT	0.64	0.60	0.65	0.63
RF	0.78	0.85	0.90	0.87

Table 8.
Performance of the classifiers on the balanced dataset.

To evaluate the overall performance of the classifiers in categorizing students into different motivation groups, we examined the AUC-ROC (Area Under the Curve - Receiver Operating Characteristics) for each motivation group and calculated the average AUC across the groups, as shown in **Figure 6**. By comparing the AUC-ROC values of the classifiers for each group and the average AUCs, it can be observed that there is no significant difference in the performance of these classifiers. All classifiers achieved excellent performance, with AUC-ROC values ranging from 0.82 to 0.94 for each group and an average AUC exceeding 0.85.

In this study, recall measures the percentage of students correctly classified by the models. From **Table 9**, we observe that recall is over 0.82 for all classifiers except SVM_L_W and SVM_R_W. Surprisingly, the accuracy of SVM_R_W is only 0.01, while that of SVM_L_M is 0.68. This indicates that the weighted SVM may over-emphasize the outliers in the dataset we used. Comparing the performance of the other four classifiers, Logistic Regression (LR) achieves the highest recall (0.83) with relatively good accuracy (0.70) and precision (0.72). The Decision Tree (DT) appears to perform better than LR in terms of accuracy (0.76) and precision (0.82). DT examines each decision rule when classifying students into the corresponding motivation groups. Moreover, DT can provide interpretable results, which can be used to explain which features are most significant to the target variable.

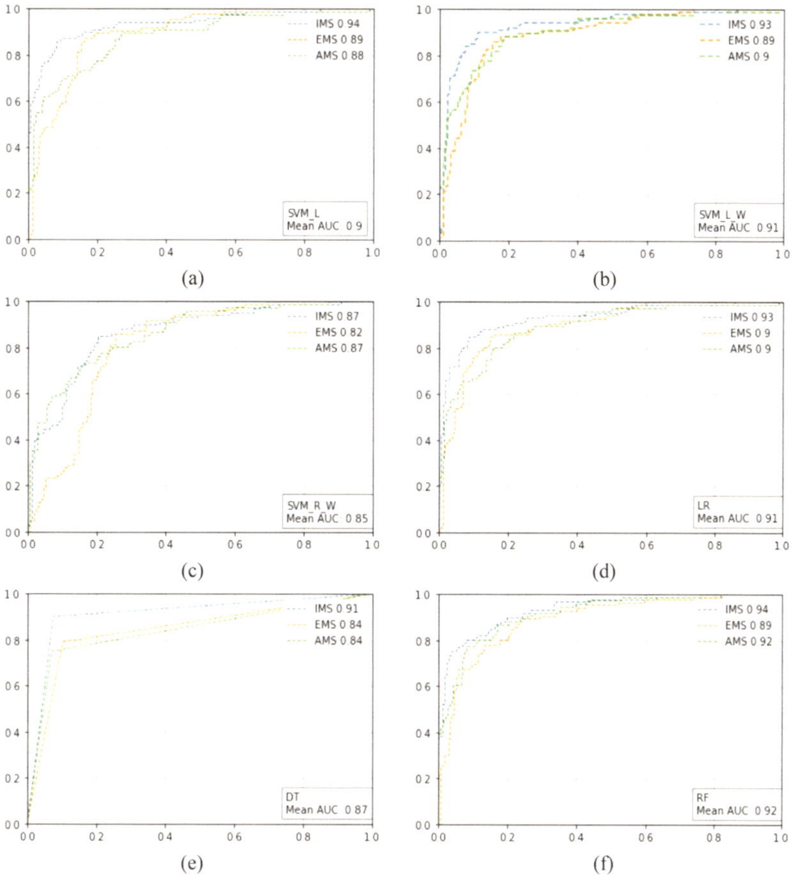

Figure 6.
The AUC-ROC of each classifier on the balanced dataset.

Classifier	Accuracy	Precision	Recall	F1-Score	AUC-ROC			avgAUC
					IMS	EMS	AMS	
SVM_L	0.66	0.69	0.82	0.75	0.94	0.89	0.88	0.90
SVM_L_W	0.66	0.84	0.75	0.79	0.93	0.89	0.90	0.91
SVM_R_W	0.01	0.86	0.50	0.58	0.87	0.82	0.87	0.85
LR	0.70	0.72	0.83	0.77	0.93	0.90	0.90	0.91
DT	0.76	0.82	0.82	0.81	0.91	0.84	0.84	0.87
RF	0.58	0.61	0.89	0.66	0.94	0.89	0.92	0.92

Table 9.
The classification performance of the classifiers.

Overall, all classifiers demonstrate sound performance on the dataset, successfully classifying students into different motivation groups at a relatively early stage, before the first assignment. This indicates that combining learning activities with demographic information can effectively identify student learning motivations, as both learning behaviors and demographic information have an association with or represent the learning motivations of students to some extent.

6. Discussion

Our study provides substantial insights into the characterization of student learning motivation in online learning settings. By utilizing metrics informed by Self-Determination Theory (SDT), we quantitatively modeled students' motivations and classified them into intrinsic, extrinsic, and Amotivated groups. The use of various machine learning algorithms validated these metrics, demonstrating their reliability and applicability in identifying distinct motivation groups based on students' online learning behaviors and demographic information.

In the context of SDT, our findings align with the theoretical framework that distinguishes between intrinsic, extrinsic, and Amotivated forms of motivation. Intrinsic motivation was evident in students who exhibited consistent learning behaviors and sound academic performance. This corresponds with previous research indicating that intrinsically motivated students are more likely to adopt deep learning approaches and exhibit persistence throughout an academic semester [5, 19]. Our results also underscore the importance of extrinsic motivation. Extrinsically motivated students initially demonstrated high engagement, which often diminished over time. This finding resonates with studies by Hsu et al. and Alamri et al., suggesting that extrinsic incentives can initially trigger motivation but may not sustain long-term engagement [7, 20]. The Amotivated group showed inconsistent behaviors and higher dropout rates, supporting previous findings that amotivation is linked to undesirable academic performance and increased dropout rates [25].

This study extends the existing literature by integrating learning behavior data with demographic information, offering a dynamic and comprehensive approach to understanding student motivations. Traditional methods, such as self-reported surveys and interviews, often fail to capture the fluid and multifaceted nature of motivation. Our approach addresses this gap by providing real-time analysis of online learning behaviors. This is particularly relevant in online learning environments, where face-to-face interactions are limited, and instructors need robust tools to monitor and support student motivation [26, 27].

Moreover, the successful application of machine learning algorithms to predict and model motivation groups based on early stage learning behaviors has significant implications. These results suggest that learning motivations can be effectively modeled and predicted, which can inform the design of online learning environments and instructional strategies. This aligns with the previous work that highlighted the potential of machine learning in enhancing educational outcomes through predictive analytics [26, 28].

7. Conclusion, limitations and future directions

In this paper, we conducted a case study to identify students' learning motivations at an early stage using demographic information and learning behaviors recorded by the VLE at the Open University. We developed a set of metrics to model students' learning motivation informed by SDT. A series of statistical analyses were then applied to identify different motivation groups among students using these metrics.

Several machine learning algorithms were employed to classify motivation groups and test the applicability of the developed metrics in our settings. The experimental results show that most classifiers demonstrated good performance in terms of accuracy, precision, recall, F1-measure, and AUCs. This indicates that learning motivations can be quantitatively characterized using a set of online learning behaviors, and students' motivation can be categorized into intrinsic, extrinsic, and Amotivated groups in alignment with SDT.

Our research contributes to existing literature by offering a novel methodological perspective for analyzing learning motivation through the lens of SDT and advanced machine learning techniques. The implications of this study are twofold. Firstly, it offers instructors an approach to conceptualizing online learning motivation guided by SDT, constructing its corresponding indicators, and validating its effectiveness, aiming to identify students' different motivation profiles and provide timely interventions to enhance their learning experience. Secondly, it highlights the potential for integrating learning behavior data with demographic information to create a more nuanced understanding of student motivations, which can significantly inform personalized instructional strategies.

However, this study also has limitations. First, the research relies on data from the Open University's Virtual Learning Environment, and the generalizability of the proposed quantitative representation method requires further validation. Future research should verify these indicators across different educational platforms and environments to assess their broad applicability and effectiveness. In addition, this study combines students' learning behaviors and demographic information but has not fully considered other factors that may influence learning motivation, such as emotional states and external incentives. To improve the accuracy of the motivation analysis model, future research should integrate more diverse data sources to more comprehensively capture the multidimensional nature of student motivation.

In addition, future research will also focus on developing personalized intervention strategies tailored to different motivation groups, conducting longitudinal studies to track changes in motivation over time, expanding demographic analyses, integrating additional data sources, and developing real-time analytics tools for immediate feedback and intervention. Exploring other motivational theories and testing the scalability of these metrics in various educational settings will further deepen our understanding of student motivations and improve personalized instructional strategies.

Author details

Bo Pei
Department of Educational and Psychological Studies, College of Education, University of South Florida, Tampa, Florida, USA

*Address all correspondence to: bpei@usf.edu

References

[1] Çebi A, Güyer T. Students' interaction patterns in different online learning activities and their relationship with motivation, self-regulated learning strategy and learning performance. Education and Information Technologies. 2020;**25**(5):3975-3993. DOI: 10.1007/s10639-020-10151-1

[2] Koyuncuoglu O. An investigation of academic motivation and career decidedness among university students. International Journal of Research in Education and Science. 2021;**7**(1):125-143. DOI: 10.3389/fpsyg.2020.00609

[3] Aldowah H, Al-Samarraie H, Alzahrani AI, Alalwan N. Factors affecting student dropout in MOOCs: A cause and effect decision-making model. Journal of Computing in Higher Education. 2020;**32**(2):429-454. DOI: 10.1007/s12528-019-09241-y

[4] Moore RL, Wang C. Influence of learner motivational dispositions on MOOC completion. Journal of Computing in Higher Education. 2021;**33**:121-134. DOI: 10.1007/s12528-020-09258-8

[5] Hartnett M. The importance of motivation in online learning. In: Moore MG, Diehl WC, editors. Handbook of Distance Education. 4th ed. New York: Routledge; 2016. pp. 145-158

[6] Akram H, Li S. Understanding the role of teacher-student relationships in students' online learning engagement: Mediating role of academic motivation. Perceptual and Motor Skills. 2024;**131**(4):1415-1438. DOI: 10.1177/00315125241248709

[7] Wei X, Saab N, Admiraal W. Do learners share the same perceived learning outcomes in MOOCs? Identifying the role of motivation, perceived learning support, learning engagement, and self-regulated learning strategies. The Internet and Higher Education. 2023;**56**:100880. DOI: 10.1016/j.iheduc.2022.100880

[8] Xhomara N, Dasho A. Online interactions and student learning outcomes in a moodle-based e-learning system. Technology, Pedagogy and Education. 2023;**32**(4):419-433. DOI: 10.1080/1475939x.2023.2214576

[9] Lee J, Song HD, Hong A. Exploring factors, and indicators for measuring students' sustainable engagement in e-learning. Sustainability. 2019;**11**(4):985. DOI: 10.3390/su11040985

[10] Ishida A, Sekiyama T. Variables influencing students' learning motivation: Critical literature review. Frontier in Education. 2024;**9**:1-6. DOI: 10.3389/feduc.2024.1445011

[11] Sigmundsson H, Haga M, Elnes M, Dybendal BH, Hermundsdottir F. Motivational factors are varying across age groups and gender. International Journal of Environmental Research and Public Health. 2022;**19**(9):5207. DOI: 10.3390/ijerph19095207

[12] Maghrifani D, Sneddon J, Liu F. Personal values and travel motivations: The moderating effects of visit experience, gender and age. Journal of Hospitality and Tourism Insights. 2024;**7**(5):3091-3109. DOI: 10.1108/JHTI-07-2023-0458

[13] Basnet RB, Johnson C, Doleck T. Dropout prediction in MOOCs using deep learning and machine learning. Education and Information Technologies.

2022;**27**(8):11499-11513. DOI: 10.1007/s10639-022-11068-7

[14] Sandiwarno S, Niu Z, Nyamawe AS. A novel hybrid machine learning model for analyzing e-learning users' satisfaction. International Journal of Human-Computer Interaction. 2023;**40**(16):4193-4214. DOI: 10.1080/10447318.2023.2209986

[15] Savchenko AV, Savchenko LV, Makarov I. Classifying emotions and engagement in online learning based on a single facial expression recognition neural network. IEEE Transactions on Affective Computing. 2022;**13**(4):2132-2143. DOI: 10.1016/j.compedu.2019.103641

[16] Elshareif E, Mohamed N. Associations between key aspects of e-learning and motivation to learn during COVID-19. Journal of Research on Technology in Education. 2021;**53**(4):488-503. DOI: 10.1080/15391523.2020.1865718

[17] Alioon Y, Delialioğlu Ö. The effect of authentic m-learning activities on student engagement and motivation. British Journal of Educational Technology. 2019;**50**(2):655-668. DOI: 10.1111/bjet.12559

[18] Guo PJ, Kim J, Rubin R. How video production affects student engagement: An empirical study of MOOC videos. In: Proceedings of the First ACM Conference on Learning @ Scale. 2014. pp. 41-50. DOI: 10.1145/2556325.2566239

[19] Chiu TK. Applying the SDT to explain student engagement in online learning during the COVID-19 pandemic. Journal of Research on Technology in Education. 2022;**54**(Suppl. 1):S14-S30

[20] Wang L. Student intrinsic motivation for online creative idea generation: Mediating effects of student online learning engagement and moderating effects of teacher emotional support. Frontiers in Psychology. 2022;**13**:954216. DOI: 10.3389/fpsyg.2022.954216

[21] Ferrer J, Ringer A, Saville K, Parris MA, Kashi K. Students' motivation and engagement in higher education: The importance of attitude to online learning. Higher Education. 2020;**83**(2):317-338. DOI: 10.1007/s10734-020-00682-0

[22] Anwer F. Activity-based teaching, student motivation, and academic achievement. Journal of Education and Educational Development. 2019;**6**(1):154-170. DOI: 10.22555/joeed.v6i1.272

[23] Zhao H, Xiong J, Zhang Z, Qi C. Growth mindset and college students' learning engagement during the COVID-19 pandemic: A serial mediation model. Frontiers in Psychology. 2021;**12**:621094. DOI: 10.3389/fpsyg.2021.621094

[24] Xu J, Moon KH, van der Schaar M. A machine learning approach for tracking and predicting student performance in degree programs. IEEE Journal of Selected Topics in Signal Processing. 2017;**11**(5):742-753. DOI: 10.1109/JSTSP.2017.2692560

[25] Hsieh P. The motivated strategies for learning questionnaire: Relationships among learning strategies, motivation, and engagement. The Journal of Educational Research. 2014;**107**(3):210-222. DOI: 10.1080/00220671.2013.832970

[26] Dsilva V, Schleiss J, Stober S. Trustworthy academic risk prediction with explainable boosting machines. In: Wang N, Rebolledo-Mendez G, Matsuda N, Santos OC, Dimitrova V, editors. Artificial Intelligence in Education: AIED 2023. Lecture Notes in Computer Science. Vol. 13916.

Cham: Springer; 2023. pp. 539-551. DOI: 10.1007/978-3-031-36272-9_38

[27] Flanagan B, Majumdar R, Ogata H. Early-warning prediction of student performance and engagement in open book assessment by reading behavior analysis. International Journal of Educational Technology in Higher Education. 2022;**19**:41. DOI: 10.1186/s41239-022-00348-4

[28] Tipple C, Linden T. Decline of student engagement in online studies: Understanding the trend. In: Cochrane T, Narayan V, Bone E, Deneen C, Saligari M, Tregloan K, et al, editors. Navigating the Terrain: Emerging Frontiers in Learning Spaces, Pedagogies, and Technologies. Proceedings ASCILITE 2024. Melbourne: Australasian Society for Computers in Learning in Tertiary Education (ASCILITE); 2024. pp. 612-617. DOI: 10.14742/apubs.2024.1418

Chapter 3

Analyzing Inhibiting Factors to E-learning Success and Effectiveness in Niger

Daouda Yacouba and Nana Aicha Goza

Abstract

This research analyzes the challenges affecting the success and effectiveness of online learning at Abdou Moumouni University (AMU) in Niger Republic, where information and communication technologies (ICT) are integrated into various aspects of social life. Despite the Nigerian government's efforts to establish a legal, institutional, and technical framework, online learning at AMU remains in its nascent phase. Existing research has not sufficiently examined how socio-economic and digital skill limitations interact to impact e-learning outcomes. Using a quantitative approach, data were collected through E-learning Readiness and Engagement Questionnaires" (ELREQ) administered via kobotoolbox to survey 599 participants across the university's eight faculties. The Pearson correlation coefficients analysis, conducted using the Statistical Package for Social Sciences (SPSS), identified key barriers such as the high cost of devices/equipment and motivational challenges through lack of personal interest and low interaction with other learners. These findings suggest that financial and motivational challenges significantly hinder the effectiveness of online learning at AMU.

Keywords: inhibiting factors, E-learning's effectiveness and success, socio-economic barriers, perception, Niger

1. Introduction

Advancements in information technology have impacted all aspects of business operations. The online world is now a tool for learning, building, and sharing knowledge. It promotes learning by enabling users to exchange data remotely and have access to a great number of online services and resources [1]. The emergence of e-learning programs has transformed the traditional learning approach worldwide, including school and university education, adult education, and other supplementary learning programs [2]. The field of E-learning is still nascent globally, with 73% of higher education institutions of about 59% offering E-Learning programs and/or training for five or fewer years. It has the potential to grow substantially [3]. In Niger Republic, where six ministries offer public education and training, and recently the virtual university of Niger (VUN) was created in 2023 by decreet No. 2022-879/PRN/MES/R of November 10, 2022, taken in accordance with the provisions of decree No. 2021-/924/PRN/MF of November 1, 2021; however, online learning is nascent [4] despite the government's efforts to establish a legal, institutional and technical framework for the development of e-learning. Sagayar [5] studied the development of distance education at Abdou Moumouni University (AMU) and found that AMU has very limited expertise in implementing distance learning. It is dominated by a variety of factors. Indeed, in the context of socio-economic constraints and geographical disparities coupled with security instability, the development of e-learning struggles to achieve its objectives. The legal and institutional framework in place, although structured, seems insufficient to meet the growing needs for infrastructure, adapted educational content, and digital skills. In addition, the low availability of technologies, combined with limited access to reliable internet connections, reduces the effectiveness of e-learning solutions. In this context, identifying and analyzing the main inhibiting factors that limit the effectiveness and success of e-learning in AMU would be of paramount importance. The aim of this research is to analyze the factors that limit the success and the efficiency of e-learning in AMU, whether they come from infrastructure, digital skills, public policies, or socio-cultural aspects. This paper presents the literature review of online learning, the methodological approach, the results, the discussion, and the conclusion as its structure before providing the list of bibliographic references used for this research.

2. Literature review

Various scientific papers discussed barriers to online learning such as Ref. [6], identified several barriers to online learning, including poor time management, lack of motivation, frustration, unclear communication regarding coursework expectations, technical challenges such as low internet connectivity, and financial constraints related to tuition costs for individual courses or full programs. Under the barriers and challenges in participating in virtual exchange program, the results of Stevens Initiative [7], indicate that the availability of funding to offer virtual exchange 48.2%, policy shifts and national-level drivers that favor physical mobility 14.9%, a digital divide or lack of technology access 13.7%, infrastructure issues such as the lack of electricity 9.5%, lack of "buy in" from key decision makers, students and potential facilitators 7.7%, Post covid factors (Burnout, enrollment, school disruptions) and staffing shortage to implement virtual exchange 3%, respectively, others 17.3% and none of the above 21.4% (p. 10). According to Ref. [8], there are nine virtual learning disadvantages for students that educators need to be aware of: students' distractions at home, adapting to new learning styles, isolation and lack of social interaction, technical difficulties, not receiving clear instructions or expectations, not receiving timely feedback, lack of communication, ineffective time management, while balancing work, family, and education are the main challenges for adults. Among the few who practice e-learning, Assagaye and Adamou [9] found that most teachers and learners have limited or no access, compounded by the challenges of remoteness and data accessibility. Hagley and Green [10] found that virtual exchange participants (teachers and students) in the world face challenges in navigating the platform; some teachers teach in war zones with no or intermittent electricity and a lack of the basic tools necessary for participation. Others are in developing countries where the socio-economic situation is such that students rarely have access to the Internet. Some have huge class sizes while others have students with varying levels of language proficiency (p. 106). Similarly, Yeh and Tsai [11] highlighted multiple obstacles in massive online teaching and learning, categorizing them into technological barriers (such as unstable Internet), internal barriers (including teachers' and parents' beliefs), design thinking barriers, and classroom management challenges. Both teachers and students struggle with inconsistent or limited internet access, which directly impacts students' right to education in online settings. Teachers face the challenge of sudden pedagogical adjustments, while parents bear the responsibility of supporting their children's online learning at home. Additionally, some students experience videoconferencing fatigue and difficulty managing an overwhelming amount of digital resources and screen time. Perera and Nalin Abeysekera [12] further examined factors influencing students' willingness to engage in e-learning, identifying performance expectancy, social influence, effort expectancy, and service quality as key determinants of their perception and intention to adopt online education. Inhibiting factors to e-learning refer to the challenges or obstacles that limit the effectiveness, accessibility, and adoption of e-learning systems. Numerous studies have been conducted about the effectiveness of online learning, its challenges, and its restrictions [13]. Kohnke et al. [14] showed the difficulty for students to communicate with the instructor and peers who were attending distance learning are some barriers to e-learning. Furthermore, they should also have good use of the technology available, including screen-sharing capabilities, video conference facilities, document sharing, image capture, and so on. A similar [15] studied the perceptions of instructors and students in a chemical engineering program on hybrid learning via virtual laboratories. Their findings highlighted in this study were that the model poses extra demands on instructors in terms of lesson preparation, feedback provision, and assessment of learning. Increasingly, Pregowska et al. [16] found that the main difficulty experienced by faculty when using HyFlex® derived from their lack of professional development needed to correctly implement the model. Specific challenges to Niger in developing distance learning, include insufficient infrastructure, lack of strategic policies, and technological readiness, which are critical factors in adopting e-learning initiatives [1]. In light of the aforementioned studies, online learning faces numerous challenges, including lack of infrastructure, lack of access to technology and internet facilities, limited teacher training, low students' engagement, socio-economic disparities, logistical issues like large class sizes, policy constraints, and inadequate institutional support, all of which hinder its success and effectiveness globally. In response to these issues, this study analyzes the factors that limit the success and effectiveness of online learning in the higher education context of Niamey-Niger. In order to reach the aim assigned to this study, a methodological approach is used.

3. The research framework

Theories and models provide the foundation upon which a study is constructed and supported. In order to analyze the challenges of online learning at Abdou Moumouni University (AMU) in Niger, it is relevant to build on Davis [17] technology acceptance model (TAM), which posits that perceived usefulness and perceived ease of use influence technology adoption. The model has been extended to incorporate external variables affecting online learning effectiveness. It integrates multiple key elements that together determine the system's adoption and effectiveness. It begins by categorizing contextual and inhibiting factors into three main barriers: technological constraints (such as lack of a stable internet connection, high cost of equipment/

devices, high cost of internet subscription, and difficulties navigating the platform (technical issues), pedagogical and learning content issues (including inadequate or insufficient learning content, language barrier, low interaction with other learners and lack of support or guidance from administrators/teachers/tutors, and psycho-social and environmental barriers (like lack of personal interest, reluctance toward digital learning, lack of time to fully engage in online learning and issues related to the learning environment (distractions, inadequate space, etc.)). These local conditions directly influence how students and lecturers perceive and engage with online platforms, shaping their views on task-technology fit, which measures the alignment of digital tools such as lecture streaming, digital assessments, and collaborative projects with academic requirements. The framework further assesses performance outcomes by examining factors like learning ease, time savings, course satisfaction, enhanced instructor decision-making, and overall system trust. It distinguishes between needs models, which evaluate how well technology meets organizational or learner needs, and acceptance models like the technology acceptance model (TAM) which focus on perceived ease of use (PEOU) and perceived usefulness (PU). These constructs, along with underlying attitudes, beliefs, and social influences from peers and institutional norms, determine users' overall attitudes and intentions toward online learning, which ultimately translate into actual usage patterns and effectiveness in teaching and learning. The extended framework (TAM) from Dillman et al. [15], systematically guides the research by first pinpointing inhibiting factors such as technological constraints, pedagogical and learning content issues, and psychosocial and environmental barriers that limit task-technology fit and hinder online learning performance. It then directs researchers to measure technology acceptance model (TAM) constructs by gathering insights on perceived usefulness, ease of use, attitudes, social influence, and usage intentions from students and lecturers, faculty, and staff through surveys or interviews. This approach is complemented by an assessment of actual usage and performance, which involves analyzing usage logs, adoption rates, and key performance outcomes like pass rates and student satisfaction to evaluate the integration of online learning. By correlating these empirical findings with the identified inhibiting factors, the framework reveals the specific variables that most strongly affect online learning success and effectiveness. Ultimately, this structured process leads to actionable recommendations such as infrastructure enhancements, digital skills training, and policy reforms that are designed to address the primary barriers and improve overall performance outcomes. By placing inhibiting factors at the forefront and weaving them into the TAM constructs, this framework captures how local conditions at AMU can directly influence the perceived usefulness, ease of use, attitudes, and, ultimately, the success and effectiveness of online learning.

4. Research methodology

The methodology of this study adopts a quantitative approach, utilizing two E-learning Readiness and Engagement Questionnaires" (ELREQ), derived from a convergence of established literature in survey design and technology acceptance from the tailored design method of Dillman et al. [15], which emphasizes the importance of clear, respondent-friendly questionnaires, prior work on e-learning readiness such as Hung et al. [18] studied the learner readiness for online learning and research in the domain of digital technology acceptance by Davis's [17] technology acceptance model, which informs aspects of ease of use and engagement.

The ELREQ questionnaire is designed to assess key factors influencing e-learning experiences by structuring its evaluation around six essential dimensions. Access to resources examines the availability of personal devices for learning and potential barriers such as equipment costs and internet connectivity. Utilization of platforms explores the types of online learning platforms used, such as WhatsApp, Zoom, and Moodle, along with the frequency of their use. Technological competencies assess learners' self-reported ease in using digital tools and any prior training received. Quality of educational content measures the adequacy and relevance of online course materials, as well as user satisfaction with content quality in meeting learning objectives. Institutional support considers the presence of regular follow-up or technical assistance from teachers and administrators, as well as the perceived effectiveness of institutional or government policies in facilitating e-learning. Finally, Learner engagement and motivation evaluates students' personal motivation to engage in e-learning and identifies potential obstacles such as technical difficulties, distractions, and language barriers. By addressing these dimensions, the ELREQ provides a comprehensive framework for understanding the challenges and opportunities in digital education at AMU. The first ELREQ was addressed to students and lecturers, while the second targeted faculty deans and the administration of AMU. A Hybrid sampling approach, including a census sampling technique and a probabilistic sampling method, was applied. A Census Sampling approach was applied to include the eight deans of the eight faculties of AMU to ensure a comprehensive representation of all the faculties. A simple random sampling was then used to select 385 students out of a total population (N) of 38,730 from the eight faculties of the institution. The same technique was also used to select 206 lecturers out of a total population (N) of 444, with a 95% confidence level ($t = 1.96$) within the margin error of ($e = 0.05$ or 5%), controlling the acceptable deviation from the actual population parameter; a proportion estimate ($p = 0.5$), used to maximize sample size; and a non-response rate (TNR = 1%), accounting for potential non-responses.

The study surveyed a total of 599 participants online via kobotoolbox. Data were collected by sending a consent statement for research participation, which introduces the researchers and their institution, explains the purpose of the study, ensures anonymity and confidentiality, states that participation is voluntary and provides an estimated time commitment, includes a kobotoolbox link to the ELREQ and it expresses gratitude for participation. This message is sent to students, lecturers, and the faculty deans WhatsApp groups from December 24, 2024, to January 6, 2025. To ensure reliability and accuracy, we deleted all data from other participants than students, lecturers and the deans of faculties. The collected data were processed statistically using Pearson correlation coefficients analysis with the Statistical Package for the Social Sciences (SPSS) software, version 25.

5. Results

The presentation and analysis of results are presented under this point. A descriptive analysis is used to highlight the frequency of the residence of participants and their regular access to Internet, while a Pearson correlation coefficients analysis is used to assess whether the relationships between online learning success and effectiveness at AMU and the socio-economic factors are closely related, providing a basis for testing the research hypothesis (**Figure 1**).

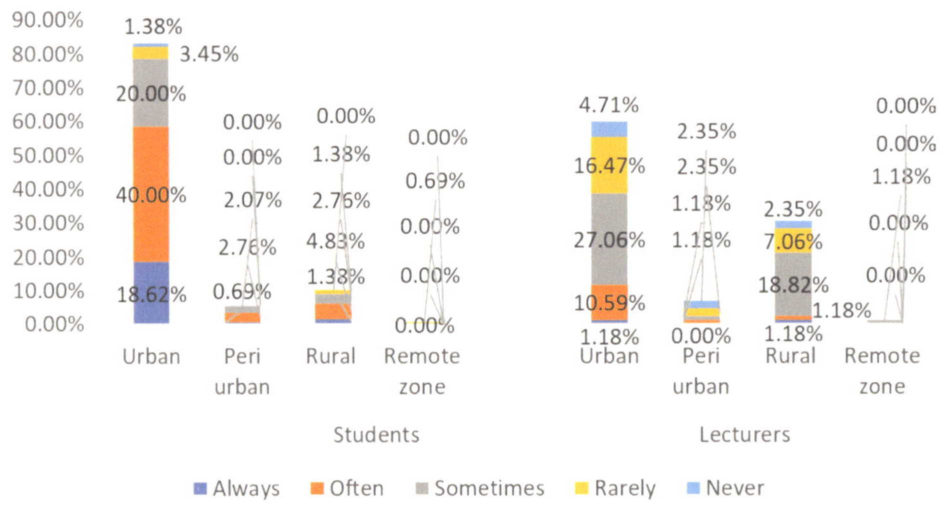

Figure 1.
Residence and regular access to Internet.

This dataset provides insights into the relationship between the place of residence of AMU students and lecturers and their regular internet access. The analysis highlights disparities in internet access, with patterns strongly influenced by geographic location. Urban areas dominate both student and lecturer populations in terms of internet access, representing 83.2% of students and 62.1% of lecturers. Among both groups, urban residents have the highest proportions of consistent internet access: "Always" access: 18.62%, "Often" access: 40.00%. Combined, these categories account for nearly 59% of urban residents across both groups. This indicates that urban residents benefit from reliable connectivity which is necessary for online education and professional development.

Peri-urban areas represent 5.6% of students and 6.9% of lecturers, with low rates of regular internet access. For example: Only 0.69% report "Always" having regular internet access, and 2.76% report "Often" access. Rural areas: Include a more substantial portion of lecturers (29.9%) compared to students (10.5%), but both groups face similar challenges: a small fraction (1.38%) has "Always" access, while a slightly larger group (4.83%) reports "Often" access. Regular internet access deteriorates further, with higher rates of "Sometimes" or "Rarely" access in rural areas compared to urban settings. The data indicates a significant digital divide, where peri-urban and rural areas lack adequate internet infrastructure to support consistent connectivity. Remote zones have the lowest representation, with only 0.7% of students and 1.1% of lecturers residing in these areas. Internet access is severely restricted: No residents report "Always" or "Often" regular internet access. A negligible 0.69% of lecturers and students combined report "Rarely" accessing the internet. These findings highlight the near-complete absence of reliable internet in remote zones. In terms of comparison students predominantly urban-based (83.2%), with significantly fewer residing in rural or remote areas (10.5% and 0.7%, respectively). They experience slightly better regular internet access than lecturers in urban and peri-urban areas, potentially due to institutional support, such as campus free Wi-Fi, initiated in 2012, and other free governmental and non-governmental organizations in and the surrounding of the capital city (Niamey). While urban-based lecturers account for 62.1%, a considerable proportion (29.9%) reside in rural areas. They report similar challenges to students in terms of limited access, with reliance on inconsistent connectivity. This analysis reveals stark inequalities in internet access based on residential location. While urban students and lecturers benefit from robust connectivity, their rural and remote counterparts face significant barriers.

5.1 Inhibiting factors to e-learning success and effectiveness

From the institutional view, AMU's partial online learning faces 62.5% of insufficient funds and 100% lack of adequate infrastructures to support online learning coupled with 62.5% high cost of equipment/devices. Here is the data that provides insights into the barriers faced by both students and lecturers in the success and effectiveness of online learning at AMU (**Table 1**).

The figure above categorizes the barriers to online learning at AMU into several groups: technological and infrastructure barriers, platform and content-related barriers, motivation, and interaction barriers, as well as additional challenges. Each barrier is accompanied by its Pearson correlation coefficient and corresponding p-value. (Recall that Pearson correlation coefficients range from −1 to +1, where +1 indicates a perfect positive correlation, −1 a perfect negative correlation, and 0 no correlation.)

5.1.1 Technological and infrastructure barriers

High cost of devices/equipment: with a correlation coefficient of 0.469 and a p-value of 0.000, this barrier shows a strong and statistically significant relationship with online learning difficulties. This suggests that students' inability to afford adequate devices significantly hampers their participation in digital learning.

Barriers to online learning	Correlation of Pearson	Significance (P-Value)
Lack of stable Internet connection	0.165	0.006
High cost of devices/equipment	0.469	0.000
High cost of the Internet subscription	0.159	0.008
Language barrier	0.011	0.434
Difficulties in navigating the platform (technical issues)	0.329	0.000
Inadequate or insufficient educational content	0.355	0.000
Lack of personal interest	0.468	0.000
Reluctance to digital learning	0.349	0.000
Lack of support or guidance from administrators/teachers/tutors	0.186	0.002
Low interaction with other learners	0.385	0.000
Lack of time to fully engage in e-learning	—	0.000
Problems related to the learning environment (distractions, inadequate space, etc.)	—	0.000

Table 1.
Inhibiting factors to online learning at AMU.

High cost of internet subscription and lack of stable internet connection: although these factors have lower correlation coefficients (0.159 and 0.165, respectively), they remain statistically significant ($p = 0.008$ and $p = 0.006$). Even moderate infrastructural challenges related to internet access can therefore negatively affect digital learning.

5.1.2 Platform and content-related barriers

Technical difficulties in navigating the platform: a correlation of 0.329 ($p = 0.000$) indicates that issues with platform navigation are a substantial barrier to effective online engagement. While inadequate or insufficient educational content: with a coefficient of 0.355 ($p = 0.000$), this barrier underlines the importance of quality content. When educational materials fail to meet learners' needs, the overall online learning experience can be significantly diminished.

5.1.3 Motivation and interaction barriers

Lack of personal interest and reluctance to digital learning: exhibiting correlation coefficients of 0.468 and 0.349, respectively (both with $p = 0.000$), these factors are among the strongest barriers. They suggest that a lack of engagement and resistance to digital learning critically impede students' progress. Low interaction with other learners has a coefficient of 0.385 ($p = 0.000$); this barrier highlights the importance of peer interaction; insufficient collaborative opportunities can reduce the effectiveness of digital learning platforms. Lack of support or guidance: a correlation of 0.186 ($p = 0.002$) indicates that limited support from administrators, teachers, or tutors is also a significant barrier, albeit to a lesser extent than the others. Support remains indispensable in guiding learners through the digital learning process.

5.1.4 Additional barriers

Lack of time to fully engage and issues with the learning environment: although specific correlation coefficients were not provided for these factors, their highly significant p-values ($p = 0.000$) suggest that external constraints such as time management and unsuitable learning spaces further complicate online learning. And language barrier, with an almost negligible correlation coefficient of 0.011 and a non-significant p-value ($p = 0.434$), language does not appear to be a barrier to digital learning at AMU.

In summary, the analysis demonstrates that technological and infrastructure constraints through the high cost of devices/equipment, motivational challenges through lack of personal interest, and low interaction with other learners are the most significant barriers to online learning at AMU.

6. Discussion

This section presents first the interpretation of the findings using the theoretical model, followed by the analysis of the causes of online learning barriers at AMU and the comparison of our findings with other studies from the literature.

The objective of this study was to analyze the challenges to the success and effectiveness of developing online learning at Abdou Moumouni University (AMU) in Niger Republic. The research aimed to uncover barriers faced by students and lecturers and evaluate their implications on the advancement of online learning at the institution. The analysis demonstrates that technological constraints through the high cost of devices/equipment and the motivational challenges through lack of personal interest and low interaction with other learners are the most significant barriers to online learning at AMU. Analyzing the causes of the current research results through utilizing the technology acceptance model (TAM) and its extended framework, along with the E-learning Readiness and Engagement Questionnaire (ELREQ). These frameworks, combined with the literature from Dillman et al. [15] tailored design method and Hung et al. [18], can help us understand the underlying factors contributing to the identified barriers.

The first result indicates that the high costs of devices and equipment are the most significant barriers to e-learning at AMU. This can be analyzed using TAM, ELREQ, and relevant literature:

6.1 TAM: Perceived ease of use (PEOU) and perceived usefulness (PU)

According to TAM, ease of use plays an indispensable role in the acceptance of technology. The high cost of devices/equipment affects learners' access to essential tools for e-learning. If learners are unable to afford or access the necessary technology, they experience difficulty in using the tools, making it harder for them to adopt and engage in online learning. This can lower the perceived ease of use of the online learning environment, thus inhibiting participation and learning success. The perceived usefulness of e-learning tools could also be compromised if learners face issues related to the quality or availability of the required equipment. If learners are unable to access devices that can adequately support the e-learning platform, they may feel that online learning is not valuable or effective for them. Thus, a high cost of devices leads to lower perceived usefulness, which hinders the adoption of e-learning.

6.2 E-learning readiness (ELREQ)

Technological readiness: based on Hung et al. [18], technological readiness is a key factor in e-learning success. The high cost of devices is a direct barrier to learners' technological readiness. If they cannot afford the required tools (such as computers, smartphones, or software), their readiness to engage with e-learning is severely limited.

Institutional readiness and support: institutional readiness plays an indispensable role in facilitating e-learning, as it includes infrastructure and technology investment. The absence of support from the university in providing affordable devices or subsidized access to technology results in inequitable access, thereby exacerbating the technological divide between learners who can afford devices and those who cannot.

6.3 Financial barriers

The financial constraints observed in the research could also stem from socio-economic factors such as learners from lower-income backgrounds struggling to access necessary devices for e-learning. Research consistently finds that access to technology in e-learning environments is a significant determinant of success [17, 18]. This can be linked to e-learning digital divides in developing countries, where affordability is a persistent barrier. This aligns with studies that show that affordable devices are foundational for the adoption and success of e-learning platforms [1]. Similarly, Kyaw et al. [19] explored the integration of e-libraries and e-textbooks in Myanmar's higher education system and found that the high cost of digital devices significantly restricts access. Similarly, Jain and Kaur [2] identified the limited availability of devices as a key obstacle to the use of online learning platforms. Beaunoyer et al. [20] further emphasized that socio-economic factors, such as the inability to afford electronics like computers or mobile phones, exacerbate disparities in accessing online education in resource-limited settings. These findings collectively underscore the critical role of the high costs of digital devices to ensure equitable access to e-learning platforms.

The second result highlights motivational challenges, including lack of personal interest and low interaction with peers, as significant barriers to e-learning at AMU. Analyzing these causes through TAM and ELREQ provides a deeper understanding of how motivation influences online learning.

6.4 TAM: Attitude toward technology use and engagement

For attitude toward technology use, TAM posits that individuals' attitudes toward using technology influence their actual use of technology. If learners do not find the e-learning system interesting or useful, they are unlikely to engage with the material. The lack of personal interest could be attributed to a low perceived usefulness (PU) of e-learning, especially if learners do not find the platform engaging or relevant to their learning goals.

As for the engagement and interaction, TAM's extended framework emphasizes the role of engagement and social interaction in technology acceptance. A lack of peer interaction and social presence in online learning environments could reduce learners' engagement, making it difficult for them to feel connected to the content or to their peers. This can lead to lower motivation, further contributing to the lack of personal interest and reduced interaction.

6.5 E-learning readiness and social presence

Social presence and learner engagement: According to Hung et al. [18], a key component of e-learning readiness is social presence, which refers to the degree to which learners feel connected to their instructors and peers in an online learning environment. Low interaction with other learners suggests weak social presence, which can decrease motivation and engagement. Without collaborative tools, discussion forums, or group projects, learners may feel isolated, which detracts from their overall learning experience.

Self-directed learning: e-learning often requires self-directed learning skills, which include self-regulation, motivation, and autonomy. Learners who lack personal interest or who struggle with self-motivation may find it difficult to engage with the content independently. This lack of engagement is a significant barrier to e-learning success, particularly when learners find e-learning devices/equipment very expensive and also if they are not provided with clear structures for peer collaboration. The key causes of the current research results can be attributed to technological constraints through the high cost of devices that leads to limited access to essential e-learning tools, which also decreases learners' perceived usefulness and ease of use of online learning platforms. This is a clear manifestation of accessibility issues and technological readiness barriers. The motivational challenges through lack of personal interest and low interaction with peers both stem from low perceived usefulness and engagement with online platforms, coupled with poor course design and limited social presence. Learners feel disconnected, leading to disengagement. These align with Sweeney [21], who explored the seven top challenges of online learning and found that lack of motivation is a common barrier that online learners face. Ref. [6] identified several barriers to online learning, including lack of motivation. Similarly, Yeh and Tsai [11] highlighted multiple obstacles in massive online teaching and learning, categorizing them into internal barriers (including teachers' and parents' beliefs). Perera and Nalin Abeysekera [12] further examined factors influencing students' willingness to engage in e-learning, identifying performance expectancy, social influence, effort expectancy, and service quality as key determinants of their perception and intention to adopt online education. Addressing these issues by implementing targeted financial support initiatives. For example, the university could introduce a subsidized loan program or grants to help learners purchase the necessary devices. Additionally, forming partnerships with technology companies to secure discounted equipment for students may further reduce this constraint. These measures would help ensure that financial limitations do not impede access to digital learning resources. The institution could also enhance collaborative learning by introducing interactive tools such as virtual breakout rooms, discussion forums, and group projects to foster peer-to-peer interaction or to organize regular virtual study groups or workshops that encourage learners to engage with one another. Providing personalized feedback and tailored learning pathways could help maintain individual interest, or offering mentorship programs or peer tutoring, where more experienced learners guide and support others, fostering a community atmosphere could substantially improve the digital learning experience.

7. Conclusion

The objective of this study was to uncover barriers faced by both learners and lecturers and evaluate their implications on the success and effectiveness of online learning at AMU. The findings revealed that technological constraints, particularly the high cost of devices/equipment, and the motivational challenges such as lack of personal interest and limited interaction with other learners are the most significant barriers to online learning at AMU. These results align with the context of the existing literature such as the theoretical and application value, supplement the research limitations, and the prospect of future research.

7.1 The theoretical value of the research

The theoretical value of this research is reflected in its extension of TAM to a new context, the integration of inhibiting factors with task-technology fit, and its contribution to broadening the scope of Technology Acceptance Research.

7.1.1 The extension of TAM in a new context

This study extends the technology acceptance model (TAM) and its extended framework to the context of AMU, contributing to the theoretical literature by validating TAM in a setting where both technological and motivational barriers are present. The findings, which emphasize the high cost of devices/equipment and motivational challenges such as lack of personal interest and limited peer interaction, provide empirical support for the idea that external factors can significantly influence core TAM constructs, including perceived ease of use (PEOU) and perceived usefulness (PU).

7.1.2 The integration of inhibiting factors with task-technology fit

The extended framework used in this study incorporates task-technology fit alongside TAM constructs, offering a deeper understanding of how infrastructural constraints and motivational challenges impact online learning. This integration helps refine theoretical models by demonstrating that barriers like high financial costs and poor learner engagement disrupt the alignment between digital tools and academic requirements, ultimately reducing overall system acceptance and performance outcomes.

7.1.3 Broadening the scope of technology acceptance research

This study broadens the scope of technology acceptance research by introducing motivational and interactional variables as key factors influencing digital learning success. It highlights that even if a technology is perceived as useful and easy to use, a lack of personal interest and limited peer interaction can hinder its effective adoption. This finding calls for future research to incorporate psychosocial and cultural dimensions as essential components of technology acceptance models.

7.2 The application value of the research

The application value of this research lies in its potential to inform policy and practice, while also providing insights for enhancing digital learning environments.

7.2.1 Informing policy and practice

The results provide clear evidence for educational institutions and policymakers that addressing technological constraints, specifically the high cost of devices and motivational barriers, is essential. Practical interventions might include establishing subsidized technology schemes, forging partnerships with device manufacturers for discounts, or implementing financial support programs to alleviate economic barriers. These steps can directly enhance learners' access to online learning platforms.

7.2.2 Enhancing digital learning environments

Recognizing motivational challenges as a major barrier suggests that online platforms need to be more engaging and interactive. Educational administrators can leverage these insights to redesign online curricula, incorporate collaborative tools, and foster virtual communities that stimulate peer interaction. By enhancing the social and interactive aspects of digital learning, institutions can improve perceived usefulness and ease of use, ultimately leading to higher adoption rates.

7.3 The research limitations

The research limitations include issues related to sampling and representativeness, reliance on quantitative methods, and the constraints of the instruments used in data collection.

7.3.1 Sampling and representativeness

Although the study employed a hybrid sampling approach using a census for faculty deans and simple random sampling for students and lecturers, the sample is restricted to Abdou Moumouni University (AMU). This context-specific sample may limit the generalizability of the findings to other universities or regions.

7.3.2 Reliance on quantitative methods

The exclusive use of quantitative methods (i.e., the ELREQ questionnaires and linear regression analysis via SPSS) may limit the depth of insights regarding the nuances of students' and lecturers' experiences. Qualitative data, such as in-depth interviews, focus groups, or class observation, might provide a richer context for interpreting the barriers identified by the technology acceptance model (TAM) and its extended framework.

7.3.3 Instrument limitations

While the ELREQ questionnaire was designed based on established literature from Refs. [1, 2, 4, 8, 10, 11, 14, 15, 18, 19], its adaptation to the local context of AMU might have introduced measurement limitations. The validity and reliability of the adapted instrument should be further scrutinized in future research.

7.4 Prospects for future research

The prospects for future research include exploring longitudinal and mixed-methods designs, expanding the study to other contexts, integrating additional theoretical constructs, and evaluating intervention strategies to further deepen the understanding of the factors influencing online learning success.

7.4.1 Longitudinal and mixed-methods designs

Future studies should consider employing longitudinal designs to track how inhibiting factors evolve over time, particularly as digital infrastructure and user competencies improve. Incorporating qualitative methods alongside quantitative surveys could provide a more comprehensive understanding of the underlying causes of technological and motivational barriers.

7.4.2 Expansion to other contexts

Extending research beyond AMU to include multiple universities or different geographical regions would enhance the external validity of the findings. Comparative studies could reveal whether the identified barriers are unique to AMU or are common across diverse educational settings, thereby enriching the theoretical scope of TAM in e-learning research.

7.4.3 Integration of additional theoretical constructs

Future research could expand the TAM framework by integrating additional constructs such as subjective norms, facilitating conditions, and user satisfaction. This integration might involve testing mediating or moderating variables that influence the relationship between inhibiting factors (e.g., high device costs and low motivation) and e-learning effectiveness.

7.4.4 Evaluation of intervention strategies

Building on the current findings, subsequent studies could investigate the efficacy of specific interventions designed to mitigate technological and motivational barriers. For instance, research could assess the impact of subsidized device programs, enhanced technical support, or initiatives to foster interactive learning environments on improving e-learning outcomes. By addressing these limitations and exploring the proposed research directions, future studies can further refine our understanding of the barriers to e-learning and enhance both the theoretical and practical applications of the technology acceptance model in the context of digital education.

Additional information

Author's ORCID verification code: https://orcid.org/0009-0008-3747-6199.

Author details

Daouda Yacouba[1*] and Nana Aicha Goza[2]

1 École Normale Supérieure (ENS) of Abdou Moumouni University of Niamey-Niger, Niamey, Niger

2 University Didactic and Pedagogy Centre (CDPU) at École Normale Supérieure (ENS) of Abdou Moumouni University, Niamey, Niger

*Address all correspondence to: bouweyyacouba@gmail.com

References

[1] Mahdavi, Ardestani SF, Adibi S, Golshan A, Sadeghian P. Factors influencing the effectiveness of e-learning in healthcare: A fuzzy ANP study. Healthcare. 2023;**11**(14) Article number 2035. DOI: 10.3390/healthcare11142035

[2] Jain S, Kaur G. Bridging the gap: The role of online learning platforms in enhancing rural education. ResearchGate. 2024. Available from: https://www.researchgate.net/publication/387603488_bridging_the_gap_the_role_of_online_learning_platforms_in_enhancing_rural_education

[3] Muhammad A, Kainat A. Learning amid the COVID-19 pandemic: Students' perspectives. Pakistan. Journal of Pedagogical Sociology and Psychology. 2020;**2**(1):45-52. DOI: 10.33902/JPSP.2020261309

[4] Galy KA, Coulibaly M. COVID-19 et les cours en ligne au Niger: enquête sur les causes de l'échec. Revue internationale des technologies en pédagogie universitaire. 2021;**18**(3):73-87. Available from: http://ritpu.org/ijthe.org. ISSN 1708-7570

[5] Moussa Mohamed Sagayar. L'enseignement à distance à l'Université au Niger: un processus en construction. Open Access Publications - Bibliothèque de l'Université de Genève Creative Commons Licence 4.0. vol. 10 n° 2 2020:252-267. DOI: 10.51186/journals/ed.2020.10-2. e349

[6] AU. 2024. Available from: https://www.athabascau.ca/news/university-news/student-life-and-support/barriers-to-online-learning-and-how-to-overcome-them.html [Accessed: June 1, 2025]

[7] Stevens Initiative. Findings from a survey of virtual exchange programs connecting young people in different countries in the world from fall 2022 through summer 2023; 2024

[8] National University. Challenges of distance learning for students [Internet]. Available from: https://www.nu.edu/blog/challenges-of-distance-learning-for-students/

[9] Agaissa Assagaye, Bouba Adamou. L'apport didactique des TIC à la continuité pédagogique lors de la COVID-19 en contexte nigérien Alternatives Éducatives, Innovations pédagogiques et Qualité de l'éducation du 13 au 14 Décembre 2021; 2023

[10] Hagley E, Green W. Helping teachers help their students participate in virtual exchange: The importance of teacher training. International Journal of TESOL Studies. 2022;**4**(3):94-110. DOI: 10.46451/ijts.2022.03.08

[11] Yeh C-Y, Tsai C-C. Massive Distance Education: Barriers and Challenges in Shifting to a Complete Online Learning Environment. Frontiers Psychology. 2022;**13**:1-8. DOI: 10.3389/fpsyg.2022.928717

[12] Perera and Nalin Abeysekera. Factors Affecting Learners' Perception of e-Learning during the COVID-19 Pandemic R.H.A.T. Nugegoda, Sri Lanka: Department of Marketing Management, Open University of Sri Lanka; 2022

[13] Basar ZM, Mansor AN, Jamaludin KA, Alias BS. The Effectiveness and Challenges of Online Learning for Secondary School Students—A Case Study. Bangi,

Selangor, Malaysia: Faculty of Education, Universiti Kebangsaan Malaysia; 2021. DOI: 10.24191/ajue.v17i3.14514

[14] Moorhouse BL, Wong KM. Blending asynchronous and synchronous digital technologies and instructional approaches to facilitate remote learning. Journal of Computers in Education. 2021;**9**:51-70. DOI: 10.1007/s40692-021-00195-8

[15] Dillman DA, Smyth JD, Christian LM. Internet, Phone, Mail, and Mixed- Mode Surveys: The Tailored Design Method. 4th ed. Hoboken, New Jersey, USA: John Wiley & Sons. Inc.; 2014. DOI: 10.1002/9781394260645

[16] Pregowska A, Masztalerz K, Olszewski R, et al. Adopting HyFlex in higher education in response to COVID-19. Open Learning: The Journal of Open, Distance and e-Learning. 2021;**36**(3):231-243

[17] Davis FD. A technology acceptance for empirically testing new end user information system: theory and results [doctoral dissertation]. Cambridge, MA: Sloan School of Management, Massachusetts Institute of technology; 1986

[18] Min-Ling Hung, Chien Chou, Chao-Hsiu Chen, Zang-Yuan Own. Learner readiness for online learning: Scale development and student perceptions. 2010. Available from: www.elsevier.com/locate/compedu. 10.1016/j.compedu.2010.05.004

[19] Kyaw KM, Mar S, Kyaw HWW, Dare R. Barriers and opportunities in adopting E-libraries and E-textbooks in Myanmar: A comprehensive survey of educational institutions. Asian Journal of Sociological Research. 2024;7(1):67-79. Available from: https://journalsociology.com/index.php/AJSR/article/view/111

[20] Beaunoyer E, Dupéré S, Guitton MJ. COVID-19 and digital inequalities: Reciprocal impacts and mitigation strategies. Computers in Human Behavior. 2020;**111**:106424. DOI: 10.1016/j.chb.2020.106424

[21] Aaron Sweeney. 7 Top Challenges of Online Learning for Students (and Solutions). 2024. Available from: https://ntinow.edu/7-top-challenges-of-online-learning-for-students-and-solutions/

Chapter 4

The Importance of e-Learning in Universities: Impact of e-Learning on Students of the Autonomous University of Tamaulipas, México

Arturo Amaya Amaya, Daniel Cantú Cervantes and Daniel García Mercado

Abstract

The Autonomous University of Tamaulipas has 25 years of experience in distance education models. This study aimed to identify the level of satisfaction in students subject to the virtual modality at the Autonomous University of Tamaulipas during the Covid-19 pandemic through the Scale of Satisfaction, Interaction, Self-sufficiency, and Self-regulated Learning in Online Courses. With a quantitative approach and a descriptive cross-sectional design with a correlational scope. The results showed that most of the students (stratified sample $n = 3604$, age $M = 20.49$, $SD \pm 0.552$, $min = 18$, $max = 28$) presented high levels of satisfaction in the online courses, and more than 80% of the participants expressed their willingness to continue studying under the virtual modality. The factors of self-efficacy in the use of the Internet and the interaction of the student-instructor showed positive and significant correlations ($p < 0.05$) concerning student satisfaction under the virtual modality; in addition, the older participants presented more satisfaction than the younger subjects. On the other hand, the gender of the participants, their employability status, and their age range do not show significant differences ($p > 0.05$) in the scores obtained.

Keywords: e-learning, virtual education, university, satisfaction, post-covid-19 education

1. Introduction

In 2020, the world underwent significant changes due to the pandemic caused by Severe Acute Respiratory Syndrome Coronavirus (SARS-CoV-2) [1]. This crisis led to the implementation of strict health protocols across all public and private agencies and organizations to protect personal health through physical isolation and protective measures. As a result, communication technologies gained prominence as essential tools for maintaining connectivity and continuity [2, 3]. These protocols transformed face-to-face social interactions into digital ones, particularly in universities, which adopted online education schemes [4, 5].

Amid the health crisis, Schianio et al. [4] highlighted that one of the key advantages of distance education is the curricular flexibility it provides to university students, many of whom balance their academic studies with part-time jobs to support their families or cover tuition and living expenses. Reimers [6] further noted that the combination of inflationary pressures and the health emergency has driven a growing number of higher education students to seek part-time employment to meet financial demands while pursuing their degrees.

A critical aspect of understanding the impact of online education on students during the Covid-19 pandemic is evaluating their perceptions and levels of satisfaction regarding essential components of interaction and pedagogical achievement in online learning [7, 8]. Identifying the factors contributing to university student satisfaction in online classes is vital for assessing the effectiveness of distance education and exploring the trends shaping a potential new academic normal. This insight will help tailor education systems to better meet the needs and interests of adult learners [9, 10].

To examine the factors influencing student satisfaction in virtual education, it is essential to focus on students as active participants in the educational process. This includes their interactions with course content, instructors, technology, and peers [11, 12]. Satisfaction can be defined as the fulfillment of a desire or need, making it a key predictor of students' willingness to repeat a positive educational experience [13, 14].

Analyzing satisfaction serves as a primary indicator for assessing the success of an educational program, especially one that considers students as its central focus [11, 15]. Student experiences often correlate with the perceived quality of a course and serve as valuable predictors for institutional evaluations [16, 17]. High levels of student satisfaction are associated with improved academic well-being, greater persistence, and higher rates of successful course completion. Understanding the benefits of student satisfaction in online learning environments will enable institutions to identify opportunities for improvement and develop targeted support strategies for students in virtual modalities [7, 18].

As mentioned, one of the key factors inherent in online educational practice is the interaction between students and teachers [17, 19]. This diverse interaction serves as a guide, enabling students to enhance their learning through clear and effective communication with their instructors. In this dynamic, the teacher's role shifts from merely transmitting content to acting as an attentive mentor who organizes and supports students' learning behaviors [20, 21].

An essential quality of an effective online teacher is their consistent availability, which fosters students' confidence in the course and their motivation to learn. Achieving this involves frequent and meaningful interactions between teachers and students, providing timely feedback, and conveying information through various channels [22, 23]. Building trust between students and instructors ensures that questions and answers flow freely in both directions. Timely interaction is crucial for maintaining effective communication between learners and educators in virtual environments [24, 25].

Another critical factor in online education is the interaction among students. While often facilitated by the teacher, peer-to-peer engagement is vital for fostering mutual feedback and co-evaluation [11, 26]. Classmates' comments and ideas reinforce each other's understanding, and respectful, open communication builds confidence, encouraging students to actively seek clarification. Various studies [27–29] indicate that greater trust and harmony within a student group lead to increased participation in discussions, enhancing collaborative learning experiences.

The relationship between students and course content represents another fundamental interaction in virtual education. Although this interaction is primarily one-way (student to content), effective segmentation of materials should facilitate an intuitive understanding of the subject matter. Well-designed content should guide students in analyzing and applying knowledge through clearly defined activities [30, 31]. Key indicators of successful student-content interaction include clear instructions, well-articulated evaluation criteria, the relevance of information, its connection to prior knowledge, and the accessibility of the materials. These indicators help students understand *what* to learn, *how* to learn it, and *why* it is essential [15, 32].

In virtual environments, self-efficacy in using technology emerges as another significant factor influencing student satisfaction. Students must possess basic digital literacy to navigate hardware, software, and online platforms effectively [33, 34]. This competency enables them to resolve common issues related to the use of information and communication technologies (ICT) [35]. While collective intelligence among teachers and students facilitates problem-solving, students' confidence in using digital tools independently is critical for their success in virtual education [35, 36].

Self-efficacy with technological tools not only promotes creativity and confidence but also equips students to complete tasks with ease in online courses. Achieving this requires intuitive resources and accessible training. The more familiar students are with the software and hardware used in their courses, the better they can work, research, and engage with the material [37]. Alongside technological self-efficacy is the equally important factor of self-regulation in learning. This involves students' awareness of their cognitive processes during learning, which allows them to prioritize class materials and stay focused despite emotional or environmental distractions [38, 39].

Self-regulation is built on understanding the importance of the content being learned, setting clear course goals, receiving formative feedback, and determining how to optimize learning strategies [40, 41]. These aspects are strongly supported by teacher guidance and peer feedback [42]. Online courses designed with a student-centered approach should emphasize self-regulation, as this autonomy enables learners to take greater responsibility for managing their education [43]. Self-regulation is crucial for academic success and student satisfaction, as it fosters the internalization of learning, which is the ultimate goal of education.

All these factors—interaction with teachers, peers, and content; technological self-efficacy; and self-regulation—are essential not only for predicting student satisfaction in online higher education but also for improving course quality and developing key learning skills [29, 44].

Various studies [11–13, 15, 16] have positively correlated online interaction with student satisfaction. Specifically, Bolliger and Martindale [11] identified that the instructor's role in fostering interactivity plays a crucial role in online student satisfaction. In their study, they surveyed over 500 online university students using a cross-sectional instrument designed to evaluate tele-courses. The evaluation focused on three key factors of interaction (measured through Likert-type items): student-instructor interaction, interaction with the technological environment, and course administration. Through correlational inferential analysis, Bolliger and Martindale [11] found that the teacher's performance as an instructor exhibited the strongest positive correlation with student satisfaction.

Similarly, Elshami et al. [45] reported that communicative interaction between teachers and students was the most significant factor influencing student satisfaction. Their study surveyed more than 300 online university students using a virtual education satisfaction questionnaire that assessed interactions between students and their instructors, the technology used, and the course's ease of navigation.

Self-efficacy with technological tools has also been identified as an important determinant of online university student satisfaction. For instance, Shyju et al. [46] emphasized the significance of proficiency in handling basic software and hardware in virtual courses. Kuo et al. [47] further reported that technological self-efficacy and student-teacher interactions were better predictors of student satisfaction than peer-to-peer interactions. In their study, 291 participants completed a questionnaire assessing technological self-efficacy, self-regulated learning, and interactions with instructors, content, and peers (measured through Likert-type items). ANOVA and Pearson correlation analyses revealed that teacher-student and student-content interactions showed stronger positive correlations with satisfaction than student-student interactions. While both technological self-efficacy and self-regulated learning were significant factors, self-efficacy demonstrated higher positive correlations with satisfaction.

Building on this, Kuo et al. [48] developed a comprehensive questionnaire to evaluate key interactions in virtual courses, including student-teacher, student-student, and student-content interactions, as well as technological self-efficacy, self-regulated learning, and the proclivity to continue in an online modality (Likert-type items). Pearson correlation analysis revealed that student-instructor and student-content interactions were the strongest predictors of satisfaction, with student-content interaction emerging as the most significant factor.

These findings align with Alqurashi [16], who identified student-content interaction as the factor most closely related to satisfaction in virtual higher education. Alqurashi's study involved 167 university students and used a 29-item Likert-scale questionnaire to assess interactions with content, instructors, and peers, as well as self-regulated learning. While this study did not include a dimension for proclivity to continue with online education, it found that student-content interaction was the most significant factor for satisfaction. Additionally, self-regulated learning recorded the highest average scores among participants.

Contrasting these findings, Chang and Smith [12] argued that interpersonal interactions—both student-teacher and student-student—were the most important predictors of satisfaction. Their study surveyed over 900 students using a questionnaire that assessed interactions with content, peers, instructors, and course technology. Correlation analysis revealed that personal interactions (student-teacher and student-student) were more strongly correlated with satisfaction than interactions with content or technology.

Similarly, another study [13] highlighted that course format and student-content interactions were less relevant to satisfaction than interpersonal interactions involving students and instructors. Lin et al. [49] further noted that while interpersonal interactions were important, only the student-teacher factor significantly impacted satisfaction, with student-student and student-content interactions being less relevant.

Most studies [11–13, 16, 21, 49, 50] have been cross-sectional and relied on validated instruments to measure student satisfaction in online contexts. However, not all included the factor of proclivity to continue with online courses, which is a crucial dimension for assessing whether students are likely to prefer virtual learning in the future. Although Rajeh et al. [50] incorporated a dimension for intention to continue, their instrument did not focus on interactions between key components of the online learning process. While satisfaction is a strong predictor of students' likelihood to continue with online education, explicitly addressing this dimension is vital for evaluating long-term preferences in a post-Covid-19 educational landscape.

Based on the reviewed literature, this study sought to address the following research question: What is the level of student satisfaction with the virtual modality at the Autonomous University of Tamaulipas during the Covid-19 pandemic?.

Accordingly, the objective of this study was to assess the level of satisfaction among students enrolled in virtual courses at the Autonomous University of Tamaulipas during the pandemic, using the Scale of Satisfaction, Interaction, Self-Efficacy, and Self-Regulated Learning in Virtual Courses developed by Kuo et al. [48].

2. Methods

We worked under a quantitative approach with a descriptive cross-sectional design and correlational scope due to the analytical approach and types of data used [51]. An ex post facto cross-sectional design was used since no variables were manipulated, and the data used was collected at a single time point [52]. This research was carried out during the third semester of 2021 at the Autonomous University of Tamaulipas, Mexico, during the Covid-19 pandemic. The viability of the study was made possible through surveys carried out through the Google Forms© platform, distributed to the participants through institutional mail [53]. The following hypotheses were established:

H1: "Interpersonal interactions (student-teacher, student-student) show significant correlations ($p < 0.05$) with student satisfaction in virtual courses".

H0: "Interpersonal interactions (student-teacher, student-student) do not show significant correlations ($p > 0.05$) with student satisfaction in virtual courses".

Ha1: "The interaction of the student with the professor and the self-efficacy in the use of the Internet show significant correlations ($p < 0.05$) with the student satisfaction in the virtual courses".

Ha2: "Self-efficacy and Internet use show significant correlations ($p < 0.05$) with student satisfaction in online courses."

H2: "The gender of the participants differs significantly ($p < 0.05$) between their results obtained."

H02: "The gender of the participants does not differ significantly ($p > 0.05$) between their results obtained."

H3: "Marital status and employability status lead to significant differences ($p < 0.05$) between the scores obtained by the participants."

H03: "Marital status and employability status do not lead to significant differences ($p > 0.05$) between the scores obtained by the participants."

H4: "Older participants show significant scores ($p < 0.05$) of greater satisfaction compared to younger participants."

H04: "Both the older and younger participants show significant scores ($p < 0.05$) of greater satisfaction."

Ha4: "Both the younger participants show significant scores ($p < 0.05$) of greater satisfaction compared to the older participants."

This research is focused on students enrolled in Facultad de Comercio y Administración Tampico (FCAV1), Facultad de Comercio y Administración Victoria (FCAV2), Facultad de Comercio, Administración y Ciencias Sociales Laredo (FCAV3), Facultad de Derecho y Ciencias Sociales Tampico (FADyCS1), Facultad de Derecho y Ciencias Sociales Victoria (FADyCS2), Facultad de Medicina Veterinaria y Zootecnia "Dr. Norberto Treviño Zapata" (FMVZ), Unidad Académica de Trabajo Social y Ciencias para el Desarrollo Humano (UAMTSC), Unidad Académica Multidisciplinaria de Ciencias, Educación y Humanidades (UAMCEH), Unidad Académica Multidisciplinaria Matamoros (UAMM), Unidad Académica Multidisciplinaria Reynosa Aztlán (UAMR1), Unidad Académica Multidisciplinaria Reynosa Rodhe (UAMR2) belonging to the Autonomous University of Tamaulipas during the fall of 2021.

The enrollment registered for each of the faculties (FCAV1 [N = 1654], FCAV2 [N = 1789], FCAV3 [N = 1256], FADyCS1 [1665], FADyCS2 [N = 1764], FMVZ [N = 808], UAMTSH [N = 1631], UAMCEH [N = 831], UAMM [N = 1466], UAMR1 [N = 1694], UAMR2 [N = 1626] and FI [N = 1101]) was 17,285 students, respectively. In that regard, the probabilistic sample (n) of the finite population (N) was stratified under the formula:

$$Z2Npq\ n = a\ E2(N-1) + Z2pq\ a$$

Where "n" makes up the sample size, "N" the population, "p" the probability in favor (50%), "q" the probability against (50%), "Z" the 95% confidence level, and "E" the acceptable error (0.05%) [54].

The complementary data of the affiliation profile are shown in **Table 1**. The research considerations on dealing with human beings established by the Code of Ethics of the Autonomous University of Tamaulipas [55] were followed, in addition to the privacy criteria of the information in studies on pedagogy proposed by Hall [56]. The Institutional Review Board (IRB) approval number assigned to this research is UAT-2021-2101-49 (internal record).

This research worked through the Scale of Satisfaction, Interaction, Self-sufficiency, and Self-regulated Learning in Virtual Courses validated by Kuo et al. [48] and developed from the Internet Self-Efficacy Scale by Eastin and LaRose [57] and the Learning Self-Regulation Questionnaire (MSLQ) by Pintrich, Smith, García, and McKeachie [58], in addition to the Scale of Satisfaction and Interaction in Virtual Environments by Kuo, Eastmond, Schroder, and Bennet [59]. The Scale of Satisfaction, Interaction, Self-sufficiency, and Self-regulated Learning in online courses by Kuo et al. [48] is made up of 43 Likert-type polytomous items with five response alternatives and distributed into six factors: Student-student interaction (SSI; reliability of Cronbach's alpha coefficient $\alpha = 0.93$), student-instructor interaction (SII, alpha coefficient of Cronbach $\alpha = 0.88$), student-content interaction (SCI, Cronbach's alpha coefficient $\alpha = 0.92$), self-efficacy in Internet use (SI, Cronbach's alpha coefficient $\alpha = 0.93$), self-regulated learning (SL, Cronbach's alpha coefficient $\alpha = 0.79$) and online course satisfaction (OS, Cronbach's alpha coefficient $\alpha = 0.93$). Items are rated on a 5-point scale ranging from 1 ("Never"), 2 ("Rarely"), 3 ("Occasionally"), 4 ("Often") to 5 ("Always"), except for frequency questions 1 and 8 of the AA factor, which were valued at 1 ("Always"), 2 ("Rarely"), 3 ("Occasionally"), 4 ("Often"), and 5 ("Always"). The factors of the Scale of Satisfaction, Interaction, Self-sufficiency, and Self-regulated Learning in Virtual

Gender	Min	Max	A	SD	n	%
Masculine					1782	49.4
Feminine					1822	50.6
General age range	18	28	20.49	± 0.552	3604	100.0
18 to 20 years	18	20	19.46	± 0.449	2570	71.3
21 to 25 years	21	25	22.61	± 0.481	882	24.5
25 years and older	26	28	26.59	± 0.494	151	4.2
Marital Status						
Single					2736	75.9
Married or domestic partners					844	23.4
Divorced, separated, or widowed					24	0.7
Work						
Work and study					1385	38.4
Unemployed					2219	61.6
Work Schedule						
Full-time					152	10.97
Half-time					1233	89.03
Previous experience in online courses					3604	100.0

It is considered from the percentage of participants who worked in parallel to their studies. Mn = minimum, Max = maximum, A = arithmetic average, SD = standard deviation, n = sample size, % = percentage. Source: Compiled by authors based on the results collected.

Table 1.
Participant filiation profile (N = 3604, SD ± 0.502).

Courses by Kuo et al. [48] allow us to measure the frequency of perceived acceptance and satisfaction about the interpersonal interaction between the key actors of the online courses (student-student and student-teacher), in addition to the student's interaction with the course materials. On the other hand, it makes it possible to understand the trust between the student and his skill regarding his self-sufficiency in the use and understanding of the Internet (based on online schooling) and his habits of control over the understanding of what he learns (self-regulation).

The items (n = 8) related to the SSI factor (α = 0.93) conform to (1) "In general, I had numerous interactions related to the content of the course with other students." (2) "I got a lot of feedback from my classmates." (3) "I communicated with my classmates about the content of the course through different electronic means, such as email, discussion forums, and instant messaging tools, among others." (4) "I answered questions from my colleagues through different electronic means, such as email, discussion forums, and instant messaging tools, among others." (5) "I shared my thoughts or ideas about lectures and their application with other students during this class." (6) "I comment on the thoughts and ideas of other students." (7) "Group activities during class allowed me to interact with my classmates"; and (8) "Class projects led to interactions with my classmates" [48].

On the other hand, the items (n = 6) linked to the SII actor (α = 0.88) are (1) "I had numerous interactions with the instructor during the class." (2) "I asked my questions to the instructor through different electronic means, such as email, discussion forums, instant messaging tools, among others." (3) "The instructor regularly posted some questions for the students to discuss in the discussion forum," (4) "The instructor answered my questions promptly," (5) "I responded to the instructor's messages," and (6) "I received enough feedback from my instructor when I needed it." Therefore, the items of the SCI factor (n = 4, α = 0.92) were (1) "The online course materials helped me to better understand the content of the class," (2) "The online course materials stimulated my interest in this course," (3) "The online course materials helped to relate my personal experience with new concepts or knowledge," and (4) "It was easy for me to access the course materials online." [48].

Furthermore, the items that made up the SI factor (n = 8, α = 0.93) were (1) "I understand the terms/words related to Internet hardware," (2) "I understand the terms/words related to Internet software," (3) "I can describe the functions of Internet hardware," (4) "I can troubleshoot Internet hardware," (5) "I can explain why a task will not run on the Internet," 6) "I can use the Internet to collect data," (7) "I can learn advanced skills within a specific Internet program," and (8) "I can go to an online discussion group when help is needed." [48].

Finally, the SL and OS factors were made up of the following items: (SL [n = 12, α = 0.79]) were (1) "During class time I often lose important points because I am thinking about other things," (2) "When I read for this course, I ask questions to help focus my reading," (3) "When I get confused about something I am reading for this class, I go back and try to understand it," (4) "If the course materials are difficult to understand, I change the way I read the material," (5) "Before I study new course material thoroughly, I often review it to see how it is organized," (6) "I ask myself questions to make sure I understand the material I have been studying in this class," (7) "I try to change the way I study to suit the course requirements and the instructor's teaching style," (8) "I often find that I have been reading for the class but I do not know what it is about," (9) "When I study, I try to think about the topic and decide what am I supposed to learn from it instead of just reading it," (10) "When I study for this course, I try to determine what concepts I do not understand well," (11) "When I study for this class, I set goals to direct my activities in each study phase," and (12) "If I get confused taking notes in class, I make sure to fix it later." SC (n = 5, α = 0.93): (1) "In general, I am satisfied with the online classes," (2) "This online course contributed to my educational development," (3) "This online course contributed to my professional development," (4) "I am satisfied with the level of interaction that happened in this online course," and (5) "In the future, I would be willing to take a completely online course again." [48].

The present investigation was carried out through three stages [60]. A previous background check on the background of the object of the problem and the key elements related to student satisfaction in virtual environments (stage 1). The Satisfaction, Interaction, Self-sufficiency, and Self-regulated Learning Scale was implemented in Virtual Courses by Kuo et al. [48] to 3604 student participants before authorization from the institutional authorities (stage 2). Due to face-to-face health restrictions due to Covid-19, the control of the instrument was limited, and the surveys were applied via institutional email through the Google Forms© tool.

The results were quantified (stage 3) in basic statistics (**Table 1**) using Microsoft Excel© software, which calculated the affiliation profile of the participants (n = 3604, SD ± 0.502), such as gender, age range, marital status, employability, working time, and previous experience with online courses. Next, the global scores (**Table 2**) of all the items of the Scale of Satisfaction, Interaction, Self-sufficiency, and Self-regulated Learning in Virtual Courses [48] were calculated with their respective statistics, such as the values of arithmetic average, standard deviations, minimum, maximum, and typical errors.

I.N	Key	N	Min	Max	A	DE	Err.T	Answers options									
								NV		RL		OC		OT		AW	
								Fr	%	Fr	%	Fr	%	Fr	%	Fr	%
1	SSI1	3604	1	5	4.45	1.005	0.017	48	1.3	179	5.0	156	4.3	815	22.6	2406	66.8
2	SSI2	3604	1	5	4.36	0.854	0.014	25	0.7	143	4.0	319	8.9	1141	31.7	1976	54.8
3	SSI3	3604	1	5	3.73	1.233	0.021	206	5.7	343	9.5	1084	30.1	544	15.1	1427	39.6
4	SSI4	3604	1	5	4.43	0.640	0.011	7	0.2	10	0.3	224	6.2	1555	43.1	1808	50.2
5	SSI5	3604	1	5	4.03	0.989	0.016	25	0.7	177	4.9	1024	28.4	807	22.4	1571	43.6
6	SSI6	3604	1	5	4.11	1.113	0.019	203	5.6	150	4.2	389	10.8	1176	32.6	1686	46.8
7	SSI7	3604	1	5	4.20	0.916	0.015	4	0.1	96	2.7	907	25.2	753	20.9	1844	51.2
8	SSI8	3604	1	5	4.26	0.869	0.014	9	0.2	143	4.0	535	14.8	1144	31.7	1773	49.2
9	SII1	3604	1	5	4.36	0.860	0.015	7	0.2	30	0.8	784	21.8	614	17.0	2169	60.2
10	SII2	3604	1	5	4.74	0.556	0.009	16	0.4	24	0.7	43	1.2	714	19.8	2807	77.9
11	SII3	3604	1	5	4.47	0.737	0.012	16	0.4	81	2.2	191	5.3	1238	34.4	2078	57.7
12	SII4	3604	1	5	4.36	0.805	0.013	23	0.6	77	2.1	380	10.5	1210	33.6	1914	53.1
13	SII5	3604	1	5	4.13	0.763	0.012	5	0.1	38	1.1	702	19.5	1597	44.3	1262	35.0
14	SII 6	3604	1	5	4.51	0.885	0.015	58	1.6	132	3.7	217	6.0	693	19.2	2504	69.5
15	SCI1	3604	1	5	3.96	0.806	0.103	28	0.8	15	0.4	1027	28.5	1527	42.4	1007	27.9
16	SCI2	3604	1	5	3.69	1.215	0.020	284	7.9	189	5.2	1121	31.1	778	21.6	1232	34.2
17	SCI3	3604	1	5	3.57	1.211	0.021	16	0.4	902	25.0	935	25.9	501	13.9	1250	34.7
18	SCI4	3604	1	5	4.55	0.709	0.012	2	0.1	9	0.2	420	11.7	760	21.2	2413	66.9
19	SI1	3604	1	5	4.67	0.614	0.010	8	0.2	13	0.4	193	5.4	733	20.3	2657	73.7
20	SI2	3604	1	5	4.80	0.466	0.008	9	0.2	10	0.3	21	0.6	627	17.4	2937	81.5

I.N	Key	N	Min	Max	A	DE	Err.T	Answers options									
								NV		RL		OC		OT		AW	
								Fr	%	Fr	%	Fr	%	Fr	%	Fr	%
21	SI3	3604	1	5	4.16	0.917	0.015	15	0.4	107	3.0	864	24.0	921	25.6	1697	47.1
22	SI4	3604	1	5	3.94	0.915	0.015	6	0.2	27	0.7	1510	41.9	701	19.4	1359	37.8
23	SI5	3604	1	5	3.87	0.914	0.015	14	0.4	70	1.9	1468	40.7	856	23.8	1196	33.2
24	SI6	3604	1	5	4.42	0.710	0.012	4	0.1	26	0.7	364	11.1	127	35.3	1937	53.7
25	SI7	3604	1	5	4.16	0.878	0.015	6	0.2	38	1.1	994	27.6	893	24.8	1673	46.4
26	SI8	3604	1	5	4.39	0.758	0.013	5	0.1	27	0.7	496	13.8	1113	30.9	1963	54.5
27	SL1	3604	1	5	3.87	0.873	0.015	994	27.6	1325	36.8	1135	31.5	135	3.7	15	0.4
28	SL2	3604	1	5	3.84	1.043	0.017	6	0.2	366	10.2	1169	32.4	732	20.3	1331	36.9
29	SL3	3604	1	5	4.09	0.971	0.016	19	0.5	237	6.6	726	20.1	1045	29.0	1577	43.8
30	SL4	3604	1	5	3.64	1.061	0.018	17	0.5	435	12.1	1508	41.8	520	14.4	1124	31.2
31	SL5	3604	1	5	3.58	1.137	0.019	65	1.8	704	19.5	915	25.4	929	25.8	991	27.5
32	SL6	3604	1	5	3.68	1.019	0.017	23	0.6	337	10.5	1363	37.8	808	22.4	1033	28.7
33	SL7	3604	1	5	3.88	0.980	0.016	14	0.4	272	7.5	1076	29.9	1016	28.2	1226	34.0
34	SL8	3604	1	5	3.58	1.044	0.017	910	25.2	829	23.0	1363	37.8	446	12.4	56	1.6
35	SL9	3604	1	5	3.87	0.960	0.016	27	0.7	133	3.7	1357	37.7	843	23.4	1244	34.5
36	SL10	3604	1	5	3.79	0.998	0.017	26	0.7	292	8.1	1224	34.0	943	26.2	1119	31.0
37	SL11	3604	1	5	3.61	0.956	0.016	34	0.9	209	5.8	1785	49.5	669	18.6	907	25.2
38	SL12	3604	1	5	3.72	1.063	0.018	76	2.1	389	10.8	1068	29.6	1018	28.2	1053	29.2
39	OS1	3604	1	5	4.71	0.603	0.010	2	0.1	4	0.1	264	7.3	481	13.3	2853	79.2
40	OS2	3604	1	5	4.23	0.971	0.015	18	0.5	288	8.0	408	11.3	1027	28.5	1863	51.7

I.N	Key	N	Min	Max	A	DE	Err.T	Answers options									
								NV		RL		OC		OT		AW	
								Fr	%	Fr	%	Fr	%	Fr	%	Fr	%
41	OS3	3604	1	5	4.25	0.747	0.012	5	0.1	8	0.2	611	17.0	1424	39.5	1556	43.2
42	OS4	3604	1	5	4.36	0.938	0.016	21	0.6	205	5.7	428	11.9	740	20.5	2210	61.3
43	OS5	3604	1	5	4.68	0.756	0.013	16	0.4	104	2.9	231	6.4	301	8.3	2952	81.9

I.N = item number, Key = factor nomenclature, SSI = student-student interaction, SII = student-instructor interaction, SCI = student-content interaction, SI = self-efficacy in internet use, SL = self-regulated learning, SO = satisfaction about the online course, N = population, Min = minimum, Max = maximum, A = arithmetic average, SD = standard deviation, Err. T = typical error, NV = never, RL = rarely, OC = occasionally, OT = often, AW = always, Fr = frequency, % = percentage. Source: Compiled by authors based on data collected from the Scale of Satisfaction, Interaction, Self-sufficiency, and Self-regulated Learning in Virtual Courses [48].

Table 2.
Basic statistics of the results of each item.

Equitable achievement levels were established for each factor of the instrument (**Table 3**), which were developed based on the range of the total score of each reagent, which had a maximum value of five points according to the intervals of response options (as it has been observed). The achievement levels were adapted into different categories: (1) Student-student interaction ("very low SSI" [R = 1–8], "low SSI" [R = 9–16], "regular SSI [R = 17–24], "high SSI" [R = 25–32], and "very high SSI" [R = 33–40]); (2) Student-instructor interaction (very low SII" [R = 1–6], "low SII" [R = 7–12], "regular SII [R = 13–18], "high SII" [R = 19–24], and "very high SII" [R = 25–30]); (3) Student-content interaction (SCI very low" [R = 1–4], "SCI low" [R = 5–8], "SCI fair [R = 9–12], "SCI high" [R = 13–16], and "very high SCI" [R = 17–20]); (4) Self-efficacy in internet use ("very low SI" [R = 1–8], "low SI" [R = 9–16], "regular SI [R = 17–24], "high SI" [R = 25–32], and "very high SI" [R = 33–40]); (5) Self-regulated learning ("SL very low" [R = 1–12], "SL low" [R = 13–24], "SL regular [R = 25–36], "SL high" [R = 37–48], and "SL very high" [R = 49–60]); (6) Satisfaction with the online course ("very low OS" [R = 1–5], "low OS" [R = 6–10], "regular OS [R = 11–15], "high OS" [R = 16–20], and "very high OS" [R = 21–25]).

Student-Student Interaction Factor (SSI)				
Achievement level	**Fr**	**%**	**% Valid**	**% Aggregated**
Student-student Interaction very low	0	0	0	0
Student-student Interaction low	0	0	0	0
Student-student Interaction regular	4	0.1	0.1	0.1
Student-student Interaction high	1193	33.1	33.1	33.2
Student-student Interaction very high	2407	66.8	66.8	100.0
Total	3604	100.0	100.0	
Student-Instructor Interaction Factor (SII)				
Student-instructor Interaction very low	0	0	0	0
Student-instructor Interaction low	0	0	0	0
Student-instructor Interaction regular	2	0.1	0.1	0.1
Student-instructor Interaction high	488	13.5	13.5	13.6
Student-instructor Interaction very high	3114	86.4	86.4	100.0
Total	3604	100.0	100.0	
Student-Content Interaction Factor (SCI)				
Student-content Interaction very low	0	0	0	0
Student-content Interaction low	2	0.1	0.1	0.1
Student-content Interaction regular	209	5.8	5.8	5.8
Student-content Interaction high	2039	56.5	56.5	62.3
Student-content Interaction very high	1354	37.6	37.6	100.0
Total	3604	100.0	100.0	
Self-efficiency of the student in the use of the Internet Factor (SI)				
Self-efficiency of the student in the use of the internet very low	0	0	0	0
Self-efficiency of the student in the use of the internet low	0	0	0	0

Student-Student Interaction Factor (SSI)				
Achievement level	**Fr**	**%**	**% Valid**	**% Aggregated**
Self-efficiency of the student in the use of the internet regular	0	0	0	0
Self-efficiency of the student in the use of the internet high	725	20.1	20.1	20.1
Self-efficiency of the student in the use of the internet very high	2879	79.9	79.9	100.0
Total	3604	100.0	100.0	
Self-regulated learning Factor (SL)				
Self-regulated learning very low	0	0	0	0
Self-regulated learning low	0	0	0	0
Self-regulated learning regular	19	0.5	0.5	0.5
Self-regulated learning high	2963	82.2	82.2	82.7
Self-regulated learning very high	622	17.3	17.3	100.0
Total	3604	100.0	100.0	
Online Course Satisfaction Factor (OS)				
Online Course Satisfaction very low	0	0	0	0
Online Course Satisfaction low	0	0	0	0
Online Course Satisfaction regular	6	0.2	0.2	0.2
Online Course Satisfaction high	627	17.4	17.4	17.6
Online Course Satisfaction very high	2971	82.4	82.4	100.0
Total	3604	100.0	100.0	

Fr = frequency, % = percentage, %Valid = valid percentage, Accumulated % = accumulated percentage. Source: Compiled by authors based on the data collected.

Table 3.
Achievement levels by factors.

The statistical software IBM SPSS© version 22 was used to perform the inferential analysis to identify the assumption of normality through the Kolmogorov-Smirnov test with bilateral asymptotic probability from the Lilliefors tables in each of the categories of the instrument, in addition to Levene's test for equality of variances. The significance value was adjusted to 0.05% [51]. If the normality criterion was met, a student's t-test was computed for independent samples to compare group scores by gender, marital status, employability status, and previous experience with online courses. In addition to this test, unidirectional ANOVA and univariate linear model analyses were performed with Scheffé's post hoc tests to find significant differences between the compared groups. In case of non-compliance with normality, the Mann-Whitney U test will be used.

Moreover, the linear relationship between quantitative variables of the analysis of covariance was calculated using Pearson's product-moment correlation coefficient (r) with post hoc tests using the partial squared eta coefficient to identify the effect size. For this analysis, the statistical program G*Power version 3.1.9.7 was used, which also calculated the size of the statistical power of the results [61]. Following Cohen [62] and Hopkins [63], a value less than 0.20 was estimated to reflect a trivial effect size, between 0.20 and 0.62 small, between 0.63 and 1.14 medium, between 1.15 and 1.99 large, and greater than or equal to 2 very great. On the other hand, as indicated by Cohen [62] and Hernández et al. [51], they interpreted that the absolute values of | r | <0.10 reflect a weak strength of association, between 0.10 and 0.25 small, between 0.26 and 0.49 medium, between 0.50 and 0.74 considerable, between 0.75 and 0.89 very strong, and ≥ 0.900 reflects unitary. After the analysis of the findings, they were contrasted with the previous evidence of primary literature, and the conclusions were presented in the manifestation of the fulfillment of the objectives and hypotheses raised.

The research considerations regarding the treatment of human subjects established by the Code of Ethics of the Autonomous University of Tamaulipas [55] were followed, as well as the information privacy criteria in pedagogy studies proposed by Hall [48]. All participants were informed about the purpose of the study, ensuring the confidentiality of the data for strictly academic purposes. All subjects expressed their willingness to provide information for the objectives of this research, with the option at any time to refrain from answering or withdraw from the survey, which was anonymous and did not collect any personal data such as first names, last names, phone numbers, email addresses, home addresses, or similar information.

3. Results

Table 1 shows the affiliation profile of the participants (N = 3604, SD ± 0.502), where 1782 men (49.4%) and 1822 women (50.6%) took part, all students enrolled in the Autonomous University of Tamaulipas, during the first half of 2021. All participants were of legal age.

Table 1 shows that the percentage of gender was equivalent and that more than 70% were students located in an age range of 18 to 20 years. A majority of the population was single, and more than 38% were employed at the time of data collection. From this percentage of the population, more than 80% worked part-time in parallel to their studies, and only a little more than 10% worked full-time. All participants agreed to have previous experience in online courses.

Table 2 shows the basic statistics of the global findings of the Scale of Satisfaction, Interaction, Self-sufficiency, and Self-regulated Learning in Virtual Courses [48].

In **Table 2**, more than 50% of the participants indicated response frequencies "Often" and "Always" for all the items of the factors SSI (student-student interaction), SII (student-instructor interaction), SCI (student-content interaction), SI (self-efficacy in Internet use), and OS (satisfaction with the online course), except for the SL factor (self-regulated learning). From these dimensions, the OS factor that showed the highest scores stands out. Outstanding in the "Always" option; in addition to the SII factor that, together with OS, showed arithmetic means above 4.0 in all its reagents. No item showed an absence of frequency in any of the intervals of the options, and no lost values were reported between the participant responses.

The levels of achievement reached by the participants in each of the factors were calculated.

As can be seen in **Table 3**, the "very high" category achievement levels reported the highest scores in each factor, highlighting the SSI, SII, SI, SL, and OS dimensions that did not indicate frequencies in the "very low" and "low" levels, except for the SCI factor, although none of the dimensions showed frequencies at the "very low" level. The self-efficacy factor SI was distinguished by the absence of frequency at the "very low," "low," and "regular" levels, and the satisfaction factor OS showed scores above 95% at the "very high" and "high" levels. This provides evidence indicating that the majority of students exhibited high levels of satisfaction with the online courses they undertook at the Autonomous University of Tamaulipas in 2021, during the COVID-19 pandemic. This finding addresses the research question: ¿What is the level of student satisfaction with the virtual modality at the Autonomous University of Tamaulipas during the COVID-19 pandemic?

To perform the inferential analysis, the Kolmogorov-Smirnov bilateral asymptotic significance test with Lilliefors correction showed a normal distribution fit in all the scale factors (IEE: $|Dmax| = 0.139$, $p > 0.05$; IEI: $|Dmax| = 0.154$, $p > 0.05$; IEC: Dmax$|$ = 0.110, $p > 0.05$; AI: $|Dmax| = 0.098$, $p > 0.05$; AA: $|Dmax| = 0.059$, $p > 0.05$; SC: $|Dmax| = 0.105$, $p > 0.05$), in addition to Levene's test ($p = 0.228$, $p > 0.05$) for equality of variances. What allowed the normality factor to compute the ANOVA analysis between the results obtained?

In this case, the student's t-test and one-way ANOVA showed that among men ($n = 1782$, $M = 33.55$, $SD \pm 2.629$) and women ($n = 1822$, $M = 33.49$, $SD \pm 2.762$) there were no significant differences with respect to the SSI Student-Student Interaction factor ($t = -0.426$, $P > 0.682$, $p > 0.05$, 95% CI [−0.218, 0.141]; ANOVA $F = 0.181$, $P = 0.670$, $p > 0.05$) in all participants, as well as for the other dimensions of SII Student-Instructor Interaction (men $M = 26.60$, $SD \pm 1.894$; women $M = 26.55$, $SD \pm 1.881$; $t = 0.768$, $P > 0.644$, $p > 0.05$, 95% CI [− 0.075, 0.172]; ANOVA $F = 0.589$, $P = 0.443$, $p > 0.05$), Student-Content Interaction (males $M = 15.81$, $SD \pm 2.036$; females $M = 15.64$, $SD \pm 2.046$; $t = 0.960$, $P > 0.337$, $p > 0.05$, 95% CI [−0.068, 0.199]; ANOVA $F = 0.922$, $P = 0.337$, $p > 0.05$), Student Self-Efficacy in Internet Use (males $M = 34.38$, $SD \pm 2.282$; females $M = 34.43$, $SD \pm 2.546$, $t = -0.616$, $P > 0.473$, $p > 0.05$, 95% CI [−0.203, 0.094], A NOVA $F = 0.514$, $P = 0.462$, $p > 0.05$), Self-Regulated Learning (males $M = 45.17$, $SD \pm 3.613$; women $M = 45.12$, $SD \pm 3.442$; $t = 0.419$, $P > 0.676$, $p > 0.05$, 95% CI [−0.181, 0.280]; ANOVA $F = 0.175$ $P = 0.676$, $p > 0.05$), Satisfaction with the online course (men $M = 22.27$, $SD \pm 1.840$; Women $M = 22.20$, $SD \pm 1.845$; $t = 0.676$, $P > 0.499$, $p > 0.05$, CI 95% [−0.079, 0.162]; ANOVA $F = 0.457$, $P = 0.499$, $p > 0.05$), which provided evidence to support.

H02 (The gender of the participants does not differ significantly ($p > 0.05$) among their results obtained).

The ANOVA test of the univariate linear model did not show significant differences ($p > 0.05$) between the three age groups (**Table 1**) in five factors (SSI, SII, SCI, SI, and SL) of the Scale of Satisfaction, Interaction, Self-sufficiency, and Self-regulated Learning in Virtual Courses [48]: (IEE [$F = 0.115$, $P = 0.995$, $p > 0.05$]; IEI [$F = 0.378$, $P = 0.685$, $p > 0.05$] IEC [$F = 0.756$, $P = 0.460$, $p > 0.05$], AI [$F = 0.646$, $P = 0.524$, $p > 0.05$], and AA [$F = 2.760$, $P = 0.062$, $p > 0.05$], except in the OS factor that did present significant differences ([$F = 3.052$, $P = 0.047$, $p > 0.05$, small effect size $\eta 2 = 0.41$, $1\text{-}\beta = .60$]) for which the Scheffé post hoc analysis was admitted for this factor, which revealed that older participants (over 25 years old) ($M = 23.68$, $SD \pm 1.760$) had significantly higher satisfaction with the online course ($P = 0.048$, $p < 0.05$) than younger students (18 to 20 years $M = 22.19$, $SD \pm 1.651$; 21 to 25 years $M = 22.23$, $SD \pm 1.823$) although, with a small effect size difference ($\eta 2 = 0.42$, $1\text{-}\beta = .80$), this provided evidence to support H4: The older participants show significant scores ($p < 0.05$) of greater satisfaction compared to younger participants.

On the other hand, marital status (**Table 1**) was not generally a differentiating aspect among the scores of the participants. The ANOVA test of the univariate linear model did not show significant differences between the three groups for each of the factors (SSI [$F = 0.042$, $P = 0.961$, $p > 0.05$]; SII [$F = 1.104$, $P = 0.332$, $p > 0.05$], SCI [$F = 0.378$, $P = 0.685$, $p > 0.05$], SI [$F = 0.141$, $P = 0.868$, $p > 0.05$],

SL [F = 1.823, P = 0.162, p > 0.05], and OS [F = 2.175, P = 0.114, p > 0.05]), so it did not admit post hoc analysis. Likewise, the employability status did not show significant differences (p > 0.05) between the groups of participants who worked parallel to their studies in part-time, full-time, or non-working modalities (SSI [F = 0.493, P = 0.611, p > 0.05]; SII [F = 1.143, P = 0.319, p > 0.05]; SCI [F = 0.522, P = 0.594, p > 0.05], SI [F = 0.805, P = 0.447, p > 0.05], SL [F = 1.924, P = 0.146, p > 0.05], and OS [F = 2.846, P = 0.053, p > 0.05]), so evidence is provided to support H03 (marital status and employability status do not lead to significant differences (p > 0.05) among scores obtained by the participants).

The correlations among the dimensions of the Scale of Satisfaction, Interaction, Self-sufficiency, and Self-regulated Learning in Virtual Courses [48] to determine the degree of relationship between these factors are presented below.

As can be seen in **Table 4**, all the factors show positive correlations with each other, although most of them are not significant (p > 0.05). However, the online

Factor	Statistics	SSI	SII	SCI	SI	SL	OS
SSI		-					
SII	*r*	.064	-				
	Sig.	.211					
	η2	.25					
	1-β	.98					
SCI	*r*	.058	.084	-			
	Sig.	.140	.223				
	η2	.24	.28				
	1-β	.98	.98				
SI	*r*	.080	.038	.113	-		
	Sig.	.181	.249	.059			
	η2	.28	.19	.34			
	1-β	.98	.96	.99			
SL	*r*	.056	.109	.068	.042	-	
	Sig.	.344	.072	.161	.229		
	η2	.22	.34	.26	.20		
	1-β	.98	.99	.98	.96		
OS	r	.115	.218*	.104	.361*	.098	-
	Sig.	.058	.042	.074	.028	.063	
	η2	.34	.41	.32	.60	.31	
	1-β	.99	1	.99	1	.98	

**p* < .05. *r* = *Pearson correlation coefficient, η2 = effect size times the squared eta coefficient (Cohen, 1992). 1-β = power test. IEI = student-instructor interaction, SII = student-content interaction, SI = self-efficacy in internet use, SL = self-regulated learning, OS = virtual course satisfaction. Source: Compiled by authors based on the results collected.*

Table 4.
Correlations between the factors of the Scale of Satisfaction, Interaction, Self-sufficiency, and Self-regulated Learning in Virtual Courses [48] (N = 3604, SD ± 0.502).

course satisfaction factor (OS) showed a medium and significant correlation ($p < 0.05$, with a small effect size $\eta 2 = .41$) with the student-instructor interaction factor (SII). This means that the interpersonal contact between the teacher and the student is a relevant aspect of their satisfaction with virtual courses. On the contrary, the link between the student-student interpersonal interaction (SSI) and the satisfaction factor (OS), although they presented positive relationships, was not significant ($p > 0.05$), nor was their correlation with the student-content interaction (SCI).

On the other hand, the OS factor presented a considerable and significant positive correlation ($p < 0.05$, median effect size $\eta 2 = .60$) with the student's self-sufficiency in the use of the Internet (SI). This means that the autonomy and self-sufficiency of the student on the Internet were the most important aspects among the participants for their satisfaction in the online course. These data provided evidence to support Ha1, which indicated that student interaction with the teacher and self-efficacy in Internet use show significant correlations ($p < 0.05$) with student satisfaction in virtual courses.

4. Discussion

The correlational findings of this study align with those reported by Bolliger and Martindale [11], Chejlyk [13], Chang and Smith [12], Lin et al. [49], and Elshami et al. [45], who identified student-instructor interaction as a key factor influencing university students' satisfaction in the virtual modality. Conversely, findings by Kuo et al. [47] and Shyju et al. [46] highlight self-efficacy in internet use as the most significant factor for student satisfaction. In this context, Eastin and LaRose [57] and Liang and Tsai [33] emphasize that proficiency in internet and software use for online courses positively affects satisfaction. They argue that a lack of digital competency can hinder effective participation, thereby reducing satisfaction.

Unlike Kuo et al. [48], who reported that both student-teacher and student-content interactions were the strongest predictors of satisfaction, this study found only the student-instructor interaction to be particularly significant. Consistent with Kuo et al. [48], however, this study also found that student-student interpersonal interactions did not significantly correlate with satisfaction in the virtual educational setting—results similar to those reported by Chejlyk [13] and Lin et al. [49].

Regarding gender, this study's results diverged from those of Alqurashi [11] by using equivalent gender samples but, like Elshami et al. [45], found no significant differences ($p > 0.05$) in satisfaction scores between male and female participants. These findings support the hypothesis H02. Additionally, no significant differences were observed between participants' marital status or employment status and their satisfaction scores, providing evidence to support hypothesis H03. This suggests that gender, marital status, and employability were not significant predictors of participant responses.

Other notable findings include that over 80% of participants expressed a willingness to take another course in the virtual modality. Furthermore, older students (aged 25 and above) demonstrated significantly higher satisfaction scores ($p < 0.05$) compared to younger students. Reimers [6] suggests that older students may exhibit greater motivation in their studies, as they are often employed concurrently with their education. However, in this study, no significant differences ($p > 0.05$) were seen between employed and unemployed students regarding their satisfaction levels. The following section presents the conclusions derived from this investigation.

5. Conclusion

This study aimed to identify the level of satisfaction in students subject to the virtual modality at the Autonomous University of Tamaulipas during the Covid-19 pandemic through the Scale of Satisfaction, Interaction, Self-sufficiency, and Self-regulated Learning in Online Courses. It is important to mention that the academic programs of the 3604 students who participated in the research were originally in-person; that is, their transition to virtual education was necessitated by the health conditions. From another perspective, this study contributes by demonstrating that students at the Autonomous University of Tamaulipas quickly adapted to the virtual modality, recognizing its benefits, ranging from the flexibility to study anywhere and at any time to developing digital communication and collaboration skills through digital platforms. In fact, most students reported high levels of satisfaction with the online courses they attended at UAT in 2021 during the Covid-19 pandemic. Additionally, more than 80% of the participating students expressed a willingness to continue studying in an online modality. These findings effectively answered the research question: ¿What is the level of student satisfaction with the virtual modality at the Autonomous University of Tamaulipas during the Covid-19 pandemic?.

The results highlighted that self-efficacy in internet use and student-instructor interaction were the most significant factors contributing to student satisfaction in the virtual modality. Furthermore, older participants demonstrated higher satisfaction levels than younger students, regardless of their employment status, alongside their education. However, no significant differences were found in satisfaction scores based on gender, employment status, or age range.

Within the study's limitations is the centrality of findings derived from a single public institution at a specific point in time, despite the large sample size employed. This may impede the generalization of the results, as the situation caused by COVID-19 has not officially concluded. Additionally, this study did not aim to correlate student satisfaction with physical or social factors, such as concerns about illness, family harmony, self-esteem levels, or participants' academic performance (grades).

To further deepen our understanding of these factors, future research should explore their correlation across diverse educational levels in both public and private institutions. Expanding this research scope could provide valuable insights into improving student satisfaction in online education, aiding the development of effective strategies to adapt to the evolving post-Covid educational landscape.

Author details

Arturo Amaya Amaya[1*], Daniel Cantú Cervantes[1] and Daniel García Mercado[2]

1 Autonomous University of Tamaulipas, México

2 Technological University of Matamoros, México

*Address all correspondence to: dcantu@docentes.uat.edu.mx

References

[1] Organización Mundial de la Salud. Brote de Enfermedad Por Coronavirus (Covid-19) [Coronavirus Disease Outbreak (Covid-19)]. Press Conference. Organización de las Naciones Unidas. NY: EE.UU; 2020

[2] Sánchez D, Morales H. Retos de la pedagogía en los tiempos de Covid-19 [Challenges of pedagogy in the times of Covid-19]. Archivos en Medicina Familiar. 2021;**23**(2):59-64

[3] López M, Ruiz P. Satisfacción con la Vida y su relación con la satisfacción académica durante el COVID-19 [Life satisfaction and its relationship with academic satisfaction during COVID-19]. Educación Social: Análisis y Reflexiones. 2023;**34**(3):50-65

[4] Schianio A, Biasutti M, Philippe R. Creative pedagogies in the time of pandemic. Music Education Research. 2021;**23**(2):167-178

[5] Arévalo M, Pérez J. Satisfacción académica y autoeficacia en estudiantes universitarios durante la pandemia [Academic satisfaction and self-efficacy in university students during the pandemic]. Revista de Educación y Aprendizaje. 2021;**33**(1):45-60

[6] Reimers F. Educación y COVID-19: Recuperarse de la Pandemia y Reconstruir Mejor [Education and Covid-19: Recovering from the Pandemic and Building Back Better]. Madrid: IBE; 2021. p. 20

[7] Salinas A, Morales J, Martínez P. Satisfacción del estudiante y calidad universitaria: un análisis exploratorio en la Unidad Académica Multidisciplinaria Agronomía y Ciencias de la Universidad Autónoma de Tamaulipas, México [Student satisfaction and university quality: An exploratory analysis in the Agronomy and Science Multidisciplinary Academic Unit of the Universidad Autónoma de Tamaulipas, Mexico]. Revista de Enseñanza Universitaria. 2008;**1**(31):39-55

[8] Castillo A, Medina R. La satisfacción académica en estudiantes de educación a distancia: Un estudio comparativo [Academic Satisfaction in Distance Education Students: A comparative study]. Dilemas Contemporáneos: Educación, Política y Valores. 2020;**8**(2):1-15

[9] González M, Pino M, Penado M. Estudio de la satisfacción percibida por los estudiantes de la UNED con su Vida universitaria [Study of satisfaction perceived by UNED students in their university life]. RIED. Iberoamerican Review of Digital Education. 2017;**20**(1):243-260

[10] Garbanzo S. Satisfacción estudiantil en la valoración de la calidad educativa: Un análisis en universidades latinoamericanas [Student satisfaction in the evaluation of educational quality: An analysis in Latin American universities]. Revista Latinoamericana de Educación Superior. 2021;**13**(2):25-40

[11] Bolliger D, Martindale T. Key factors for determining student satisfaction in online courses. International Journal on E-Learning. 2004;**3**(1):61-67

[12] Chang SH, Smith R. Effectiveness of personal interaction in a learner-centered paradigm distance education class based on student satisfaction. Journal of Research on Technology in Education. 2008;**40**(4):407-426

[13] Chejlyk S. The Effects of Online Course Format and Three Components of Student Perceived Interactions on Overall Course Satisfaction. Minneapolis: Cappella University; 2006. p. 64

[14] González L, Martínez F. Propiedades psicométricas de la escala de satisfacción académica en estudiantes universitarios españoles [Psychometric Properties of the Academic Satisfaction Scale in Spanish University Students]. Revista Internacional de Educación y Psicología. 2022;**69**(1):12-28

[15] Battalio J. Interaction online: A reevaluation. Quarterly Review of Distance Education. 2007;**8**(4):339-352

[16] Alqurashi E. Predicting student satisfaction and perceived learning within online learning environments. Distance Education. 2018;**40**(1): 133-148

[17] Martínez J, Torres C. Análisis de la satisfacción académica de los estudiantes de la Facultad de Administración y Contaduría [Analysis of academic satisfaction among students of the Faculty of Administration and Accounting]. Revista de Ciencias Administrativas. 2020;**15**(1):30-44

[18] Morales M. Estudio Descriptivo de la Calidad de Vida Laboral en Profesionistas de la contaduría de la Ciudad de Toluca [Descriptive Study of the Quality of Work Life of the Accounting Office of the City of Toluca]. Toluca: Universidad Autónoma del Estado de México; 2016. p. 84

[19] Barnard L, Paton V, Lan W. Online self-regulatory learning behaviors as a mediator in the relationship between online course perceptions with achievement. International Review of Research in Open & Distance Learning. 2008;**9**(2):1-11

[20] Palmer A, Koenig-Lewis N. The effects of pre-enrolment emotions and peer group interaction on students' satisfaction. Journal of Marketing Management. 2012;**27**(1):1208-1231

[21] Medrano J, Pérez A. Evaluación de la satisfacción académica en estudiantes universitarios: Un enfoque psicométrico [Evaluation of academic satisfaction in university students: A psychometric approach]. Psicología Educativa. 2019;**25**(4):200-215

[22] Liao PW, Hsieh JY. What influences internet-based learning? Social Behavior and Personality. 2011;**39**(7):887-896

[23] Silva-Ramos M, Tacca E. La relación entre autoeficacia y satisfacción académica en estudiantes online: Un estudio empírico [The relationship between self-efficacy and academic satisfaction in online students: An empirical study]. Revista Internacional de Educación a Distancia. 2021;**24**(2):75-89

[24] Reinhart J, Schneider P. Student satisfaction, self-efficacy, and the perception of the two-way audio/ video distance learning environment: A preliminary examination. Quarterly Review of Distance Education. 2001;**2**(4):357-365

[25] Zúñiga R, Castillo A. Satisfacción académica y su relación con el rendimiento académico en educación superior: Un estudio empírico en Chile y Perú [Academic satisfaction and its relationship with academic performance in higher education: An empirical study in Chile and Peru]. Revista Latinoamericana de Estudios Educativos. 2019;**12**(2):55-70

[26] Benítez C, López MA. Impacto del aprendizaje autorregulado en la satisfacción académica en cursos online:

Un estudio correlacional en estudiantes universitarios españoles [The impact of self-regulated learning on academic satisfaction in online courses: A correlational study in Spanish university students]. Revista Internacional de Educación a Distancia. 2021;**24**(1): 15-29

[27] Artino AR. Online military training: Using a social cognitive view of motivation and self-regulation to understand students' satisfaction, perceived learning, and choice. Quarterly Review of Distance Education. 2007;**8**(3):191-202

[28] Chu R, Tsai C. Self-directed learning readiness, internet self-efficacy and preferences towards constructivist internet-based learning environments among higher-aged adults. Journal of Computer Assisted Learning. 2009;**25**(1):489-501

[29] Peterson S. Self-Regulation and Online Course Satisfaction in High School. Los Angeles: University of Southern California; 2011. p. 48

[30] Moore M, Kearsley G. Distance Education: A Systems View. New York: Wadsworth; 1996

[31] González-Pérez E, Tello-Carrasco A. La influencia del diseño instruccional en la satisfacción académica de los estudiantes online [The influence of instructional design on academic satisfaction in online students]. Educación a Distancia: Investigación y Prácticas. 2022;**18**(3):30-47

[32] Anderson T. Modes of interaction in distance education: Recent developments and research questions. In: Moore MG, Anderson WG, editors. Handbook of Distance Education. Mahwah, NJ: Erlbaum; 2003. pp. 129-144

[33] Liang JC, Tsai CC. Internet self-efficacy and preferences toward constructivist internet-based learning environments: A study of pre-school teachers in Taiwan. Educational Technology & Society. 2008;**11**(1):226-237

[34] Jara LM. Calidad en educación virtual y satisfacción académica en los estudiantes de una universidad de Chiclayo [Quality in Virtual Education and Academic Satisfaction Among Students at a University in Chiclayo]. Perú: Universidad de Chiclayo; 2023

[35] Kaminski K, Switzer J, Gloeckner G. Workforce readiness: A study of university students' fluency with information technology. Computers & Education. 2009;**53**(2):228-233

[36] Manrique C, Sánchez A. La satisfacción estudiantil en la educación virtual [Student satisfaction in virtual education]. Revista de Educación a Distancia. 2022;**22**(1):1-15

[37] Alenezi A, Karim A, Veloo A. An empirical investigation into the role of enjoyment, computer anxiety, computer self-efficacy and internet experience in influencing the students' intention to use e-learning: A case study from Saudi Arabian government universities. The Turkish Online Journal of Educational Technology. 2010;**9**(4):22-34

[38] Moller L, Huett J. The Next Generation of Distance Education: Unconstrained Learning. New York: Springer; 2012. p. 64

[39] Morales J, Saldarriaga F. Satisfacción estudiantil en la educación virtual universitaria [Student satisfaction in Virtual University Education]. Producción Científica Luz. 2024;**14**(3): 45-60

[40] Schunk D. Self-regulated learning. Educational Psychologist. 2005;**40**(2):85-94

[41] Pérez R, González M. Educación virtual y satisfacción académica en estudiantes universitarios de Puno, Perú [Virtual Education and Academic Satisfaction in University Students From Puno, Peru]. Dialnet. 2025;**15**(1):25-40

[42] Artino A. Promoting academic motivation and self-regulation: Practical guidelines for online instructors. TechTrends. 2008;**52**(3):37-45

[43] McManus T. Individualizing instruction in a web-based hypermedia learning environment: Non-linearity, advance organizers, and self-regulated learners. Journal of Interactive Learning Research. 2000;**11**(3):219-251

[44] Hargis J. The self-regulated learner advantage: Learning science on the internet. Electronic Journal of Science Education. 2000;**4**(4):1-8

[45] Elshami W, Taha M, Abuzaid M, Saravanan C, Al Kawas S, Abdalla M. Satisfaction with online learning in the new normal: The perspective of students and faculty at medical and health sciences colleges. Medical Education Online. 2021;**26**(1):1920-1929

[46] Shyju P, Vinodan A, Sadekar P, Sethu M, Lama R. Determinants of online learning efficacy and satisfaction of tourism and hospitality management students during the COVID-19 pandemic. Journal of Teaching in Travel & Tourism. 2021;**21**(4):403-427

[47] Kuo Y, Walker A, Belland B, Schroder K. A predictive study of student satisfaction in online education programs. The International Review of Research in Open and Distance Learning. 2013;**14**(1):16-39

[48] Kuo Y, Walker A, Schroder K, Belland B. Interaction, internet self-efficacy, and self-regulated learning as predictors of student satisfaction in online education courses. The Internet and Higher Education. 2014;**20**(1):35-50

[49] Lin C, Zheng B, Zhang Y. Interaction, Satisfaction, and Perceived Progress in Online Language Courses. Las Vegas: Association for the Advancement of Computing in Education (AACE); 2015

[50] Rajeh M, Abduljabbar F, Alqahtani S, Waly F. Students' satisfaction and continued intention toward e-learning: A theory-based study. Medical Education Online. 2021;**26**(1):2-6

[51] Hernández R, Fernández C, Baptista M. Metodología de la investigación [Investigation methodology]. 6th ed. México: McGraw Hill; 2014. p. 534

[52] Vega C. Papel de trabajo, Aspectos epistemológicos de la estimación estadística de modelos: Investigación Ex-post-Facto [Working paper, epistemological aspects of the statistical estimation of models: Ex-post-facto research]. Carabobo: Instituto de Matemática y Cálculo Aplicado; 2015. p. 4

[53] Balderas J, Roque R, López A, Salazar R, Juárez C. ¿Cómo cambió la enseñanza-aprendizaje de las asignaturas prácticas en el área de tecnologías de la información con la COVID-19? [How did teaching-learning change in the area of information technology with COVID-19?]. RIDE. Iberoamerican Journal for Educational Research and Development. 2021;**11**(22):e116. DOI: 10.23913/ride.v11i22.826

[54] Levine D, Krehbiel T, Berenson M. Estadística [Statistics]. México: Pearson; 2006. p. 68

[55] Universidad Autónoma de Tamaulipas. Código ética en la investigación [Code of Ethics in Research]. Victoria: Universidad Autónoma de Tamaulipas; 2018. p. 44

[56] Hall R. Ética de la investigación Social [Ethics of social research]. Querétaro: Universidad Autónoma de Querétaro; 2016. p. 54

[57] Eastin MS, LaRose R. Internet self-efficacy and the psychology of the digital divide. Journal of Computer Mediated Communication. 2000;**6**(1):611-618

[58] Pintrich PR, Smith DA, Garcia T, McKeachie WJ. Reliability and predictive validity of the motivated strategies for learning questionnaire (MSLQ). Educational and Psychological Measurement. 1993;**53**(3):801-813

[59] Kuo Y, Eastmond J, Schroder K, Bennett LJ. Student Perceptions of Interactions and Course Satisfaction in a Blended Learning Environment. Jackson: Jackson State University; 2009. p. 15

[60] Pérez Z. Los diseños de método mixto en la investigación en educación: Una experiencia concreta [Mixed method designs in education research: A concrete experience]. Revista de Electrónica Educare. 2011;**15**(1):15-29

[61] Cárdenas M, Arancibia H. Statistical power and effect size calculating in G*power: Complementary analysis of statistical significance testing and its application in psychology. Salud & Sociedad. 2014;**5**(2):210-224

[62] Cohen J. Statistical Power Analysis for the Behavioral Sciences. 2nd ed. Hillsdale: Lawrence Erlbaum Associates; 1988. p. 14

[63] Hopkins W. A Scale of Magnitudes for Effect Statistics. Auckland: Auckland University; 2006. p. 13

Chapter 5

Virtual Reality in Vocational Education: Integrating Technology to Strengthen Student Character

Hendra Jaya, Badaruddin Anwar, Rina Febriana, Sapto Haryoko and Sutarsi Suhaeb

Abstract

Virtual reality (VR) offers transformative potential in vocational education by bridging gaps in technical skill development and character building. This chapter explores the integration of VR technology to enhance vocational education outcomes through immersive simulations. These simulations provide students with realistic environments for practicing technical skills, such as machinery operation or engineering tasks, in a safe, interactive, and cost-effective manner. Beyond technical proficiency, VR also plays a pivotal role in fostering character traits like responsibility, teamwork, and ethical decision-making through tailored scenarios. The discussion highlights the dual benefits of VR in addressing industry demands for skilled professionals while instilling values crucial for workplace success. By leveraging VR, educators can create engaging, adaptive, and inclusive learning experiences that prepare students for future challenges. The study concludes that integrating VR into vocational education is not only an innovative pedagogical approach but also a strategic step toward producing well-rounded graduates with strong technical capabilities and moral integrity.

Keywords: virtual reality, vocational education, immersive learning, character building, technical skill development

1. Introduction

Immersive technology offers an extraordinary experience for its users, making them feel as if they are truly present in a virtual environment [1]. With its ability to create highly realistic simulations, this innovation allows individuals to interact directly with objects and scenarios within the virtual world [2]. In the field of education, this approach introduces a fresh perspective, offering a new way of learning—one that is more engaging, dynamic, and emphasizes real-life experiences through profound visualizations [3]. For educators, this technology serves as a bridge to deliver learning in a more relevant and meaningful way, even in situations that are challenging to replicate in traditional classrooms [4]. Moreover, this innovation creates significant opportunities to overcome various limitations, such as access to physical facilities or real-life scenarios that are difficult to bring into a learning environment [5].

In vocational education, such as in Vocational High Schools (SMK), virtual reality technology holds great potential in enhancing students' competencies in practical skills [6]. Vocational education, which often relies on hands-on learning, requires an approach that can provide realistic simulations without high risks or significant costs [7]. Through this technology, students can practice technical skills in a digital environment, such as repairing machinery, operating heavy equipment, or performing medical procedures, without the risk of accidents or equipment damage [8]. Moreover, the integration of virtual simulations also allows students to learn in a more adaptive and independent way, where they can repeat practices until they fully understand each step of the process [9].

Beyond focusing on the development of technical skills, the integration of VR in vocational education also plays a crucial role in shaping students' character [10]. Through interactive and participatory learning experiences, students are encouraged to develop a sense of responsibility, discipline, and teamwork [11]. VR-based simulations can be designed to train ethical decision-making, conflict management, and leadership, all of which are important aspects of the workplace [6]. Therefore, VR not only serves as a learning tool but also as a medium for instilling character values that are relevant to the needs of both industry and modern society [12]. This makes VR an innovative solution for building a generation that is both skilled and strong in character [7].

This study employs both qualitative and quantitative methods to explore the integration of Virtual reality (VR) technology in vocational education, particularly in developing students' character and enhancing their technical competencies. The qualitative approach involves in-depth interviews with educators and students in vocational schools to understand their experiences in using VR for learning. Additionally, direct observations are conducted on the use of VR in learning activities, including students' interactions with VR-based work simulations. The quantitative approach is applied through educational experiments using pre-test and post-test methods to measure the effectiveness of VR technology in improving concept comprehension, technical skills, and character development. Quantitative data are collected through questionnaires and statistical analysis to identify skill improvements and character values developed during VR-based learning. This study also adopts a case study design in several Vocational High Schools and vocational education institutions that have implemented VR technology. The collected data are analyzed using thematic analysis techniques to uncover key patterns related to VR's impact on character education, while the quantitative results are tested with descriptive and inferential statistical analysis.

2. Increase learning interest and concept understanding

The use of Virtual Reality (VR) in education has become one of the technological innovations that play a crucial role in increasing student engagement [13]. VR technology shows great potential in enriching learning experiences and enhancing educational outcomes across various educational contexts. As an innovation, VR enables the creation of immersive and interactive learning experiences, helping

DOI: http://dx.doi.org/10.5772/intechopen.1010718

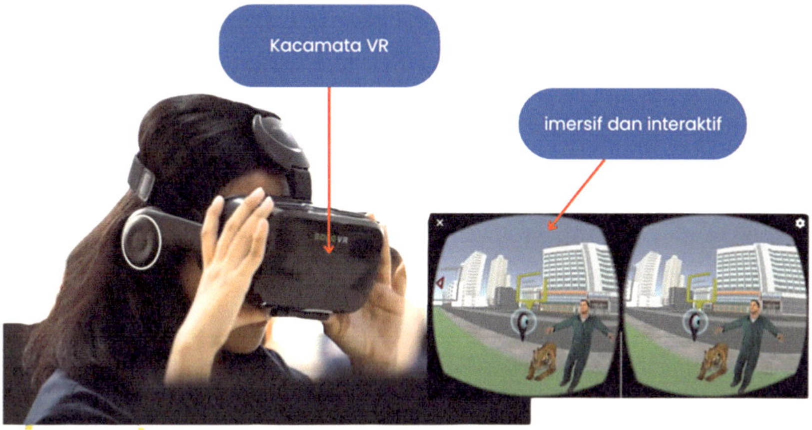

Figure 1.
VR that can create immersive and interactive learning experiences.

students grasp abstract concepts in a more tangible and understandable way [13]. **Figure 1** illustrates a student using a VR device that enables immersive and interactive learning experiences. The image also shows a virtual city environment, providing a realistic representation to help students better understand abstract concepts in a concrete manner.

This technology has become one of the most significant breakthroughs in modern education. It offers a range of benefits that not only simplify but also enrich the way students learn [13]. With its ability to create realistic 3D simulations, VR takes the learning experience to an entirely new level, making it more engaging and enjoyable [14]. **Figure 2** illustrates a virtual laboratory environment where VR creates realistic 3D simulations for practical learning using VR Box Video 360 3D. The image demonstrates a simulation of an AND-gate circuit, enabling students to interactively explore

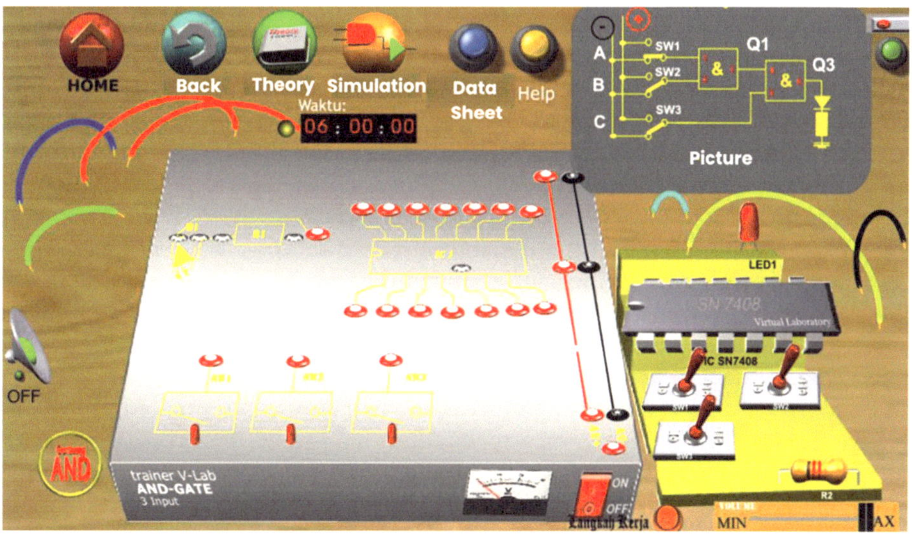

Figure 2.
VR creates realistic 3D simulations in Practicum.

and understand the functionality of electronic components in a highly visual and engaging manner.

One of the primary advantages of VR is its ability to enhance students' interest in learning. When education becomes more immersive, students feel directly connected to the material they are studying. Moreover, VR significantly boosts students' motivation to actively engage in the learning process. They no longer remain passive listeners but transform into active and enthusiastic participants in every learning session [15].

This technology paves the way for more dynamic and meaningful teaching experiences. For instance, through VR, students can explore environments they could previously only imagine, such as walking on the surface of Mars, gaining a deep understanding of human anatomy, or visiting historical sites that are otherwise hard to access. These capabilities not only broaden their horizons but also provide enjoyable and unforgettable learning experiences. With such immense potential, VR is not merely a tool but an innovative solution that can transform the paradigm of education to be more relevant and adaptive [14]. This technology invites educators to keep experimenting, fostering learning experiences that are inspiring, interactive, and beneficial for future generations [15].

One of the key advantages of Virtual reality (VR) is its ability to facilitate active learning. Through immersive simulations, students can "experience" concepts firsthand, allowing them to gain a deeper understanding of the material while strengthening their memory retention. For example, students can study human anatomy by exploring detailed structures of organs or visit historical sites as if they were physically present. Moreover, VR opens doors to environments that are otherwise hard to reach. This technology enables students to explore other planets, dive into the complexities of modern technology, or practice in fields requiring safe simulation, such as medicine and engineering. All of these can be achieved without real-world risks, providing students with the opportunity to experiment and learn through experience.

The ability of VR to tailor learning experiences to individual needs makes it a highly personal and flexible tool. In a virtual environment, students can learn at their own pace and in their preferred style. Moreover, VR supports cross-location collaboration, creating interactive shared learning spaces without geographical limitations. This is particularly relevant for fostering communication and cooperation among individuals in an increasingly connected world. However, the implementation of VR in education also faces challenges. The high cost of devices, limited availability of relevant educational content, and the need to adapt curricula pose significant hurdles. Additionally, technical issues such as infrastructure and technological support require careful attention. Even so, these challenges should not deter us from harnessing VR's immense potential to create enhanced learning experiences.

In its application, VR has the potential to enrich education across various fields. This technology significantly impacts learning in STEM, vocational training, language acquisition, as well as the exploration of history and geography. Moreover, VR contributes to inclusive education by supporting students with special needs through interactive and adaptive approaches. With proper integration, VR has the power to transform the teaching and learning process, making it more relevant, engaging, and effective. This technology paves the way for education to advance, creating immersive, meaningful, and joyful learning experiences. Ultimately, VR becomes more than just a tool; it serves as a partner in shaping a generation better equipped to face the challenges of the future.

Figure 3 is a chart illustrating hypothetical research findings on the impact of Virtual Reality (VR) technology in education. The graph highlights improvements in

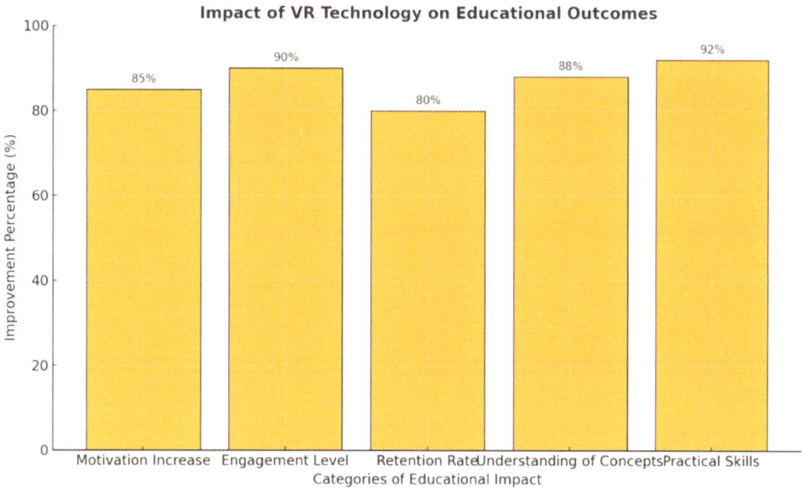

Figure 3.
Percentage Increase in Learning Outcomes Based on the Impact Categories of VR Usage.

motivation, engagement levels, material retention, conceptual understanding, and practical skills among students who use VR as a learning medium.

This study combines qualitative and quantitative approaches to understand how Virtual Reality (VR) can enhance learning in vocational schools. A total of 100 students from various technical disciplines were carefully selected using purposive sampling to ensure a diverse representation. In data collection, in-depth interviews were conducted with educators and students to explore their experiences in using VR, while direct observations provided insights into how they interacted within simulations. Additionally, pre-tests and post-tests were administered to measure improvements in technical skills and character development, supplemented by surveys capturing students' perceptions of VR's effectiveness in learning.

Over 8 weeks, students participated in VR-based training modules, starting with a pre-test to assess their initial competencies and concluding with a post-test to determine the extent of their progress. To gain deeper insights into the results, statistical analyses such as paired t-tests and ANOVA were used to examine differences before and after VR implementation. Meanwhile, a thematic approach in qualitative analysis helped uncover patterns in students' experiences and impressions throughout their journey with this technology. By integrating both numerical data and real-life narratives, this study not only presents statistical findings but also provides a comprehensive picture of how VR shapes students' learning and development. Based on the results of the One-Way ANOVA analysis of post-test scores across three skill categories—technical skills, teamwork and collaboration, and ethical decision-making. With a total of 100 respondents, an F-statistic value of 5.0621 and a p-value of 0.0069 were obtained. Using a significance level of 0.05, the p-value being less than 0.05 indicates that the results are statistically significant. These findings suggest that there is a meaningful difference in the average post-test scores among the three skill categories analyzed (**Table 1**). This means that one or more of the skill categories demonstrated a significant difference in learning outcomes after the training or intervention was provided.

Table 1 presents a comparative analysis of the pre-test and post-test results, highlighting improvements in technical skills and character development among students.

Metric	Pre-test Score	Post-test Score	Improvement (%)
Technical skills	62.5	85.3	36.5%
Teamwork and collaboration	58.2	81.7	40.4%
Ethical decision-making	60.1	83.2	38.4%

Table 1.
Comparison of pre-test and post-test scores across various skills.

These results indicate a significant improvement in both technical skills and soft skills after students were exposed to the VR-based learning modules.

In the ever-evolving field of education, Virtual Reality (VR) technology emerges as an innovation that elevates learning experiences to a higher level. Research has proven that the implementation of VR-based learning significantly enhances students' motivation and academic performance compared to conventional teaching methods [16]. In Indonesia, the use of Virtual Reality (VR) technology in educational research involving students must comply with ethical research standards set by the government and relevant institutions. This technology offers a more engaging and interactive approach, surpassing the limitations of traditional methods, which often fail to deeply involve students.

In vocational education, particularly in the field of automotive technology, VR offers significant opportunities through realistic simulations. For instance, students can learn to disassemble and reassemble an engine virtually, without the need for a physical machine. This process allows them to clearly observe how each engine component operates and interacts within a system. Such simulations not only enhance students' understanding but also provide a safe and efficient practical experience.

Another advantage of VR technology lies in its immersive nature. The learning environments created through VR can transport students into interactive and engaging worlds. This is particularly beneficial for visualizing complex concepts that were previously difficult to grasp using traditional teaching methods [17]. Moreover, VR has been proven to enhance conceptual understanding, train critical thinking skills, and foster students' creativity in tackling learning challenges [18].

However, like any other new technology, implementing VR in education requires careful planning. Teacher training is crucial to ensure the successful integration of this technology into the learning process. Additionally, there are technical and ethical challenges that must be addressed, such as the availability of devices, accessibility, and the impact on students' social interactions [17, 18].

Ultimately, Virtual reality technology offers immense opportunities to create deeper, more interactive, and relevant learning experiences across various subjects. By utilizing VR thoughtfully and strategically, education can progress, shaping a generation better prepared to navigate the complexities of the modern world. As educators and education practitioners, now is the time to step into a new, more innovative era where technology serves as a partner in fostering meaningful learning experiences.

The use of VR allows students to learn through a highly detailed and interactive visual approach [7]. This experience enables students to not only gain theoretical understanding but also acquire practical experiences that closely resemble real-world scenarios [6]. This approach significantly helps students grasp complex concepts more easily [12] Moreover, VR provides students with the opportunity to learn without the fear of making major mistakes, as all simulations are conducted within a safe virtual environment [10].

The engaging learning experience offered by VR fosters a higher level of interest among students [10]. This interest serves as a crucial foundation for developing positive character traits such as perseverance, curiosity, and problem-solving skills [12]. Students' perseverance in completing challenging virtual tasks and their curiosity to explore further can positively impact their learning outcomes [6]. Therefore, integrating VR technology in education, particularly in vocational fields, not only enhances students' understanding but also supports the development of strong character traits that align with the demands of the future workforce [7].

3. Practical skills and soft skills development

In addition to providing a profound theoretical understanding, virtual reality (VR) technology supports the development of practical skills that are highly essential for vocational high school (SMK) students [19]. Through VR-based learning, students can practice and refine their skills in a virtual environment designed to replicate real-world conditions [20]. This approach allows students to engage in active learning and participate directly in simulations relevant to their areas of expertise, without requiring complex physical facilities or incurring high operational costs [21].

Learning through virtual reality (VR) also strengthens students' character development, including empathy and care, particularly through virtual interactions that enable a deeper understanding of patients' needs. Studies have shown that VR-based approaches in nursing education can enhance students' empathy by simulating patient experiences. For instance, Dean et al. [22] highlight that VR can teach sensitivity to patients' unique needs while stimulating curiosity [22]. Additionally, research by Liu et al. [23] reports a significant increase in empathy scores among nursing students after using VR simulations to understand the conditions of patients with cognitive impairments [23]. In the context of nursing education, Collier et al. [24] found that VR-based simulations enable students to adopt patients' perspectives, positively influencing their understanding of patients' emotional experiences [24]. However, as Dean et al. [22] emphasize, it is crucial to integrate VR-based learning with direct guidance from experienced mentors, as profound empathy is often more effectively developed through interpersonal and contextual interactions.

This experience not only helps students understand patients' emotional needs but also enhances their confidence in providing care. As highlighted by Kim and Chun [25], participation in virtual reality (VR)-based learning programs significantly improves clinical skills [25]. In conclusion, VR learning is not just a technical tool for skill acquisition; it is also an effective platform for fostering students' character and empathy, which are critical in service-oriented professions.

Virtual reality technology offers students the opportunity to make mistakes in a controlled environment, which is a crucial element of learning. According to Dean et al. [22], immersive technology-based simulations create a safe space where students can practice without the real-world consequences of errors, allowing them to try various approaches to problem-solving [22]. This is supported by Liu et al. [23], who observed that such simulation experiences boost students' confidence, as they can experiment and learn from their mistakes without facing tangible repercussions [23].

The ability also enhances problem-solving skills, which are essential in the workplace. In a study conducted by Collier et al. [24], students reported that they were able to develop new approaches to solving problems after using VR technology, as they were encouraged to reflect on their mistakes and seek better solutions with guidance from instructors [24]. This process also fosters deep reflection, as reported by Kim and Chun [25], who found that students using VR simulations gained a better understanding of their weaknesses, enabling them to progressively improve their skills [25].

The integration of virtual reality (VR) in vocational education offers numerous benefits for both technical skills and character development. VR simulations provide immersive and interactive learning experiences that enhance student engagement, motivation, and critical thinking skills [18]. In vocational high schools, virtual laboratories can improve students' cognitive and psychomotor competencies while facilitating character education without time and place constraints [26]. The integration of character education in vocational programs aims to develop both hard and soft skills, preparing students to meet industry demands through innovative teaching strategies and extracurricular activities [27]. Students generally perceive VR positively in laboratory practice, finding it more engaging and effective than conventional methods, despite some technical challenges [28]. Overall, VR technology in vocational education supports student success by providing relevant industry knowledge, fostering ethical and professional values, and preparing them for increasingly complex work environments.

The integration of immersive simulation technology into vocational education offers significant benefits in both technical aspects and the development of students' character. According to Liu et al. [23], virtual reality-based experiences enable students to engage in learning that closely mirrors real-life situations, effectively enhancing their knowledge and practical skills relevant to industry needs. This is further supported by the study of [22], which found that implementing such technology in education not only improves technical abilities but also encourages students to internalize ethical values and professionalism through simulations designed to reflect real-world scenarios. Kim and Chun [25] highlighted that VR-based simulations help students build confidence and improve decision-making abilities, particularly when dealing with complex or high-risk situations in the workplace. Additionally, research by Collier et al. [24] demonstrated that VR allows students to explore creative solutions to problems, a crucial competency in today's modern work environment.

4. Character building through work environment simulation

Virtual reality-based work environment simulations have become a pivotal innovation in the field of education. This approach allows students to experience realistic workplace dynamics, including challenges, pressures, and teamwork. Research by Melinda and Widjaja [29] highlights that virtual reality-based experiences provide a realistic effect to support learning. This aligns with the study by Xiang-yi [30], which revealed that technology-based simulations effectively replicate real-world environments to create interactive learning experiences.

Through these simulations, students not only acquire technical knowledge but also develop essential attitudes and values. Byrne and Furness [31] explain that virtual reality technology facilitates understanding of abstract concepts through direct interaction with information presented in 3D formats. Virtual-world-based learning environments yield positive outcomes for training and education in safe and controlled conditions [32]. Moreover, the integration of immersive technology into education presents significant opportunities to shape students' character, preparing them for the demands of the modern industrial world. Rafiq et al. [9] demonstrated that simulation-based approaches enhance student engagement and motivation in vocational education, providing intensive and immersive experiences.

Virtual reality (VR) technology is effectively utilized in mechanical engineering education, providing students with realistic and safe learning experiences. In factory simulations, learners are taught to understand workflow, adhere to safety regulations, and work collaboratively. Studies have shown that this innovation enhances students' communication and problem-solving skills [33]. The system is also used to simulate emergency scenarios or production errors in a controlled environment, equipping students with the ability to tackle challenges critically [34]. Moreover, this simulation-based approach improves students' understanding of mechanical principles through safe experimentation, enabling them to practice skills more effectively [35].

VR technology has broad relevance across various fields of study, including nursing training and design. In nursing training, this technology allows students to practice patient interactions in realistic emergency situations, significantly enhancing their clinical knowledge and skills [36, 37]. In the context of design, the use of digital simulations enables students to create and test prototypes in a virtual environment, providing hands-on experience without physical limitations [38].

Virtual reality (VR) experiences also train students to develop adaptive and innovative character traits through complex and multidisciplinary scenarios [39]. Furthermore, VR facilitates the teaching of professional values such as responsibility, integrity, and collaboration through practical simulations that enhance students' interpersonal skills and decision-making abilities [40].

The primary advantage of VR technology lies in its ability to create a safe and controlled learning environment, allowing students to learn from mistakes without facing serious consequences, particularly in high-risk or financially costly situations [41]. This technology-driven simulation has been proven to reduce students' anxiety during the learning process and increase emotional engagement relevant to the topics being studied [42]. Additionally, VR is effective in fostering students' self-reflection by enabling immediate evaluation of their performance within simulation scenarios [43]. In the context of lifelong learning, this virtual reality-based approach facilitates the development of practical skills, enhances information retention, and nurtures a reflective mindset essential for long-term personal growth [44].

The integration of VR into education represents a strategic step in bridging the curriculum with the demands of the workforce. Its application allows students to gain hands-on experience in simulated work environments, effectively building technical skills while strengthening work ethics. Research has shown that VR significantly enhances students' technical and cognitive abilities, as evidenced by a meta-analysis on its use in vocational education [45]. Moreover, it fosters confidence and resilience through immersive simulations that replicate real-world workplace challenges [46].

Character development through VR includes fostering soft skills such as empathy and self-reflection. Studies indicate that VR use enhances learners' empathy, as highlighted in research on VR-based professional training [47]. Additionally, this technology has been proven to boost students' motivation to learn, with immersive experiences facilitating deep and active learning [48]. By leveraging VR, educational institutions can produce graduates who are not only technically competent but also possess strong character foundations to navigate the evolving challenges of the industry [49].

5. Strengthening the value of togetherness and collaboration

Technology-based virtual reality (VR) learning offers an immersive educational experience while fostering an environment that strengthens values of unity and collaboration. Within the context of collaborative learning, this approach enables students to enhance their interpersonal skills through social interaction, resource sharing, and joint knowledge construction [50]. Furthermore, utilizing this technology significantly boosts students' motivation and engagement in collaborative learning scenarios, supporting the development of communication and teamwork skills that are critical in the future workforce [51].

Simulation environments also provide opportunities for complex training, such as medical operations, which substantially improve both technical and non-technical skills through collaborative-based exercises [52]. In interprofessional education, technology-driven simulations have proven effective in enhancing cross-disciplinary collaboration by fostering better communication and teamwork learning [53].

Collaboration in virtual environments presents various challenges, enabling students to learn constructive conflict resolution. Research highlights that such technology creates a collaborative learning atmosphere that facilitates social interactions, resource sharing, and knowledge building. This, in turn, helps students develop crucial conflict-resolution skills [50]. Additionally, simulation-based virtual training has demonstrated its ability to improve mediation and conflict-resolution abilities among students, enabling them to overcome collaborative challenges more effectively [54].

Virtual reality simulations provide a safe platform for students to practice conflict resolution without facing real-world risks. This supports the development of their social and emotional skills [55]. This approach is also relevant for enhancing student engagement in cross-disciplinary and cross-geographical collaboration, where virtual technology facilitates more immersive and meaningful learning experiences [56].

Virtual reality technology enables cross-cultural and geographical collaboration, a crucial aspect in this era of globalization. In education, this technology opens opportunities for students to interact with peers from diverse backgrounds, broadening their perspectives and fostering inclusive character development. Research supports this, showing that collaborative and interactive learning improves through a constructivist approach [48]. Moreover, virtual reality-based learning environments allow students from varied backgrounds to work together in settings that promote collaboration [57]. Thus, the use of virtual reality not only enhances student engagement but also equips them with the ability to work in multicultural teams and tackle challenges in a global environment [49].

Immersive technology provides a collaborative learning experience, helping students develop qualities such as adaptability, flexibility, and teamwork, which are crucial in various aspects of life [10]. In the educational context, this approach significantly enhances student engagement, motivation, and learning outcomes compared to traditional methods [4]. Furthermore, technology-based learning allows for exploration and experimentation within a supportive environment, positively influencing students' emotions and motivation [25]. Overall, the application of cutting-edge technology in education plays a pivotal role in preparing future generations to face upcoming challenges [58].

Technology-driven immersive learning creates innovative educational experiences by promoting collaboration through interaction and active student participation [59]. In education, this approach enhances social skills, facilitates resource sharing, and enables the construction of knowledge among students [50]. Additionally, the use of immersive technology fosters character development through simulations of real-life situations, encouraging teamwork and ethical decision-making [10].

Virtual reality technology has proven effective in language learning by creating immersive environments that allow students to engage more deeply in cross-cultural collaboration and acquire language skills more naturally [60]. By integrating this innovation, education not only improves in technical aspects but also significantly contributes to the holistic development of students' character. This includes fostering empathy, teamwork, and communication skills, which are essential in a globally interconnected world [61].

6. Learning ethics and morals through decision making simulation

By utilizing immersive technology, teachers can create simulation scenarios that require students to make decisions based on specific situations, such as ethical dilemmas in business or workplace safety. This approach enhances students' critical thinking skills, as demonstrated by research showing that virtual reality-based methods significantly improve students' cognitive and critical thinking abilities compared to traditional teaching methods [62]. Additionally, these simulation media provide an interactive and immersive learning experience, strengthening students' decision-making skills and their understanding of the ethical implications of their actions [63]. This approach also fosters character development by engaging students in real-life scenarios that require moral considerations. As highlighted by Harrison [10], this technology supports character education through opportunities for deep and autonomous learning.

Teaching ethics and morality through decision-making simulations using immersive technology represents a significant innovation in modern education. Studies indicate that interactive digital experiences enable students to deeply engage with real-world situations, thus enhancing the effectiveness of learning by presenting real-life ethical dilemmas, such as those in business scenarios or workplace safety [64]. This technology has proven to make business ethics education more engaging and to improve students' ability to navigate moral dilemmas by creating practically relevant learning environments [65]. Furthermore, other research has found that virtual reality-based approaches can be employed to explore the ethical and social dimensions of education in a more interactive and in-depth manner [66].

This approach is also relevant to bioethics education, where simulation technology is employed to recreate complex ethical scenarios in remote environments, equipping students with strong ethical reasoning skills [67]. Virtual scenarios are designed to require students to make decisions based on specific ethical values, offering them the opportunity to grasp the moral complexities tied to real-world consequences of their choices [68]. For instance, in a business context, students may face situations requiring them to choose between upholding corporate integrity or pursuing mere profit, supporting practical and interactive ethics learning [69]. Additionally, simulations involving workplace safety dilemmas allow students to prioritize between operational efficiency and employee safety, helping them explore decisions grounded in life values [70]. Thus, virtual reality technology becomes an effective pedagogical tool for honing decision-making skills that encompass ethical principles as well as the moral and social implications of every choice made [71].

The use of immersive technology in learning encourages students to develop critical thinking skills by analyzing complex scenarios, evaluating alternative solutions, and understanding the consequences of their actions [72]. This learning process enables students to better comprehend the material through realistic simulation experiences, positively influencing their ability to make more responsible decisions [73]. Moreover, this approach provides opportunities for students to reflect on their actions and improve their approach to ethical issues in the future [47]. This strategy has also been proven to enhance students' motivation in understanding abstract concepts and improve reflective skills [62].

Decision-making-based simulations provide students with hands-on experiences to understand moral and ethical values, strengthen their integrity, and enhance empathy when faced with complex dilemmas [74]. Through this approach, students not only learn abstract concepts but also internalize values that support community life, such as maintaining a balance between personal interests and the common good [75]. Research findings indicate that using simulations significantly improves students' ability to make responsible decisions [76].

Teaching ethics and morals through technology-driven immersive simulations offers transformative experiences for students. This approach creates an interactive and challenging learning environment, allowing students to engage more deeply in moral dilemmas [64]. Simulation methods in moral education provide a better understanding of ethical issues compared to traditional methods [77]. Moreover, virtual reality-based approaches facilitate character and moral value development through realistic experiences that closely mimic real-life conditions [78]. Studies show that this technology enhances students' ethical awareness by presenting real-world dilemmas, enabling them to practice responsible decision-making [66].

7. Real-time character learning and evaluation

One of the key advantages of virtual reality (VR) technology is its ability to collect data and evaluate student performance in real-time. For instance, research shows that immersive simulation-based platforms enable the collection of performance data that can be used to enhance teaching strategies and create more adaptive approaches [79]. Teachers can observe students' interactions within digital environments designed to mirror real-world scenarios and provide relevant feedback, as demonstrated by studies assessing the effectiveness of these tools in teacher training through various realistic scenarios [47]. Additionally, evaluations using immersive technology have been shown to boost students' confidence in data collection and overall skill development [80]. This process not only helps students understand the development of their character but also enables them to identify areas needing improvement [81].

Learning through VR technology offers immense potential to develop students' character more effectively and efficiently by leveraging innovations that provide real-time data on student performance within educational simulations. In traditional learning environments, student evaluations often take time and rely heavily on manual teacher observation. However, digital simulation-based approaches allow for immediate data collection and analysis, providing deeper insights into students' learning processes [82]. This technology also creates immersive and interactive learning environments, which enhance student engagement and motivation by representing real-world scenarios in a simulated space [9]. Furthermore, the application of VR-based tools in education enables personalization and interactivity in teaching, offering richer and more adaptive learning experiences tailored to individual student needs [83].

The use of virtual reality technology in education allows students to engage in simulations that test their character traits, such as courage, cooperation, and honesty, within a safe and controlled environment [10]. Teachers can observe students' interactions within these digital environments and collect quantitative data, such as the time taken to make decisions, choices of actions, and the outcomes of decisions within the simulation. This provides a more objective evaluation compared to conventional methods [84]. In this context, interactive simulation technology not only enhances student engagement but also facilitates profound experiential learning through realistic simulation scenarios [4].

The ability of simulation technology to provide real-time feedback significantly supports adaptive and personalized learning processes. When students make mistakes or exhibit behaviors misaligned with expected values, the system can immediately deliver corrective information. Studies show that simulation-based approaches enable adjustments based on performance, needs, and student profiles while offering relevant feedback to foster understanding and the development of positive values [85, 86]. Additionally, teachers can leverage this data to provide more tailored and focused guidance. This is evident in the development of immersive digital environments designed to monitor users' physiological and cognitive responses while dynamically adjusting task difficulty levels in real time [87].

With adaptive feedback, students can gain insights into how their actions reflect their character and learn steps to improve or develop positive values. Research indicates that data-driven adaptations in VR systems enhance learning by reducing errors and improving cognitive performance [88, 89]. The implementation of this technology allows the creation of more effective character-based learning systems, helping students become more independent learners who are responsive to corrections.

Virtual Reality (VR)-based assessments also enable students to directly observe their character development over time. By recording performance and behavior data across various learning sessions, teachers can show students areas they have improved on and aspects requiring further attention [10]. This creates a reflective learning experience where students recognize the importance of character development and its impact on their daily lives in the real world [4]. Such data-driven evaluations are also transparent and motivate students to keep learning and growing [90].

The Virtual Reality (VR) application developed using MilleaLab incorporates several key technological aspects that support immersive learning interactions. Technologically, VR in MilleaLab-based learning leverages real-time graphic rendering, motion sensors for user interaction, and artificial intelligence (AI) algorithms to tailor the learning experience. From a pedagogical perspective, adaptive learning algorithms are utilized to adjust the difficulty level and content based on user responses. These algorithms analyze user interaction data, such as task completion speed or errors made, to provide challenges suited to students' abilities. This technology is often combined with machine learning to enhance personalized learning experiences.

Ultimately, immersive technology-based learning opens doors to deeply integrating character development into the curriculum. With this approach, character education can become a continuously evaluated and reinforced element, rather than just a supplementary component [91]. Teachers can design scenarios aligned with local, national, or global values, allowing students to understand the significance of character in various dimensions of life [46]. In this way, simulation-based digital learning experiences not only help students grasp academic material but also shape them into individuals with strong character, ready to face future challenges [58].

8. Conclusions

The integration of immersive technology in vocational education presents a significant opportunity to strengthen character-based learning. Simulation-based solutions allow students to learn through virtual experiences that closely mimic real-world situations. This approach enables students to practice technical skills in a safe, interactive, and risk-free environment. Not only does this enhance their understanding and mastery of skills relevant to industry needs, but it also provides a profound experience for honing soft skills such as communication, teamwork, and problem-solving. Furthermore, simulation technology can serve as an effective tool for instilling the character traits necessary for the workplace and social life. Through virtual scenarios, students can engage in ethical decision-making, conflict management, or leadership simulations, all designed to internalize values like integrity, responsibility, and empathy. This method helps students grasp not only the technical consequences of their decisions but also their social and moral implications.

The implementation of virtual reality technology in vocational education becomes even more effective when combined with teaching methods that promote positive values and strong character. For instance, project-based learning approaches leveraging this technology can provide students with opportunities to tackle real-world challenges while adopting values such as hard work, perseverance, and honesty. Additionally, involving students in workplace simulations within a virtual environment can better prepare them to face the pressures and dynamics of the working world in a more directed and meaningful way.

With this integration, vocational education can produce graduates who are not only technically proficient but also possess strong character traits, such as high integrity, a commitment to quality, and a deep sense of responsibility. The combination of technical expertise and character development is crucial for addressing the challenges of the modern era, where technical skills alone are insufficient without the support of good character qualities. Thus, virtual reality technology acts as a catalyst for transforming vocational education, making it more relevant, inclusive, and future-oriented.

Acknowledgements

This chapter has been made possible through the support and collaboration of many parties. First and foremost, I would like to express my deepest gratitude to the Directorate of Research, Technology, and Community Service (DRTPM) of the Directorate General of Higher Education, Research, and Technology (DIKTI) for providing the research grant that has supported this project. I extend my heartfelt appreciation to the Rector of Universitas Negeri Makassar (UNM), who has continuously supported and encouraged academic pursuits that contribute to educational development. I am also sincerely grateful to the Chairperson of LP2M UNM for facilitating and guiding this research project, as well as to the Dean of the Faculty of Engineering (FT) UNM and the Head of the Department of Electronics Engineering Education, Faculty of Engineering, UNM, for their invaluable administrative and academic support. Lastly, I would like to acknowledge the efforts of my colleagues, collaborators, and reviewers whose feedback has enriched the quality of this chapter. Your dedication and contributions have been instrumental in bringing this work to fruition. Thank you all for your continued support and commitment to advancing the field of education through technology integration.

Author details

Hendra Jaya[1*], Badaruddin Anwar[1], Rina Febriana[2], Sapto Haryoko[1]
and Sutarsi Suhaeb[1]

1 State University of Makassar, Makassar, Indonesia

2 State University of Jakarta, Jakarta, Indonesia

*Address all correspondence to: hendra.jaya@unm.ac.id

References

[1] Slater M, Sanchez-Vives MV. Enhancing our lives with immersive virtual reality. Nature Reviews. Neuroscience. 2016;**17**(5):348-355. DOI: 10.1038/nrn3903

[2] Bailenson JN. Experience on demand: What virtual reality is, how it works, and what it can do. Current Directions in Psychological Science. 2018;**27**(1):7-13

[3] Freina L, Ott M. A literature review on immersive virtual reality in education: State of the art and perspectives. eLearning and Software for Education (eLSE). 2015;**1**:133-141

[4] Makransky G, Lilleholt L. A structural equation modeling investigation of the emotional value of immersive virtual reality in education. Computers in Human Behavior. 2018;**83**:123-135. DOI: 10.1016/j.chb.2018.02.010

[5] Radianti J, Majchrzak TA, Fromm J, Wohlgenannt I. A systematic review of immersive virtual reality applications for higher education: Design elements, lessons learned, and research agenda. Interactive Learning Environments. 2020;**28**(6):1-21

[6] Ravichandran R, Mahapatra J. Virtual reality in vocational education and training: Challenges and possibilities. Journal of Digital Learning and Education. 2023;**3**(1):25-31. DOI: 10.52562/jdle.v3i1.602

[7] Huang L, Sheng Y. Research on the application of virtual reality technology in vocational education. In: Proceedings of the 2019 International Conference on Education Technology and Economic Management (ICETEM 2019). UK: Francis Academic Press; 2019. DOI: 10.25236/icetem.2019.282

[8] Mulders M. Vocational training in virtual reality: A case study using the 4C/ID model. Multimodal Technologies and Interaction (MTI). 2022;**6**(7):49. DOI: 10.3390/mti6070049

[9] Rafiq A, Triyono M, Djatmiko IW. Enhancing student engagement in vocational education by using virtual reality. Waikato Journal of Education. 2022;**27**(3):175-188. DOI: 10.15663/wje.v27i3.964

[10] Harrison T. Virtual reality and character education: Learning opportunities and risks. Journal of Moral Education. 2023;**53**:219-239. DOI: 10.1080/03057240.2023.2206553

[11] Jaya H, Haryoko S. Integrating Virtual Training Environment into Vocational High School to Facilitate Character Education to Deliver a Professional Workforce. Yogya karta: UNY Press; 2011

[12] Golubeva O, Shutov I. Virtual reality as a didactic tool for the development of professional competencies. Transport Technician: Education and Transport. 2021;**2**:61-70. DOI: 10.46684/2687-1033.2021.1.61-70

[13] Vats S, Joshi R. The impact of virtual reality in education: A comprehensive research study. In: Transfer, Diffusion and Adoption of Next-Generation Digital Technologies. Switzerland: Springer Nature; 2023. pp. 126-136. DOI: 10.1007/978-3-031-50204-0_11

[14] Marougkas A, Troussas C, Krouska A, Sgouropoulou C. How personalized and effective is immersive virtual reality in education? A systematic literature review for the last decade. Multimedia Tools and Applications.

2024;**83**:18185-18233. DOI: 10.1007/s11042-023-15986-7

[15] Oubibi M, Hryshayeva K. Effects of virtual reality technology on primary school students' creativity performance, learning engagement and mental flow. Education and Information Technologies. 2024;**29**:22609-22628. DOI: 10.1007/s10639-024-12766-0

[16] Handayani NR. Pengembangan aplikasi pembelajaran berbasis teknologi virtual reality untuk meningkatkan motivasi dan hasil belajar siswa di sekolah menengah. Jurnal Ekonomi dan Bisnis. 2022;**14**(2). DOI: 10.55049/jeb.v14i2.186

[17] Putra LD, Shiddiq AJ, Khafi I, Nugroho BB. Integrasi teknologi immersive learning dalam pembelajaran sekolah dasar. Jurnal Riset Madrasah Ibtidaiyah (JURMIA). 2024;**4**(2):218-230. DOI: 10.32665/jurmia.v4i2.3349

[18] Yulianti SD, Arini RE, Fildansyah R. Merangkul Teknologi: Mengintegrasikan Realitas Virtual dalam Pengalaman Pembelajaran. Jurnal Pendidikan West Science. Jun 2023;**1**(6):350-356. DOI: 10.58812/jpdws.v1i6.458

[19] Gonzalez J, Gonzalez F, Rivera M. Virtual reality as a practical training tool in vocational education: An emerging trend. International Journal of Educational Technology. 2024;**31**(2):89-104

[20] Zainuddin Z, Idrus R, Razali M. Bridging the skills gap through VR-based learning in vocational schools. Journal of Vocational and Technical Education. 2024;**43**(3):205-223

[21] Rahman A, Syamsuddin S. Penerapan Virtual Reality dalam Pembelajaran Kejuruan: Studi Kasus SMK Indonesia. Jurnal Pendidikan Teknologi dan Kejuruan. 2023;**12**(1):45-59

[22] Dean S, Halpern J, McAllister M, Lazenby M. Nursing education, virtual reality and empathy? Nursing Open. 2020;**7**:2056-2059. DOI: 10.1002/nop2.551

[23] Liu J, Mak PY, Chan K, Cheung D, Cheung K, Fong KNK, et al. The effects of immersive virtual reality–assisted experiential learning on enhancing empathy in undergraduate health care students toward older adults with cognitive impairment. JMIR. Medical Education. 2024;**10**. DOI: 10.2196/48566

[24] Collier R, Darling R, Sprague L, Murphy J. The Development and Feasibility of an Empathy Virtual Reality Scenario in Healthcare Education. Computers, Informatics, Nursing: CIN; 2023. DOI: 10.1097/CIN.0000000000001034

[25] Kim HY, Chun J. Effects of a patient experience–based virtual reality blended learning program on nursing students. Computers, Informatics, Nursing: CIN. 2021;**40**:438-446. DOI: 10.1097/CIN.0000000000000817

[26] Jaya H. Pengembangan Laboratorium Virtual untuk Kegiatan Praktikum dan Memfasilitasi Pendidikan Karakter di SMK. Jurnal Pendidikan Vokasi. 2013;**2**. DOI: 10.21831/JPV.V2I1.1019

[27] Nugroho W. Integrasi Pendidikan Karakter pada Pendidikan Vokasi di Sekolah Menengah Kejuruan. Vocational: Jurnal Inovasi Pendidikan Kejuruan. 2022;**2**(1):73-84. DOI: 10.51878/vocational.v2i1.936

[28] Siyamsih D. Persepsi Mahasiswa Terhadap Penggunaan Virtual Reality dalam Pembelajaran Praktikum Laboratorium. EduTech Journal. 2024;**1**(1):25-29. DOI: 10.62872/12tsrd26

[29] Melinda V, Widjaja AE. Virtual reality applications in education. International Transactions on Education Technology (ITEE). Nov 2022;**1**(1): 68-72. DOI: 10.34306/itee.v1i1.194

[30] Xiang-Yi L. Application of virtual reality in educational training. Computer Simulation. 2005. Link

[31] Byrne CM, Furness T. Virtual reality and education. IEEE Proceedings. 1994. Link

[32] Carruth DW. Virtual reality for education and workforce training. In: 15th International Conference on Emerging eLearning Technologies and Applications (ICETA). 2017. DOI: 10.1109/ICETA.2017.8102472

[33] Halabi O. Immersive virtual reality to enforce teaching in engineering education. Multimedia Tools and Applications. 2019;**79**:2987-3004. DOI: 10.1007/s11042-019-08214-8

[34] Bell JT, Fogler HS. The application of virtual reality to chemical engineering education. IEEE Virtual Reality. 2004:217-218. DOI: 10.1109/VR.2004.75

[35] Wei N, Song T, Luo F. Application of virtual simulation technology in teaching complex engineering mechanics problems. Frontiers in Educational Research. 2023. DOI: 10.25236/fer.2023.062903

[36] Chen FQ, Leng YF, Ge JF, Wang DW, Li C, Chen B, et al. Effectiveness of virtual reality in nursing education: Meta-analysis. Journal of Medical Internet Research. 2020;**22**. DOI: 10.2196/18290

[37] Scott AJS, McCuaig F, Lim V, Watkins W, Wang J, Strachan G. Revolutionizing nurse practitioner training: Integrating virtual reality and large language models for enhanced clinical education. Studies in Health Technology and Informatics. 2024;**315**:671-672. DOI: 10.3233/SHTI240272

[38] Singh A, Ferry D, Ramakrishnan A, Balasubramanian S. Using virtual reality in biomedical engineering education. Journal of Biomechanical Engineering. 2020. DOI: 10.1115/1.4048005

[39] Hong C, Wang L. Virtual reality technology in nursing professional skills training: Bibliometric analysis. JMIR Serious Games. 2023;**11**. DOI: 10.2196/44766

[40] Rourke S. How does virtual reality simulation compare to simulated practice in the acquisition of clinical psychomotor skills for pre-registration student nurses? International Journal of Nursing Studies. 2019;**102**:103466. DOI: 10.1016/j.ijnurstu.2019.103466

[41] Parsons T, Riva G, Parsons S, Mantovani F, Newbutt N, Lin L, et al. Virtual reality in pediatric psychology. Pediatrics. 2017;**140**:S86-S91. DOI: 10.1542/peds.2016-1758I

[42] Maheshwari I, Maheshwari P. Effectiveness of immersive VR in STEM education. In: 2020 Seventh International Conference on Information Technology Trends (ITT). 2020. pp. 7-12. DOI: 10.1109/ITT51279.2020.9320779

[43] van der Want AC, Visscher A. Virtual reality in preservice teacher education: Core features, advantages, and effects. Education in Science. 2024. DOI: 10.3390/educsci14060635

[44] Holuša V, Vaněk M, Beneš F, Švub J, Staša P. Virtual reality as a tool for sustainable training and education of employees in industrial enterprises.

Sustainability. 2023. DOI: 10.3390/su151712886

[45] Ma Y, Zhang L, Wu M. Research on the influence of virtual reality on the learning effect of technical skills of science and engineering college students: Meta-analysis based on 32 empirical studies. International Journal of Digital Multimedia Broadcasting. 2022. DOI: 10.1155/2022/6202370

[46] Predescu SL, Caramihai S, Moisescu M. Impact of VR application in an academic context. Applied Sciences. 2023. DOI: 10.3390/app13084748

[47] Stavroulia K-E, Lanitis A. Enhancing reflection and empathy skills via using a virtual reality-based learning framework. International Journal of Emerging Technologies in Learning. 2019. DOI: 10.3991/IJET.V14I07.9946

[48] Mallek F, Mazhar T, Shah SFA, Ghadi Y, Hamam H. A review on cultivating effective learning: Synthesizing educational theories and virtual reality for enhanced educational experiences. PeerJ Computer Science. 2024. DOI: 10.7717/peerj-cs.2000

[49] Animashaun ES, Familoni BT, Onyebuchi NC. The role of virtual reality in enhancing educational outcomes across disciplines. International Journal of Applied Research in Social Sciences. 2024;**6**(6):1178. DOI: 10.51594/ijarss.v6i6.1178

[50] Zheng L, Xie T, Liu G. Affordances of virtual reality for collaborative learning. In: 2018 Int Jt Conf Inf Media Eng (ICIME). 2018. DOI: 10.1109/ICIME.2018.00011

[51] van der Meer N, van der Werf V, Brinkman W-P, Specht M. Virtual reality and collaborative learning: A systematic literature review. Front Virtual Real. 2023;**4**:1-9. DOI: 10.3389/frvir.2023.1159905

[52] Edwards T, Soussi D, Gupta S, Khan S, Patel A, Patil A, et al. Collaborative team training in virtual reality is superior to individual learning for performing complex open surgery. Annals of Surgery. 2023. DOI: 10.1097/SLA.0000000000006079

[53] Qiao J, Xu J, Li L, Ouyang Y-Q. The integration of immersive virtual reality simulation in interprofessional education: A scoping review. Nurse Education Today. 2021. DOI: 10.1016/j.nedt.2021.104773

[54] Bradley J, Monda-Amaya L. Conflict resolution: Preparing preservice special educators to work in collaborative settings. Teacher Education and Special Education. 2005;**28**(4):171-184. DOI: 10.1177/088840640502800404

[55] Stewart C, Edwards H. Online collaboration: Using roleplay to develop skills in resolving conflict. International Education Studies. 2012;**5**(6):1-10. DOI: 10.5539/IES.V5N6P1

[56] Prasolova-Førland E, McCallum S, Estrada JG. Collaborative learning in VR for cross-disciplinary distributed student teams. In: 2021 IEEE Conf Virtual Reality 3D User Interfaces Abstracts Workshops (VRW). 2021. pp. 320-325. DOI: 10.1109/VRW52623.2021.00064

[57] Wehrmann F, Zender R. Inclusive virtual reality learning: Review and 'best-fit' framework for universal learning. The Electronic Journal of e-Learning. 2023;**22**(3):74-89. DOI: 10.34190/ejel.21.6.3265

[58] Yu Z. A meta-analysis of the effect of virtual reality technology use in education. Interactive Learning Environments. 2021;**31**:4956-4976. DOI: 10.1080/10494820.2021.1989466

[59] Tataru M, Berzescu S, Vert S, Mihaescu V, Stamatoiu R. Designing Applications for Collaborative Learning in Virtual Reality2022. DOI: 10.1109/ISETC56213.2022.10010175

[60] Huang X, He J, Wang H. A Case Study: Students' Perception of a Collaborative Game-Based Virtual Learning Environment2020. DOI: 10.23919/ilrn47897.2020.9155159

[61] Papanastasiou GP, Drigas A, Skianis C, Lytras MD, Papanastasiou E. Virtual and Augmented Reality Effects on K-12, Higher and Tertiary Education Students' Twenty-First Century Skills2018. DOI: 10.1007/s10055-018-0363-2

[62] Al-Said KM, Berestova A, Ismailova N, Pronkin N. The impact of video-based virtual reality training on critical thinking and cognitive load. International Journal of Evaluation and Research in Education (IJERE). 2024;**13**(5). DOI: 10.11591/ijere.v13i5.28109

[63] Cieslowski BJ, Haas T. Innovative learning: Implementing virtual reality in a large class of prelicensure students using limited equipment, time, and resources. Nursing Education Perspectives. 2023. DOI: 10.1097/01.NEP.0000000000001110

[64] Kang S, Chanenson J, Ghate P, Cowal P, Weaver M, Krum D. Advancing ethical decision making in virtual reality. In: 2019 IEEE Conf Virtual Reality 3D User Interfaces (VR). 2019. pp. 1008-1009. DOI: 10.1109/VR.2019.8798151

[65] Sholihin M, Sari R, Yuniarti N, Ilyana S. A new way of teaching business ethics: The evaluation of virtual reality-based learning media. The International Journal of Management Education. 2020;**18**:100428. DOI: 10.1016/j.ijme.2020.100428

[66] Prokopenko O, Sapinski A. Using virtual reality in education: Ethical and social dimensions. E-Learning Innovations Journal. 2024. DOI: 10.57125/elij.2024.03.25.03

[67] Harfouche A, Nakhle F. Creating bioethics distance learning through virtual reality. Trends in Biotechnology. 2020;**38**:1187-1195. DOI: 10.1016/j.tibtech.2020.05.005

[68] Brey P. The ethics of representation and action in virtual reality. Ethics and Information Technology. 2020;**1**:5-14. DOI: 10.1023/A:1010069907461

[69] Carneiro JAS, Cardoso A, Santos FP, Milagre S, Lamounier E, Oliveira LC. Ethical aspects in a virtual reality environment. In: 2023 18th Iberian Conference on Information Systems and Technologies (CISTI). 2023. pp. 1-4. DOI: 10.23919/CISTI58278.2023.10211445

[70] Sütfeld LR, Gast R, König P, Pipa G. Using virtual reality to assess ethical decisions in road traffic scenarios. Frontiers in Behavioral Neuroscience. 2017;**11**. DOI: 10.3389/fnbeh.2017.00122

[71] Ramirez E, LaBarge S. Real moral problems in the use of virtual reality. Ethics and Information Technology. 2018;**20**:249-263. DOI: 10.1007/s10676-018-9473-5

[72] Alifteria FA, Prastowo T, Suprapto N. Analysis of students' critical thinking skills on virtual reality learning media. IJORER International Journal of Recent Educational Research. 2023;**4**(1):275. DOI: 10.46245/ijorer.v4i1.275

[73] Ikhsan J, Sugiyarto K, Nur AT. Fostering student's critical thinking through a virtual reality laboratory.

International Journal of Interactive Mobile Technologies (iJIM). 2020;**14**(8). DOI: 10.3991/ijim.v14i08.13069

[74] Amri F, Djatmika E, Wahyono H, Widjaja S. The effect of using simulation on developing students' character education in learning economics. International Journal of Instruction. 2020. DOI: 10.29333/IJI.2020.13424A

[75] Gibbons B, Fernando M, Spedding T. Innovation through developing a Total Enterprise computer simulation: Teaching responsible decision making. Journal of Management Education. 2021;**46**:16-42. DOI: 10.1177/1052562920987591

[76] Rahmadini N, Rasyid T. Student character building methods on distance education. International Journal of Ethno-Sciences and Education Research. 2021. DOI: 10.46336/ijeer.v1i4.243

[77] Niforatos E, Palma A, Gluszny R, Vourvopoulos A, Liarokapis F. Would you do it?: Enacting moral dilemmas in virtual reality for understanding ethical decision-making. In: Proc 2020 CHI Conf Hum Factors Comput Syst. 2020. DOI: 10.1145/3313831.3376788

[78] Benvegnù G, Pluchino P, Gamberini L. Virtual morality: Using virtual reality to study moral behavior in extreme accident situations. In: 2021 IEEE Virtual Reality 3D User Interfaces (VR). 2021. pp. 316-325. DOI: 10.1109/VR50410.2021.00054

[79] Mdaghri-Alaoui G, Khabbachi I, Zouhair A, En-naimi E. Exploring learner achievement analysis using K-means, SVM, and EM clustering in a Unity-based virtual reality learning environment. In: 2024 International Conference on Computing, Internet of Things and Microwave Systems (ICCIMS). 2024. DOI: 10.1109/ICCIMS61672.2024.10690759

[80] King S, Dzenga C, Burch T, Kennedy K. Teaching partial-interval recording of problem behavior with virtual reality. Journal of Behavioral Education. 2020;**30**:202-225. DOI: 10.1007/s10864-019-09363-4

[81] Meeder R, Mcbride R. Improving student performance in higher education instructional design courses using virtual reality integration. Journal of Applied Instructional Design. 2024. DOI: 10.59668/1269.15638

[82] Kyaw BM, Saxena N, Posadzki P, Vseteckova J, Nikolaou CK, George PP, et al. Virtual reality for health professions education: Systematic review and meta-analysis by the digital health education collaboration. Journal of Medical Internet Research. 2019;**21**(1):e12959. DOI: 10.2196/12959

[83] Lei X. Design and optimization algorithm of interactive education system based on virtual reality technology. In: 3rd International Conference on Artificial Intelligence and Autonomous Robot Systems (AIARS). 2024. DOI: 10.1109/AIARS63200.2024.00033

[84] Ke F, Xu X. Virtual reality simulation-based learning of teaching with alternative perspectives taking. British Journal of Educational Technology. 2020;**51**(6):2544-2557. DOI: 10.1111/bjet.12936

[85] Zahabi M, Razak A. Adaptive virtual reality-based training: A systematic literature review and framework. Virtual Real. 2020;**24**:725-752. DOI: 10.1007/s10055-020-00434-w

[86] Eaves D, Breslin G, Van Schaik P, Robinson E, Spears I. The short-term effects of real-time virtual reality

feedback on motor learning in dance. Presence Teleoperators Virtual Environ. 2011;**20**(1):62-77. DOI: 10.1162/pres_a_00035

[87] Dey A, Chatburn A, Billinghurst M. Exploration of an EEG-based cognitively adaptive training system in virtual reality. In: 2019 IEEE Conference on Virtual Reality and 3D User Interfaces (VR). 2019. pp. 220-226. DOI: 10.1109/VR.2019.8797840

[88] Hubbard R, Sipolins A, Zhou L. Enhancing learning through virtual reality and neurofeedback: A first step. In: Proceedings of the Seventh International Learning Analytics and Knowledge Conference. 2017. DOI: 10.1145/3027385.3027390

[89] Fujimoto Y, Zhou H, Sawabe T, Kanbara M, Kato H. Stop bad real-time feedback!: Estimation of the timing of feedback that negatively impacts presenters for presentation training in virtual reality. In: 2023 IEEE International Symposium on Mixed and Augmented Reality Adjunct (ISMAR-Adjunct). 2023. pp. 405-410. DOI: 10.1109/ismar-adjunct60411.2023.00087

[90] Yu Z, Xu W. A meta-analysis and systematic review of the effect of virtual reality technology on users' learning outcomes. Computer Applications in Engineering Education. 2022;**30**:1470-1484. DOI: 10.1002/cae.22532

[91] Slavova Y, Mu M. A comparative study of the learning outcomes and experience of VR in education. In: 2018 IEEE Conf Virtual Reality 3D User Interfaces. 2018. pp. 685-686. DOI: 10.1109/VR.2018.8446486

Chapter 6

Education 4.0 and eLearning: Revolutionizing Digital Learning Environments

Mihai Caramihai, Irina Severin and Nicoleta Radu

Abstract

The chapter focuses on the intersection of Education 4.0 and eLearning, investigating how cutting-edge technologies are reshaping digital education. It emphasizes the potential of smart, personalized, and technology-integrated learning experiences to meet the demands of the twenty-first-century learner. The chapter explores the tools and methodologies of eLearning within the Education 4.0 framework, analyzing their effectiveness and highlighting best practices, challenges, and potential future advancements. It aims to provide a roadmap for educators, policymakers, and technologists who are committed to advancing digital learning environments. A case study on students' perception about eLearning is discussed.

Keywords: Education 4.0, eLearning, personalization, adaptive learning, learning analytics

1. Introduction

Industry 4.0, or the 4th Industrial Revolution (4IR), marks a transformative phase where computers, data, and automation converge to revolutionize industries, particularly manufacturing. Building on the 3rd Industrial Revolution's introduction of personal computers and the Internet, Industry 4.0 integrates digital and physical systems through technologies like artificial intelligence (AI), automation, and the Internet of Things (IoT). Unlike earlier revolutions that focused on developing new technologies, Industry 4.0 emphasizes their evolution and profound impact on daily life, transforming industrial production and systems [1].

This technological revolution necessitates a parallel evolution in educational paradigms, as traditional models struggle to prepare learners for the rapidly changing demands of the digital age. As technology advances rapidly, globalization increases, and societal priorities shift, education must also evolve. Traditional models, rooted in the industrial age, emphasize rote learning and standardized testing, which inadequately prepare students for today's dynamic world. To address this, education should prioritize critical thinking, adaptability, creativity, and emotional intelligence alongside foundational knowledge [1]. The digital revolution has reshaped work, communication, and problem-solving, making it essential for education systems to equip learners with skills for continuous adaptation and upskilling. Approaches such as project-based learning, interdisciplinary studies, and personalized education using technology can foster these abilities.

Modern challenges, like climate change, inequality, and global health crises, demand innovative solutions. Education must cultivate global citizenship by promoting empathy, cultural awareness, and ethical reasoning. Collaborative learning and real-world problem-solving are key. Furthermore, blurring boundaries between subjects call for integrating technology, arts, humanities, and sciences. Reimagining education as holistic and flexible is not just a response to technological change but a moral imperative to empower individuals to lead fulfilling lives and contribute meaningfully to society. This represents a global shift in how we value education.

2. Understanding Education 4.0

Personalized learning engages students by aligning with their interests, promoting active participation, and fostering cognitive and social skills. Guided learning, a key approach, involves teachers providing hints and feedback during self-directed exploration, known as scaffolding, which effectively builds cognitive abilities [2]. Closely related is inquiry-based learning, where open-ended questions introduce educational material, proving especially effective for math and science concepts [2].

These pedagogical approaches form the foundation of personalized learning ecosystems, which must be further enriched by considering students' diverse backgrounds and experiences.

Ideally, personalized learning considers a student's cultural, personal, and socioeconomic background, creating inclusive and impactful experiences [2]. It empowers students to become co-creators of their learning journey by selecting content and shaping instructional methods [3]. To meet the demand for individualized education, innovative pedagogical models and tools have been developed, fostering teamwork and new perspectives on learning [3].

Knowledge Space Theory is integral to personalized learning, mapping a learner's knowledge in specific domains and enabling customized modules based on problem-solving abilities [3]. While only a third of participants are currently familiar with personalized learning, nearly 70% believe it will grow in relevance, reflecting a shift toward learner-centered education [3]. Education 4.0 is based on some features and principles which aim to provide a comprehensive and holistic approach to learning. According to the World Economic Forum, these features and principles are seen in **Figure 1**.

The principles of personalized learning directly inform the comprehensive Education 4.0 framework, which expands these concepts into a holistic educational model designed to meet the challenges of the digital era.

Education 4.0 framework advocates equipping students with the skills essential for thriving in the Industry 4.0 era and succeeding in the digital age.

This includes proficiency in using digital technologies, such as data analysis and automated systems, alongside the ability to interpret data and interact effectively with digital devices. Central to Education 4.0 is fostering creativity and innovation, enabling students to devise solutions to emerging challenges.

Through project-based learning, students engage in real-world projects, allowing them to acquire skills that can be immediately applied. Education 4.0 also stresses

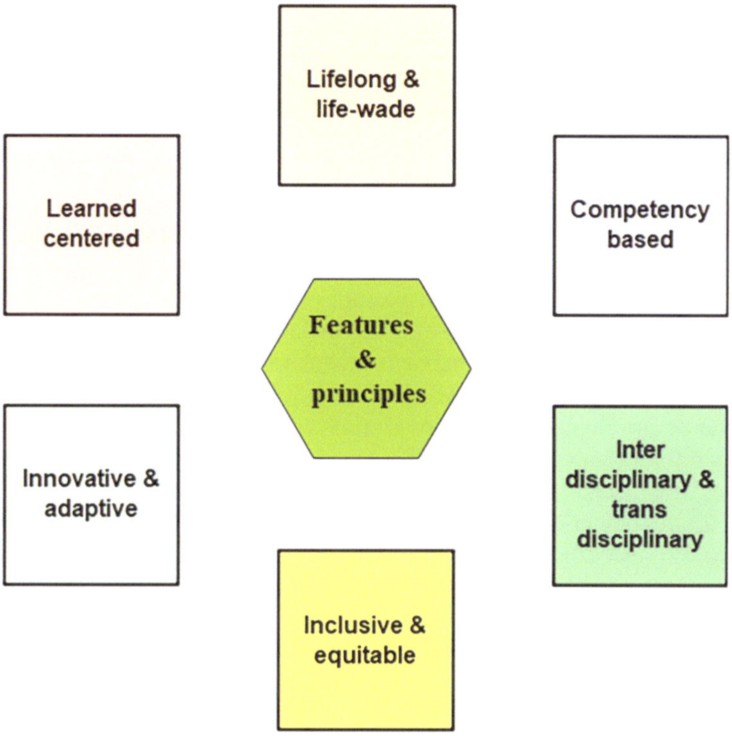

Figure 1.
Features and principles of Education 4.0.

the importance of critical evaluation of information and data, independent thinking, problem-solving, and the cultivation of computational thinking [4].

In the work of Norton et al. [5], a description of the digital transformation is given as a shift in organizational work structures driven by emerging digital technologies and innovative business models. Similarly, Mahlow and Hediger [6] emphasize that digital transformation fosters new skills and strategic models through the profound integration of digital technologies.

In the context of Education 4.0 and the knowledge economy, there is an increasing emphasis on how individuals apply digital skills, knowledge, and technologies in an interoperable manner, rather than merely focusing on theoretical concepts. Education 4.0 underpins a new educational paradigm that prioritizes the practical application of relevant skills and the ongoing processes of upskilling, reskilling, unlearning, and relearning [7].

Key outcomes for education in response to the demands of Industry 4.0 include equipping citizens with digital technology proficiency in a highly interconnected and multifaceted world, where continuous advancements in digital tools are the norm. Schools are tasked with preparing students to contribute to a more inclusive, cohesive, and competitive society. This involves fostering digital skills for both educators and students to facilitate human-centered, problem- and project-based learning and adopting innovative pedagogical approaches that encourage students to actively develop and exercise lifelong learning [7].

Understanding the theoretical framework of Education 4.0 requires examination of the technological innovations driving this educational transformation.

2.1 Key drivers

Artificial intelligence (AI) in education leverages tools like chatbots, data analytics, intelligent teaching systems (ITS), and predictive modeling to transform learning. ITS frameworks include four key components: student, domain, pedagogical, and inference engines [8]. The student model assesses prior knowledge, learning style, and comprehension, while the domain model structures instructional content. The pedagogical model identifies optimal teaching strategies, and the inference engine provides personalized feedback.

Adaptive Learning Systems (ALS) enhance engagement and motivation through continuous evaluation and adjustments, also utilizing the same core components as ITS [8]. While AI transforms the instructional experience through personalization and adaptive systems, broader Industry 4.0 technologies create the infrastructure necessary for comprehensive educational transformation.

Industry 4.0 integrates Internet of Things (IoT) and Internet of Services (IoS) technologies into manufacturing, enabling seamless connectivity and automation [9]. IoT facilitates object-to-object communication and controls aspects like heating, lighting, and machinery [10]. Complementing these IoT connections, big data analytics emerges as another essential component of Industry 4.0 ecosystem, particularly in educational contexts. Big data analytics plays a critical role in Industry 4.0, addressing the vast amounts of information generated daily, characterized by volume, variety, value, and velocity [10]. Traditional methods cannot efficiently process this data, making big data a cornerstone of modern industrial technology.

Education 4.0 aligns with Industry 4.0 demands by integrating digital technologies and cyber systems into learning [11]. Though lacking a universal definition, it focuses on equipping students with self-learning, critical thinking, digital literacy, and problem-solving skills. By implementing digital transformation in education, Education 4.0 aims to prepare future employees for an automated, technology-driven world. This approach emphasizes advanced technology integration and skill development to meet evolving societal and industrial needs.

2.2 Comparison with previous educational paradigms

Before Industry 4.0, three major industrial revolutions transformed manufacturing paradigms, each marked by significant technological advancements: mechanization with water and steam power (*Industry 1.0*), mass production via assembly lines (*Industry 2.0*), and automation enabled by information technology (*Industry 3.0*) [10].

Industry 3.0, often associated with the Digital Revolution of the twentieth century, introduced the use of computers and information and communication technologies (ICT) in production processes. This transformation, familiar to most people today, brought automation and efficiency to new levels, fueled by rapid advancements in computing technology and digital connectivity [10].

Building upon these technological foundations, Industry 4.0 represents a quantum leap in both capability and complexity. *Industry 4.0*, the current phase, represents a holistic transformation driven by digitalization and automation across all facets of business and manufacturing. This era compels individuals to adapt not only to evolving tasks but also to the pervasive integration of high-tech tools and devices, which are increasingly critical to professional life [10]. Industry 4.0 paradigm is characterized by the integration of cyber-physical systems, IoT, and Big Data into production and business operations. Companies that prioritize continuous improvement and

Paradigm	Era	Focus	Characteristics
Education 1.0	Pre-industrial	Basic literacy and rote memorization	Teacher-centered, rigid curriculums, limited resources
Education 2.0	Industrial Revolution	Standardized education for mass production	Uniform assessments, focus on compliance and discipline
Education 3.0	Information Age	Knowledge acquisition through technology	Internet-based learning, multimedia integration
Education 4.0	Industry 4.0	Skill development for the digital workforce	Personalized learning, techintegration, lifelong learning

Table 1.
Education evolution.

maintain robust research and development standards are well-positioned to adopt Industry 4.0 practices, enhancing their competitiveness (**Table 1**) [10].

This evolutionary progression illustrates how educational paradigms continuously adapt to align with changing societal and economic demands, with each stage building upon yet transforming its predecessor.

The Industrial Revolution introduced both small-scale and large-scale transformations that significantly influenced nearly every aspect of life. These changes in production methods altered workforce competencies and economic demands, compelling societal adaptation. Himmetoglu et al. [7] contextualize these shifts through the progression of Society 1.0, Society 2.0, and Society 3.0, which correspond to Industry 1.0, Industry 2.0, and Industry 3.0. Education belongs among the societal sub-systems profoundly affected by these transformations. As production processes evolved and their societal impacts emerged, the concepts and content of education underwent significant redefinition.

These industrial transformations have directly shaped educational paradigms, creating parallel evolutions in how learning is conceptualized and delivered.

Scholars have categorized these educational transformations as Education 1.0, 2.0, 3.0, and 4.0. *Education 1.0* aligns with the agricultural society, focusing on teacher-centered knowledge transfer, where students primarily absorbed information from teachers' explanations. *Education 2.0* emerged to address the needs of industrial society, emphasizing the acquisition of technologies relevant to the workplace. *Education 3.0* leveraged technology to further align education with societal needs, fostering innovation and technological proficiency [7]. Finally, *Education 4.0* aims to address the demands of the innovation age. It emphasizes preparing students to create and adapt new technologies that advance societal development. Same authors conceptualize these stages, as follows: Education 1.0 represents "download education," Education 2.0 as "open access education," Education 3.0 as "knowledge-producing education," and Education 4.0 as "innovation-producing education" [7].

As these educational paradigms evolve in response to Industry 4.0, eLearning methodologies have similarly transformed to implement these new approaches to knowledge acquisition and skill development.

3. Evolution of eLearning

The evolution of distance learning reflects a dynamic pedagogical approach that combines traditional, unconventional, and emerging communication methods to deliver instructional content across geographical boundaries. Since its inception, distance education has undergone significant transformations, transitioning from mail-based correspondence and printed materials to electronic broadcasts, mobile integration, and virtual classrooms [3]. While distance education has existed for centuries, the advent of eLearning in the 1960s marked a pivotal turning point, expanding its influence across corporations, academic institutions, training programs, and military applications [3].

Digital learning platforms have become essential tools in online education, offering versatile ecosystems that enrich the learning experience. These platforms go beyond textual content, incorporating interactive multimedia elements such as video lectures, simulations, and animations to clarify complex concepts by engaging multiple senses. They also streamline online assessments with instant feedback mechanisms, enabling students to identify areas for improvement promptly. The real-time data generated supports educators in making informed, data-driven adjustments to their teaching strategies, fostering continuous improvement [12].

Integrated collaborative tools further enhance the online learning experience. Features like discussion forums, group projects, and virtual classrooms facilitate meaningful interaction, overcoming geographical limitations. Both asynchronous and synchronous communication options strengthen interactions between students and instructors, cultivating a sense of community in the online environment [12].

Extending the capabilities of these digital platforms, Mobile Learning (M-Learning) further democratizes access to educational content by leveraging the ubiquity of personal mobile devices. Mobile Learning (M-Learning) represents an innovative extension of eLearning, emphasizing learning through mobile devices. Defined as "learning across multiple contexts, through social and content interaction, using personal electronic devices," M-Learning enables learners to access educational content anytime and anywhere [13]. Technologies involved include smartphones, tablets, laptops, and specialized software. This method not only highlights learner mobility but also encourages the creation of on-the-spot, field-based learning materials, positioning mobile tools as integral to informal educational resources [13]. Studies show that M-Learning enhances learning outcomes, improving exam scores and reducing dropout rates in technical fields.

This shift toward mobility and accessibility aligns naturally with connectivism, a learning theory that conceptualizes knowledge acquisition as a networked phenomenon rather than an individual pursuit.

Connectivism, a modern learning paradigm, aligns closely with the principles of digital education. It posits that knowledge exists within networks and communities, emphasizing the importance of connections and interactions in the learning process [14]. Online learning environments are particularly suited for enhancing connectivist learning, providing access to vast information resources while fostering interactions with experts, peers, and global communities. Platforms like MOOCs allow students to participate in worldwide discussions, attend lectures by renowned experts, and engage with diverse learning communities. Social media, online forums, and professional networks further support this paradigm by enabling continuous engagement and knowledge exchange [15].

Connectivist principles find their practical application in Massive Open Online Courses (MOOCs), which serve as digital hubs for global knowledge exchange and community learning. Most MOOCs offered by prestigious institutions are free and self-paced, allowing learners to access content flexibly using their preferred devices [16]. This accessibility democratizes education, enabling learners to select courses aligned with their interests and schedules.

Microlearning and nano-learning are emerging trends in education, focusing on delivering concise, targeted lessons. Microlearning isolates essential content into bite-sized formats, often using quizzes, videos, and gamified elements. Nano-learning takes this concept further, offering ultra-short lessons (typically 3–5 minutes), enhancing flexibility and maintaining attention for time-constrained learners [17].

Artificial intelligence (AI) plays a crucial role in eLearning by leveraging machine learning algorithms to identify learners' strengths and weaknesses, enabling personalized training content [17]. Another enduring trend is gamification, which integrates game-like features, such as points, levels, rewards, and competitions, to boost engagement and motivation. When thoughtfully designed, gamification enhances learner participation and outcomes, ensuring alignment with educational objectives.

Overall, the seamless integration of mobile learning, AI, microlearning, and gamification into broader online ecosystems underscores the potential of digital tools to transcend traditional boundaries. By fostering collaborative, networked, and personalized approaches, these innovations empower learners to thrive in an interconnected world.

4. Revolutionizing digital learning environments

Digital learning environments are undergoing the transformation driven by integration of advanced technologies, personalization of learning pathways, and enhanced opportunities for collaboration. These innovations aim to make education more accessible, engaging, and effective in preparing learners for the challenges (**Figure 2**).

4.1 Integration of advanced technologies

Artificial intelligence (AI) and Machine learning (ML) revolve around making data-driven decisions, a principle that aligns closely with the core aspects of education.

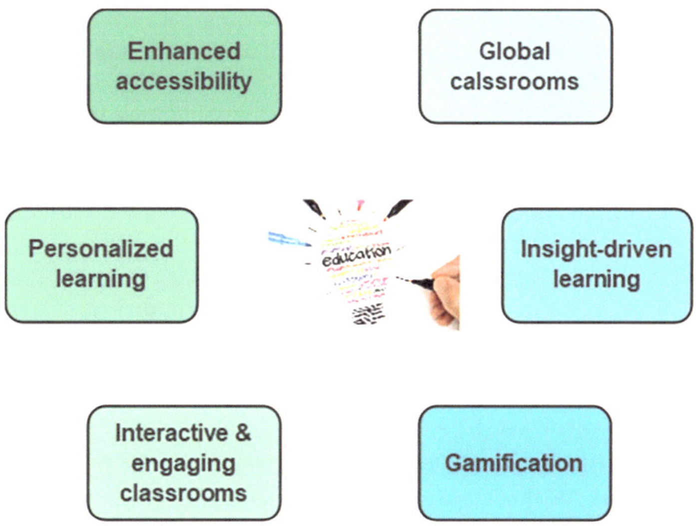

Figure 2.
Application of technology in education.

Currently, various experimental applications of AI and ML are being explored across the higher education value chain. These initiatives are often specialized and tailored, including tools for scientific research, chatbots for student assistance, systems for connecting learners to suitable universities, platforms matching students with career coaches, and solutions for optimizing health and fitness facilities on campus [18].

Many of these innovations leverage the increasing connectivity of student devices to campus infrastructure and cloud services, with a common goal of delivering personalized learning experiences. As adoption becomes widespread, significantly larger datasets will become available for analysis, further enhancing the potential of AI and ML to transform educational practices and outcomes [18].

Regarding AI, some ethical considerations related to educational assessment can be considered:

i. Data privacy and security: The collection, storage, and use of student data raise critical ethical concerns about privacy and security.

Learning analytics involves gathering data on student performance, behavior, and preferences. This data can include personal information, learning styles, and performance metrics. It is essential to ensure this data is securely stored and protected from unauthorized access. Ethical questions arise around who has access to this data, how it is used, and whether students and parents have control over their data. GDPR and similar regulations emphasize the need for informed consent, data minimization, and transparency in data processing, which are highly relevant in Education 4.0.

Example: Without proper safeguards, student data could be vulnerable to breaches, leading to identity theft or misuse of sensitive information.

ii. Bias and fairness in algorithms: AI-driven assessment tools and adaptive learning systems (ALS) are used to personalize learning. However, algorithms can perpetuate biases present in the data they are trained on, leading to unfair or discriminatory outcomes.

ALS assesses student knowledge and adjusts learning paths in real time. If the algorithms used are biased (e.g., trained on data that favors certain demographic groups), they may provide unequal learning opportunities. Algorithmic bias can result in skewed assessment outcomes, reinforcing existing inequalities in education. There is an ethical imperative to ensure that assessment algorithms are fair, transparent, and regularly audited for bias.

Example: An AI-driven grading system might unfairly penalize students from certain backgrounds due to biased training data.

iii. Transparency and explainability: As assessment becomes more automated, it is important to ensure transparency and explainability. Students and educators need to understand how assessments are made and why certain decisions are reached.

Black-box algorithms can make it difficult to understand the reasoning behind assessment outcomes. Without transparency, students may not trust the assessment process, and educators may struggle to provide meaningful feedback. Ethical AI principles emphasize the need for explainable AI (XAI), which makes the decision-making processes of algorithms more transparent.

Example: If a student receives a low grade from an automated assessment system without understanding the reasoning, it can undermine their confidence and motivation.

iv. Digital divide and accessibility: The increasing reliance on eLearning and digitalassessment can exacerbate the digital divide, disadvantaging students who lack access to technology or reliable internet connectivity.

Students from low-income families or rural areas may not have the same access to digital devices and internet as their peers, thus creating unequal learning opportunities. Assessments conducted online may not be accessible to students with disabilities if they are not designed with accessibility in mind. Ethical considerations include ensuring equitable access to technology and designing assessments that are inclusive of all learners.

Example: Students without reliable internet access may struggle to participate in online assessments, leading to lower grades and reduced educational opportunities.

v. Authenticity and plagiarism: Online assessments can be more susceptible to plagiarism and cheating, raising questions about the authenticity of student work.

Students may find it easier to copy answers or collaborate inappropriately on online assessments. There is a need for robust mechanisms to detect and prevent plagiarism, such as plagiarism detection software and proctoring tools. Ethical considerations include promoting academic integrity and ensuring that assessments accurately reflect student learning.

Example: Without proper safeguards, students may plagiarize answers from online sources or collaborate inappropriately during online exams, undermining the validity of the assessment.

Finally, it can be considered that the integration of AI technology in assessment raises important questions about data privacy, algorithmic bias, transparency, over-reliance on technology, the digital divide, and authenticity. Addressing these ethical considerations is essential to ensure that Education 4.0 and eLearning promote equitable, fair, and meaningful learning opportunities for all students.

Augmented reality (AR) and Virtual reality (VR) offer highly immersive experiences that enhance the effectiveness of eLearning. These technologies create a safe environment where students can engage in risk-free simulations and exercises. For professionals in fields such as heavy machinery operation, construction, healthcare, and emergency response, AR and VR enable practical training without exposing them to real-world dangers [19]. By incorporating simulations, AR and VR maintain learners' attention and foster a dynamic and effective learning environment. These tools are particularly beneficial for training and game-based learning, addressing traditional limitations while delivering immersive and interactive educational experiences [17].

The integration of Virtual Reality (VR) and Augmented Reality (AR) technologies has transformed online education, offering immersive and interactive learning experiences. VR transports learners into simulated environments that replicate real-world scenarios or create entirely imaginative landscapes. For example, in science education, students can navigate a 3D model of the human body, fostering a deeper understanding of anatomy and physiology. This vivid immersion enhances engagement and retention by providing memorable sensory experiences [12].

AR, on the other hand, superimposes digital information onto the physical world, blending virtual and real environments. In geography, for instance, AR applications can project historical maps onto present-day landscapes, allowing students to observe the evolution of cities and terrains. This fusion of digital and physical elements bridges the gap between theory and practical application, making abstract concepts more accessible and tangible [12].

Moreover, VR and AR facilitate collaborative learning by enabling students to interact with each other and the virtual environment simultaneously. In history classes, for example, learners can explore historical events together within a shared VR setting, fostering real-time discussion and analysis. These technologies not only deepen comprehension but also encourage the development of critical thinking and problem-solving skills [12].

Internet of Things (IoT) as it was presented above, Industry 4.0 represents the strategic incorporation of the IoT technologies into the manufacturing sector. Meanwhile, it can be understood as a system that connects a diverse range of devices to the internet via standardized protocols, making use of advanced sensor technologies to facilitate seamless communication and real-time data exchange. This enables intelligent functions such as recognition, positioning, monitoring, and management. With the rise of IoT, internet connectivity now extends to physical objects that are not traditional computers but serve a range of other purposes. The primary goal of IoT is to ensure seamless connectivity between things, places, people, networks, and services. IoT operates on three key principles: (1) a shared understanding between users and devices, (2) the role of software architects, and (3) distributed communication networks that process and transmit relevant contextual information. These principles support the development of autonomous and intelligent systems. Ultimately, the IoT represents the convergence of wired and wireless control, communication, and information technologies, connecting diverse technologies and sub-systems within a unified, intelligently managed platform [14].

4.2 Personalized learning pathways

Data analytics plays a pivotal role in creating and enhancing learning profiles by enabling a deeper understanding of individual students' progress, preferences, and challenges. Through the collection and analysis of data from a variety of sources, such as learning management systems (LMS), online assessments, and student interactions, educators can gain valuable insights into each learner's strengths, areas for improvement, and engagement patterns. Data analytics provides a comprehensive view of a student's learning journey by tracking metrics like completion rates, time spent on tasks, assessment results, etc.

One key advantage of using data analytics for learning profiles is the ability to personalize learning experiences. Analytics allow educators to identify students' unique learning styles, pace, and knowledge gaps. This information can then be used to tailor instructional content and strategies to meet the specific needs of each student. For instance, if data shows that a student is struggling with a particular concept, targeted resources or additional support can be provided to overcome the challenge. Additionally, analytics can identify high-performing students, enabling educators to provide enrichment activities to keep them engaged and challenged.

Moreover, data analytics for learning profiles can promote a more proactive approach to student support. By monitoring students' progress in real time, educators can quickly identify at-risk learners and intervene early, offering personalized feedback or additional guidance before issues escalate. This predictive capability helps prevent students from falling behind and ensures that they receive the necessary support to stay on track. Additionally, learning analytics can facilitate communication between instructors, students, and even parents, creating a collaborative approach to supporting student success.

In the broader context, learning profile data analytics can contribute to institutional decision-making by providing insights into teaching effectiveness and curriculum design. By analyzing trends across a larger cohort, educational institutions can identify effective teaching strategies, resources, or technologies.

Customizable content and assessments are key elements in creating personalized and adaptive learning experiences that cater to the diverse needs and abilities of students. By enabling educators to tailor materials and evaluations based on individual student profiles, customizable content ensures that learners engage with relevant, challenging, and appropriate resources. This personalization can range from adjusting materials to suit different reading levels, to providing alternative formats such as videos, interactive simulations, or podcasts to cater to various learning styles. Such flexibility enhances engagement and accessibility.

In addition to content, assessments can also be customized to better align with individual learning goals and abilities. Traditional one-size-fits-all assessments can often fail to capture the full spectrum of students' understanding, especially when they vary widely in their learning needs and strengths. Using adaptable assessments, such as formative quizzes, assignments with varying difficulty levels, or project-based evaluations, educators can ensure that students are challenged to demonstrate their learning in a way that is most suitable for them. Furthermore, the ability to adjust the frequency, type, and scope of assessments allows educators to provide ongoing feedback, enabling students to monitor their progress and adjust their learning strategies accordingly.

The use of customizable content and assessments also enhances student motivation and engagement, allowing them to feel confident and invested in their learning process. This sense of mastery and progress helps to foster a growth mindset, encouraging students to take ownership of their learning and persist through challenges. Additionally, the ability to customize assessments enables educators to create opportunities for differentiated instruction, ensuring that all learners are appropriately challenged.

On a broader scale, the integration of customizable content and assessments contributes to more equitable learning environments. Considering each student unique, with strengths, challenges, and learning preferences, educators can support diverse learners and design more inclusive experiences. This personalized approach promotes a sense of belonging and equity, as students feel valued.

4.3 Collaborative and social learning

Discussion forums and online communities enable peer-to-peer learning by providing a platform for students to share ideas, collaboratively solve problems, and explore diverse perspectives on course materials. In addition, real-time collaboration tools support synchronous interactions, such as live debates, brainstorming sessions, and Q&A with instructors. Together, these elements create a dynamic and engaging learning environment that fosters critical thinking, problem-solving, and communication skills.

One of the main benefits of online learning platforms is their ability to support asynchronous learning. Students have the flexibility to access course materials, lectures, and assignments at their own pace and convenience, making it easier to accommodate varying schedules and learning preferences. This autonomy empowers students to take charge of their educational journeys, promoting self-regulation and independence.

The shift toward *collaborative online spaces* not only increased student engagement but also created a sense of community within virtual classrooms. Additionally, the integration of *Learning Management Systems* (LMS) played a pivotal role in reshaping teaching strategies, inspiring educators to adopt innovative methods. Instructors could design interactive, multimedia-rich content, incorporating quizzes, discussions, and multimedia presentations. The flexibility of these systems allows for the use of various media formats, catering to different learning styles and enhancing student engagement.

Overall, online learning platforms and LMS systems have become essential components of modern education, providing numerous opportunities for flexible, interactive, and collaborative learning experiences [20].

5. Benefits of Education 4.0 and eLearning

Developing interactive multimedia content involves several steps: collecting materials and information, crafting content that integrates teaching methodologies with multimedia elements, creating media and interactive components, and finalizing the course in multiple formats. This process ensures the course is engaging and relevant, fostering effective learning and student commitment [17].

In the implementation phase, the course is delivered to students via integration into a learning management system (LMS). The educational process is facilitated under the guidance of a tutor, who provides management and support to students. This stage focuses on managing and facilitating the learning process to ensure that the course runs effectively, and educational goals are achieved [17].

The evaluation phase assesses student responses, learning outcomes, and the achievement of educational goals. It includes gathering and analyzing student feedback, evaluating the content and teaching methods, and determining whether learning outcomes are reached. This phase is essential for measuring the program's success and identifying areas for improvement, enabling adaptations to content or methods to better meet students' needs [17].

Gamification in education integrates game design principles and experiences into teaching methods. This approach enhances learning, fostering positive attitudes, behaviors, and activities across diverse contexts and subjects [8]. It emphasizes participatory strategies, collaborative learning, self-guided study, task completion, efficient assessment, exploratory techniques, and student creativity and retention.

In recent years, learning through gaming has gained significant popularity. The primary goal of gamifying education is to make it enjoyable and more engaging for a wider audience. Research indicates that video games can improve hand-eye coordination and enhance overall IQ and cognitive abilities [21].

The digital age has revolutionized the way people access education, making learning more accessible and flexible than ever before. Online platforms, mobile apps, and cloud-based tools have enabled individuals to learn from anywhere.

One of the key advantages of *increased accessibility* is the ability to customize learning experiences to fit individual schedules. Unlike traditional classroom settings that require fixed times and locations, digital learning platforms offer on-demand access to courses, lectures, and materials. This flexibility empowers learners to study at their own pace, making it easier to balance education with work, family, and other commitments. For instance, a parent can dive into a coding tutorial after putting their children to bed, while a traveler can brush up on language skills during a layover. The *"anytime, anywhere"* model is particularly impactful in reaching underserved communities.

With the rise of mobile internet and affordable devices, people in remote or poor regions can now access high-quality education. Platforms offering free or low-cost resources further level the playing field, opening doors to opportunities previously out of reach. This *democratization of learning* promotes social and economic development on a broader scale.

Moreover, the *flexibility* to learn from diverse locations enriches the educational experience itself. Being able to choose where to study—whether at a coffee shop, a library, or a quiet park—allows learners to create environments that enhance focus and creativity. Combined with adaptive technologies that tailor content to individual needs, the ability to learn anytime and anywhere ensures a truly personalized educational journey, making knowledge acquisition more engaging, effective, and inclusive than ever before. Every aspect of each school is intentionally designed with inclusion in mind, from the materials students use to the content they engage with and the art they create. Classes are structured to promote inclusivity and diversity, balancing factors such as race, ethnicity, language proficiency, gender identity, and sexual orientation among students [22].

Beyond advancing inclusion and diversity, the schools incorporate real-world applications into learning, emphasizing *global citizenship skills*. For instance, students may tackle projects such as designing sustainable alternatives to single-use plastics [22].

As we advance into the future, the workforce is evolving at an unprecedented rate. Technological innovations, globalization, and shifting societal needs are reshaping industries and redefining the skills required for success. These skills are not only crucial for individual career growth but also for fostering *innovation, adaptability, and collaboration* in the global economy.

Among the most vital twenty-first-century skills are problem-solving, critical thinking, and creativity. As automation and artificial intelligence take over many routine tasks, operators must be able to think outside the box, adapt to new situations, and solve complex problems that machines cannot easily address. Additionally, digital literacy has become a foundational skill, with an increasing reliance on technology in virtually every field. Understanding how to navigate digital tools, data analysis, and online platforms is crucial for the success of future employees.

Another key area of focus is communication and collaboration. The globalized nature of the workforce means that teams are often diverse, geographically dispersed, and multi-disciplinary. Effective communication, both verbal and written, along with the ability to collaborate across cultures and time zones, is crucial in this environment. Furthermore, emotional intelligence (EQ)—the ability to understand and manage emotions, both one's own and others'—is becoming increasingly recognized as a critical skill for leadership and teamwork. As industries move toward more collaborative and fluid work structures, individuals must be able to navigate interpersonal relationships, manage conflict, and share working goals.

Briefly, the preparation for the future workforce relies heavily on the cultivation of critical thinking, digital literacy, communication, emotional intelligence, and commitment to lifelong learning [22].

6. Challenges and solutions

One of the most significant challenges [23] is the lack of access to essential tools such as laptops, tablets, or smartphones. In rural areas, where infrastructure is often underdeveloped, students may face additional challenges, such as unreliable electricity or non-existent broadband networks. For instance, in many parts of Eastern Europe or rural Africa, families often rely on a single mobile phone with limited data to meet all their connectivity needs.

In urban environments, the challenge shifts toward affordability. Low-income families may struggle to afford the latest devices or pay for monthly internet subscriptions. Even when schools attempt to address these issues by providing shared access, such as computer labs, the lack of personalized access at home remains a critical gap. The impact of these disparities becomes especially evident during crises, such as the COVID-19 pandemic, where online learning became the primary mode of education.

6.1 Strategies for bridging the gaps

Some strategies may be identified to bridge the gaps and valorize the potential advantages of Education 4.0 [24], such as:

6.1.1 Affordable devices for students

Governments and non-profit organizations can implement programs to provide affordable or free devices for students. For example, Romania's "Euro 200" program, which subsidizes computers for low-income families, is a step toward reducing this gap. Similarly, partnerships with tech companies can help schools procure discounted or refurbished devices.

6.1.2 Community wi-fi and internet subsidies

In areas where home internet is unaffordable, setting up public Wi-Fi hotspots in schools, libraries, and community centers can give students a space to study and participate in online activities. Mobile network operators can also offer special educational data packages, ensuring students can access educational platforms without incurring high costs.

6.1.3 Rural infrastructure development

Governments and private companies must invest in expanding broadband infrastructure to rural areas. For example, initiatives like Elon Musk's Starlink aim to provide satellite-based internet in remote locations, which could be a game-changer for rural education globally.

6.1.4 Teacher training on digital tools

Teachers play a crucial role in bridging the digital divide. Training programs can equip educators with the skills to integrate digital tools into their teaching effectively. This could include learning to use online platforms, adapting content for digital delivery, and teaching students how to navigate and utilize digital resources in secure and responsible conditions.

6.1.5 Creating digital learning hubs

Schools and community centers can be transformed into digital learning hubs, equipped with computers, reliable internet, and educational software. For example, in rural India, "Smart Classrooms" have been established to provide students with access to digital resources and enhance their learning experiences.

6.1.6 Digital literacy campaigns

Beyond providing access, it is essential to ensure students and families understand how to use technology effectively. Digital literacy campaigns can teach basic skills, such as navigating the internet, using educational apps, and understanding online safety.

6.2 Data privacy and security

The management of student data within educational technology systems must adhere to strict data privacy regulations, such as GDPR and COPPA. Educational institutions have a responsibility to implement robust data protection measures to secure sensitive student information, as non-compliance can lead to serious legal and ethical consequences. These systems are vulnerable to cybersecurity risks, including data breaches and ransomware attacks. Safeguarding student data against such threats requires continuous monitoring, frequent security audits, and the adoption of strong cybersecurity protocols [12].

Ethical considerations are equally critical when handling student data. Institutions must establish transparent guidelines and policies to ensure the responsible and ethical use of data. This includes prohibiting the use of data for commercial purposes without explicit informed consent and consistently upholding student privacy rights [12]. Addressing privacy and security concerns in educational technology is essential. Institutions must comply with relevant data privacy laws, invest in comprehensive protection strategies, and actively defend against cybersecurity threats. Ethical principles should underpin all data practices, prioritizing the respect of student rights and privacy.

6.3 Teacher training and readiness

Teacher training and readiness are critical components of modern education, especially in a technology-driven world. Professional development programs play a vital role in equipping educators with the skills and knowledge needed to thrive in a digital classroom. These programs go beyond traditional pedagogy, introducing teachers to innovative teaching methods, such as blended learning, flipped classrooms, and the use of learning management systems (LMS). For teachers to effectively use technology, they must first understand its potential to enhance learning outcomes. Workshops, certifications, and ongoing training initiatives provide educators with hands-on experience using digital tools, such as interactive whiteboards, educational apps, and collaborative platforms like Google Workspace or Microsoft Teams.

Moreover, professional development programs need to be continuous and adaptable to address the ever-evolving nature of technology. Training sessions should include not only foundational skills but also advanced techniques, such as data-driven instruction, adaptive learning systems, and artificial intelligence in education.

Collaborative learning environments, where teachers can share experiences and best practices, further enrich professional development. These programs must also be inclusive, catering to teachers with varying levels of technological expertise, ensuring no educator is left behind in the digital transition.

While training programs provide the foundation, teachers also require robust support systems to effectively integrate technology into their classrooms. Integrating technology is not merely about knowing how to use a device; it is about weaving these tools seamlessly into the curriculum to enhance teaching and learning. Schools and educational institutions must provide teachers with access to reliable hardware, software, and internet connectivity to ensure they can implement their training effectively. Support staff, such as IT specialists and instructional coaches, can assist teachers in troubleshooting technical issues and designing tech-enabled lesson plans.

Additionally, teachers benefit from clear guidelines and frameworks that align technology use with educational standards and objectives. For example, schools can adopt models like TPACK (Technological Pedagogical Content Knowledge) or SAMR (Substitution, Augmentation, Modification, Redefinition) to help educators plan and evaluate their use of digital tools [25]. Providing access to curated digital resources, such as pre-approved educational software and lesson templates, can also reduce the time teachers spend searching for or creating materials.

Emotional and institutional support is equally important. Transitioning to a technology integrated classroom can be challenging and intimidating for some educators. Regular check-ins, peer mentorship programs, and a culture of collaboration can help teachers feel more confident and motivated. Schools should also consider offering incentives, such as recognition programs or stipends, for teachers who excel in integrating technology. By addressing both the technical and human aspects of technology adoption, support systems ensure that educators are not only prepared but also empowered to deliver high-quality, tech-enhanced education. A better valorization of the profession itself as a highly vocational one appears essential in the context on Education 4.0 challenges.

6.4 Student engagement and self-discipline

In online learning environments, combating isolation requires deliberate strategies to foster community and interpersonal connections. A sense of belonging is vital for student well-being and academic success. Instructors can prioritize synchronous activities, such as live discussions, Q&A sessions, and virtual office hours, to ensure that students feel seen and heard. These real-time interactions create opportunities for immediate feedback and help replicate the interactive nature of in-person learning. Group assignments, collaborative tools like shared documents, and platforms like Slack or Discord can encourage teamwork and continuous communication among students.

Moreover, creating small learning communities or cohorts can help students form meaningful connections. Teachers can also use icebreaker activities and team-building exercises, especially at the start of a course, to promote familiarity and trust. Another way to reduce isolation is to acknowledge and celebrate diversity within the classroom. Facilitating cultural exchanges, showcasing student achievements, and creating opportunities for storytelling allow students to share their experiences and relate to one another.

Technology can also play a pivotal role in reducing feelings of disconnection. Features like discussion forums, polls, and chat functions during lectures provide students with avenues to express their thoughts and interact, even in large virtual classrooms. Virtual events, such as online debates, talent shows, or trivia games, offer informal spaces for students to engage socially.

Maintaining student motivation in an online setting requires a mix of creativity, structure, and emotional support. One effective approach is to make learning dynamic and immersive. Interactive content, such as simulations, virtual reality (VR) activities, or scenario-based learning, can make lessons feel more engaging and relevant. Teachers can use storytelling techniques to weave lessons into captivating narratives, making abstract concepts more relatable and memorable. Incorporating multimedia elements like podcasts, infographics, or short videos further diversifies the learning experience, catering to various preferences and learning styles.

Providing regular structure and accountability is another key strategy. Online learners often struggle with time management and focus, so creating a clear, predictable schedule with milestone-based progress tracking can help them stay on course. Digital tools like progress dashboards or apps that send reminders for upcoming tasks can reinforce a sense of direction. Teachers can also integrate regular goal-setting exercises, encouraging students to reflect on their academic objectives and celebrate small wins along the way. Gamification techniques, such as earning badges, leveling up, or engaging in friendly competitions, tap into students' intrinsic desire for achievement and recognition.

Emotional and psychological support is equally critical for maintaining motivation. Online learning can feel overwhelming, especially when students face distractions or technical challenges. Teachers can foster resilience by normalizing challenges and encouraging a growth mindset. For example, using phrases like "mistakes are opportunities to learn" can inspire perseverance. Building a culture of positivity through frequent praise, empathy, and understanding creates an environment where students feel valued and inspired to participate.

Creating opportunities for autonomy and ownership can significantly boost motivation. Allowing students to have a say in their learning journey—such as choosing their project topics, assessment methods, or learning pace—instills a sense of control and responsibility. Integrating real-world applications of lessons, like solving local problems or designing practical projects, helps students see the tangible value of their efforts. Recognizing and celebrating individual achievements—whether through virtual certificates or peer acknowledgment—further reinforces students' motivation to keep advancing.

6.5 Challenges and solutions: A deeper analysis

While the strategies outlined earlier provide a roadmap for addressing the challenges associated with Education 4.0 and eLearning, there is a need for a more in-depth exploration of the difficulties and potential risks involved in their implementation, particularly across diverse regions. Additionally, assessing the cost-effectiveness of these strategies is crucial to ensure they are feasible and sustainable in various contexts.

6.5.1 Regional disparities and implementation difficulties

The effectiveness of strategies such as providing affordable devices, establishing community Wi-Fi, and developing rural infrastructure varies significantly depending on the region. For instance, urban areas may face affordability challenges due to high population density and income inequality, whereas rural areas often struggle with underdeveloped infrastructure, including unreliable electricity and limited broadband access. These disparities necessitate tailored approaches that account for local conditions.

a. Urban challenges: In cities, the primary barrier is often the cost of devices and internet subscriptions. However, ensuring equitable distribution and addressing the digital literacy gap among users remains a challenge.

b. Rural challenges: Rural regions require substantial investment in infrastructure development. However, the high initial costs and maintenance requirements must be carefully evaluated against long-term benefits.

6.5.2 Assessing risks

Implementing these strategies also carries inherent risks that must be considered:

a. Technological dependence: Over-reliance on technology can exacerbate existing inequalities if not managed properly. Ensuring that traditional teaching methods remain accessible is essential to avoid marginalizing those without consistent access to digital tools.

b. Cultural resistance: In some communities, there may be resistance to adopting new technologies due to cultural or generational differences. Addressing this requires stakeholder engagement and awareness campaigns to highlight the benefits of digital education.

c. Cybersecurity threats: As educational institutions increasingly rely on digital platforms, the risk of data breaches and cyberattacks grows. Robust cybersecurity measures and regular training for educators and students are mandatory.

d. Cost-effectiveness analysis: Evaluating the cost-effectiveness of each strategy is critical to ensure resources are allocated efficiently. This involves analyzing both short-term expenses and long-term returns:

  i. Affordable devices: Providing subsidized or free devices can reduce immediate barriers but requires ongoing funding for repairs, replacements, and software updates. Partnerships with tech companies can help offset costs.

  ii. Community Wi-Fi and internet subsidies: While setting up public Wi-Fi hotspots or offering educational data packages is relatively inexpensive, maintaining these services over time may prove challenging. Public-private partnerships can help distribute costs and responsibilities.

  iii. Teacher training: Investing in professional development programs for educators yields significant long-term benefits, improving teaching quality and student outcomes. The initial investment in training materials, workshops, and mentorship programs should be weighed against the improvements in learning effectiveness.

iv. Digital learning hubs: Establishing digital learning hubs in schools and community centers offers a centralized solution but requires substantial upfront investment (grants, government funding, corporate sponsorships, other initiatives).

6.5.3 Recommendations for effective implementation

To overcome these challenges and maximize the impact of the proposed strategies, the following recommendations are suggested:

a. Contextual adaptation: The stakeholders must tailor strategies to fit the specific needs and constraints of each region. Conduct thorough assessments of local infrastructure, economic conditions, and cultural factors before implementation.

b. Stakeholder collaboration: It is necessary to engage all stakeholders—governments, private sector partners, educators, parents, and students—in the planning and execution process. This fosters buy-in and ensures alignment with community priorities.

c. Pilot programs: It is necessary to launch pilot programs to test the feasibility and effectiveness of strategies in controlled environments before scaling up. Data from these pilots should be used to refine approaches and allocate resources effectively.

d. Continuous monitoring and evaluation: It is necessary to implement systems for ongoing monitoring and evaluation to track progress, identify issues early, and make necessary adjustments. Regular feedback loops involving all stakeholders will enhance adaptability and responsiveness.

e. Focus on sustainability: Solutions that are financially and environmentally sustainable in the long term should be prioritized, such as renewable energy sources for powering digital learning hubs and device management using circular economy principles.

Hence, based on these ideas, developing more robust and adaptable strategies for advancing Education 4.0 and eLearning is facilitated. This approach ensures that no learner is left behind as society moves toward a more technologically integrated educational landscape.

To contextualize these theoretical frameworks within current educational practices, we examine student perceptions of eLearning through a comprehensive case study.

7. A case study

In order to see how eLearning has affected students nowadays, a survey [26] was conducted on a sample of students from Faculty of Automatic Control and Computers/National University of Science & Technology POLITEHNICA Bucharest, Romania, collecting 93 replies.

Five aspects were analyzed as follows: Curricular area, Spatial analysis of the courses, Evaluation, Temporal analysis of the courses, and Social opportunities. A scale from 0 to 5, where 1 means least significant and 5 most significant, was considered to complete the survey.

Students expected more from the curriculum of courses. The expectations of the majority were not fulfilled; only 34.4% believed that curricular area was in line with their expectations, considering only the grades of 4 and 5. The other 65% of students did not have a strong opinion about it, or they do not even consider the subject presented in class to be relevant. But on the other hand, 52.68% believed that online teaching methods are more appropriate than traditional ones.

The statistic can be seen in **Table 2**.

Most of the students believed that online teaching methods are appropriate, so their needs are fulfilled by using virtual environment. On the other hand, they have high expectations regarding the curricular area, and this problem should be taken into consideration. Traditional learning has its benefits, but it must adapt to virtual requirements, so as the curricular area, to achieve academic performance.

Cognitive analysis of the courses was done by asking the students to grade 5 topics regarding some cognitive factors. The results are shown in the **Table 3**. As it can be seen, 77.42% of students believe that laboratory tasks should be based more on the interaction between students and virtual work environments. This problem can be solved by taking into consideration how does the curricular need and how it can benefit the students by using virtual environments to perform the laboratories such as virtual machines or tools for remote access, communication and control some devices as Microsoft Teams.

No	Topics	Agree (%)	Disagree (%)
1	It is in line with my expectations.	34.41	65.59
2	It allows me to further develop my knowledge.	43.01	56.99
3	Online teaching methods are appropriate.	52.69	47.31
4	Exercises/homework/quizzes are appropriate.	41.94	58.06

Table 2.
Curricular area results of questionnaire.

No	Topics	Agree (%)	Disagree (%)
1	While going through the courses, visual elements are more important than narrative ones.	67.74	32.26
2	While going through the courses, you prefer to resume the ideas in the form of written notes or diagrams.	70.97	29.03
3	Laboratory tasks should be based on the interaction between the student and the virtual work environment.	77.42	22.58
4	The virtual learning environment needs to be more visually inclined rather than narrative.	73.12	26.88
5	Because of the richer visual content, the virtual learning environment allows me to better accumulate knowledge.	56.99	43.01

Table 3.
Analysis of the courses questionnaire results.

Some lacks are seen regarding the accumulation of knowledge as students believe this environment is not allowing them to achieve better information using visualization tools. That depends on the subject and how well it is prepared. Overall, the spatial analysis tells that the virtual environment is a good option regarding the learning process, as there are analyzed factors as visualization tools (charts, diagrams). Students agreed that visualization is important to achieve knowledge.

Another topic taken into consideration regarding eLearning is the methods of evaluation. The study shows that 61.29% of students disagree with the fact that information presented is related to the structure of methods of evaluation, such as exercises, homework, and quizzes. In fact, here is a big problem that should be monitored, as by learning online, teachers tend to believe that information is everywhere, so all of it should be taken into consideration when an evaluation is needed, and that is a huge disadvantage of eLearning for the moment (**Table 4**). As previously discussed, curricular area needs to adapt to the needs of human being, both students and academic personnel.

Most of the students believed that the criteria used to evaluate are clear and there is a need to take into account students' capabilities; over 60% believed that.

Regarding a temporal analysis, a total of 8 topics were reviewed. The results are shown in **Table 5**, and some statistics were made for a better overview on the subject. Nearly 96.77% of students need the courses available on online platforms. On the other hand, the need of human interaction can be underlined in their disagreement on the fact that online activity should be better planned than class learning.

Last, but not least, social opportunities are a huge factor regarding eLearning as this environment is socially permissive than an in-class environment. It is important to mention that not only the student, but also academic personnel can benefit from opportunities from all around the world, as the internet is the tool that is making the world connected at a click distance. The results of the questionnaire regarding this topic on eLearning students' perspective are shown in **Table 6**.

An overall comment would be that students need improvements regarding social opportunities, as for now, they are not offering what they need, or at least do not meet their expectations. For example, a substantial disagreement percentage of 78.5% believe that online courses do not offer more opportunities for interaction with other students.

Finally, it can be concluded that students are aware of the benefits and disadvantages regarding eLearning versus traditional learning. Following a temporal approach,

No.	Topics	Agree (%)	Disagree (%)
1	Information related to the structure of exercises/homework/quizzes is appropriate.	38.71	61.29
2	The evaluation criteria are clear.	60.22	39.78
3	The professor's evaluation is in line with the results of auto-evaluation.	41.94	58.06
4	During solving exercises/homework/quizzes, I have used my own notes from the courses.	44.09	55.91
5	The evaluation should take into account the student's capability to solve exercises/homework/quizzes.	62.37	37.63
6	The evaluation should consider the student's capability to synthesize gathered knowledge.	59.14	40.86

Table 4.
Evaluation questionnaire results.

No.	Topics	Agree (%)	Disagree (%)
1	The online course should always be available to the student.	96.77	3.23
2	When I go through an online course, the only limitation I have is my own learning schedule.	75.27	24.73
3	Online learning should be based on regularly going through the materials.	61.29	38.71
4	The online learning activity should be better planned than the class learning.	37.63	62.37
5	The advantage of online courses is that they can be tackled in any order.	63.44	36.56
6	The advantage of online courses is that you can study whenever you feel like it.	73.12	26.88
7	Exercises/homework/quizzes should only be solved when the student feels prepared.	51.61	48.39
8	Student-teacher interaction should be lower in the eLearning environment.	19.35	80.65

Table 5.
Temporal analysis of the courses questionnaire results.

No.	Topics	Agree (%)	Disagree (%)
1	Online courses offered me more opportunities to interact with other students.	21.51	78.49
2	I am part of a group of students that exchange ideas/solving techniques for exercises/homework/quizzes.	36.56	63.44
3	The time spent within the online community is higher than the time dedicated to individual study.	22.58	77.42
4	It is important that, within the online community, we share any individual notes of the course that we might have.	48.39	51.61

Table 6.
Social opportunities questionnaire results.

most of them realized the importance of availability, since in a virtual environment everything should be easily accessible no matter the period or the place you are studying from. On the other hand, following a spatial approach, students are inclined to emphasize the importance of visual representation of data to better assimilate knowledge.

These empirical insights, combined with the theoretical foundations previously established, provide a holistic understanding of Education 4.0's current implementation and future potential.

8. Conclusions

The chapter explores how the Education 4.0 paradigm and eLearning have revolutionized education, emphasizing the adaptability and relevance of educational systems in an era of accelerated digitalization. Starting with the challenges brought by the 4th Industrial Revolution, which has transformed entire sectors through technologies like Artificial Intelligence (AI), the Internet of Things (IoT), and Big Data, it highlights the need for profound changes in education to prepare students for an ever-changing job market.

Education 4.0 redefines the learning process, shifting from traditional, teacher-centered approaches to personalized models tailored to each student's individual needs. Emerging technologies, such as Artificial Intelligence (AI) and Machine Learning (ML), enable adaptive learning systems and intelligent tutoring that monitor student progress and adjust content to their learning styles. Technologies like Augmented Reality (AR) and Virtual Reality (VR) offer immersive educational experiences, facilitating practical learning and safe simulations, particularly in fields like medicine, construction, and emergency response.

Internet of Things (IoT) also contributes to the development of smart classrooms, connecting devices to create interactive and efficient learning environments. Data analytics supports the personalization of learning pathways by identifying gaps and strengths for each student, enabling the development of customized content and assessments that promote inclusive and equitable education.

The chapter also examines recent trends in eLearning, such as microlearning, mobile learning (mLearning), and the widespread use of Massive Open Online Courses (MOOCs). These approaches democratize access to education, allowing "anytime, anywhere" learning that eliminates geographical and socio-economic barriers. Moreover, gamifying the educational process adds playful elements that enhance students' motivation and engagement.

Despite these clear benefits, the chapter addresses significant challenges that remain unresolved. The digital divide is one of the most pressing issues, limiting access to technology and the internet in disadvantaged communities. Gaps in teacher training to adopt modern technologies represent another obstacle, underscoring the need for ongoing professional development programs. Additionally, concerns regarding the privacy and security of student data, given the extensive use of digital technologies, require strict compliance with standards.

The case study included in the chapter provides students' perception about Curricular area, Spatial analysis of the courses, Evaluation, Temporal analysis of the courses, and Social opportunities in eLearning environment.

In conclusion, Education 4.0 and eLearning are not merely responses to technological changes but opportunities to rethink education as a flexible, inclusive, and future-oriented process. The implications for stakeholders—educators, students, policymakers, and technology developers—are profound, requiring continued collaboration to overcome challenges and maximize benefits.

Looking ahead, the transition to Education 5.0 promises a deeper integration of emerging technologies, such as blockchain and 5G networks, alongside human-centric approaches that emphasize emotional intelligence, collaboration, and social responsibility. The education of the future must not only be a process of knowledge accumulation but also a means of shaping global citizens capable of navigating an interconnected and complex world.

Acknowledgements

This work has been funded from the Erasmus+ project No 2023-1-RO01-KA220-HED-000154433, entitled "Gender, Digitization, Green: Ensuring a Sustainable Future for All in Europe". The European Commission has no responsibility concerning the content of this deliverable.

Author details

Mihai Caramihai[1*], Irina Severin[1] and Nicoleta Radu[2,3]

1 National University of Science and Technology Politehnica Bucharest, Romania

2 University of Agronomic Sciences and Veterinary Medicine of Bucharest, Bucharest, Romania

3 National Institute of Chemistry and Petrochemistry, R&D of Bucharest, Bucharest, Romania

*Address all correspondence to: m.caramihai@yahoo.com

References

[1] Bekmurzaeva R, Kovalev GS. Industry 4.0: The fourth industrial revolution. SHS Web of Conferences. 2023;**172**:02011. DOI: 10.1051/shsconf/202317202011

[2] Genesis E, Till L, Andrew S. Defining Education 4.0: A Taxonomy for the Future of Learning. 2023. pp. 1-27. Available from: https://www.weforum.org/publications/defining-education-4-0-a-taxonomy-for-the-future-oflearning/

[3] Bezhovski Z, Poorani S. The evolution of E-learning and new trends. Information and Knowledge Management. 2016;**6**(3):50-57. Available from: www.iiste.org

[4] Udvaros J et al. Industry 4.0 from the perspective of education 4.0. International Journal of Advanced Natural Sciences and Engineering Researches. 2023;**7**(4):230-234. DOI: 10.59287/ijanser.705

[5] Norton A, Shroff S, Edwards N. Digital Transformation: An Enterprise Architecture Perspective. UK: Publish Nation Limited; 2020

[6] Mahlow C, Hediger A. Digital transformation in higher education—Buzzword or opportunity? eLearn. 2019;**2019**(5):13. DOI: 10.1145/3329488/3331171

[7] Himmetoglu B, Aydug D, Bayrak C. Education 4.0: Defining the teacher, the student, and the school manager aspects of the revolution. Turkish Online Journal of Distance Education. 2021;**21**:12-28. DOI: 10.17718/TOJDE.770896

[8] Khanduri V, Teotia DA. Revolutionizing learning: An exploratory study on the impact of technology-enhanced learning using digital learning platforms and AI tools on the study habits of university students through focus group discussions. International Journal of Research Publication and Reviews. 2023;**4**(6):663-672. DOI: 10.55248/gengpi.4.623.44407

[9] Kagermann H, Wahlster W, Helbig J. Securing the Future of German Manufacturing Industry: Recommendations for Implementing the Strategic Initiative Industrie 4.0. Final Report of the Industrie 4.0 Working Group. Acatech—National Academy of Science and Engineering; 2013

[10] Tay SI et al. An overview of industry 4.0: Definition, components, and government initiatives. Journal of Advanced Research in Dynamical and Control Systems. 2018;**10**(14):1379-1387

[11] Akturk C, Talan T, Cerasi CC. Education 4.0 and university 4.0 from society 5.0 perspective. In: Proceedings of the 2022 12th International Conference on Advanced Computer Information Technologies (ACIT), Ruzomberok, Slovakia, 26-28 September. 2022. pp. 577-582. DOI: 10.1109/ACIT54803.2022.9913099

[12] Zhang Z. Revolutionizing education: The transformative power of educational Technology in Online Learning. Atlantis Press SARL. 2024. pp. 523-529. DOI: 10.2991/978-2-38476-253-8_62

[13] Afifi MA. The evolution of the e-learning process and its future. Al Dar Research Journal For Sustainability. May 2017;**2**:1-13

[14] Buckner CA et al. Complementary and alternative medicine use in patients

before and after a cancer diagnosis. Current Oncology. 2018;**25**(4):e275-e281. DOI: 10.3747/co.25.3884

[15] Maspul KA. Revolutionizing Online Higher Education: A Theoretical Approach. Insights: Journal of Primary Education Research. 2024;**1**(2):44-52. DOI: 10.59923/insights.v1i2.162

[16] Hussin AA. Education 4.0 made simple: Ideas for teaching. International Journal of Education and Literacy Studies. 2018;**6**(3):92-98. Available from: https://journals.aiac.org.au/index.php/IJELS/article/view/4616

[17] Pribilová K, Beňo M. New trends in E-learning and new approaches to the development of E-learning educational materials. R&E-Source. 2024;**1**(s1): 193-206. DOI: 10.53349/resource.2024.is1.a1255

[18] Salmon G. May the fourth be with you: Creating education 4.0. Journal of Learning for Development. 2019;**6**(2):95-115. DOI: 10.56059/jl4d.v6i2.352

[19] Solmaz S, Dominguez AJL, Santos P, Van Puyvelde P, Van Gerven T. A practical development of engineering simulation-assisted educational AR environments. Education for Chemical Engineers. 2021;**35**:81-93. DOI: 10.1016/j.ece.2021.01.007

[20] Kokkinos L. Revolutionizing education: The dynamic intersection of technology and learning. International Journal of Multidisciplinary and Current Educational Research (IJMCER). 2024;**6**(1):26-32

[21] Brodsky M. E-learning Trends, Today and Beyond. Learning and Training Innovations Magazine. 2003. Available from: http://www.elearningmag.com/ltimagazine/article/articleDetail.jsp?id=56219

[22] World Economic Forum. Schools of the future: Defining new models of education for the fourth industrial revolution. World Economic Forum Reports. 2020;**2020**(January):1-33. Available from: www.weforum.org

[23] Katyeudo KK, de Souza RAC. Digital transformation towards Education 4.0. Informatics in Education. 2022;**21**(2):283-309. DOI: 10.15388/infedu.2022.13

[24] Pinto CAS, Reis ADC. Characteristics of education 4.0 and its application in industry 4.0. Journal of Engineering Education Transformations. 2023;**37**(1):51-61. DOI: 10.16920/jeet/2023/v37i1/23131

[25] Retana RC. Technology integration models into adult education: TPACK and SAMR. Actualidades Investigativas En Educación. 2021;**21**(1):1-27. DOI: 10.15517/aie.v21i1.42411

[26] Caramihai M, Severin I, Bogatu AM. An assessment algorithm for evaluating students' satisfaction in e-learning environments: A case study. In: Arai K, Kapoor S, Bhatia R, editors. Intelligent Computing. SAI 2020. Advances in Intelligent Systems and Computing, Vol. 1230. Cham: Springer; 2020. DOI: 10.1007/978-3-030-52243-8_45

Chapter 7

Challenges Facing E-Learning and Solutions

Jehad Ali Tawfiq Almomani

Abstract

This chapter aims to present and clarify the challenges and difficulties facing the widespread spread and application of e-learning at present in various fields, in addition to the future challenges that e-learning may face hereafter. The content of the chapter is presented in the form of three main axes: the concept and importance of e-learning, and the axis of the challenges facing e-learning. These challenges are multiple and varied and can be classified into technical, educational, social, economic, and future challenges. In this axis, these challenges are presented in some detail, and their various aspects and impact on the educational process are shown. In the third axis, solutions are presented and proposed that can be worked on to confront each challenge facing e-learning, starting with employing investment to develop the infrastructure, organizing awareness campaigns for community members, preparing and training teachers and students to deal with e-learning, and ending with strategic planning for e-learning and developing evaluation and accreditation systems, preparing for change, and adopting a culture of continuous learning. By adopting these diverse solutions, the challenges of e-learning can be overcome, its spread can be expanded in various educational institutions, and its benefits can be increased in various areas of life, with the need to take into account the difficulty of relying entirely on distance education and the need to continue adopting hybrid education in educational institutions, which ensures the continuity of the existence of traditional classes alongside virtual classes in a systematic, organized, and integrated manner.

Keywords: e-learning challenges, distance education, solutions to challenges, synchronous e-learning, information security, blended learning, evaluation of e-learning

1. Introduction

E-learning in our world today has become one of the modern education models that have contributed to shaping the contemporary education system in light of the rapid technological development to keep pace with the accompanying changes in different lifestyles and enhance learning opportunities for all without spatial and temporal restrictions. The focus on e-learning has increased more after the spread of the Corona pandemic (Covid-19) and the cessation of traditional education. Through e-learning, it has become possible to access lessons, lectures and learn at any time that suits learners without the need to adhere to a specific time and place through different methods represented in distance education, interactive education and educational platforms through which scientific content is presented in the form of texts, video clips, graphics, live or recorded lectures, which encouraged everyone to learn and acquire all new knowledge and experiences, and develop their skills in ways that suit their needs and learning methods regardless of their circumstances, conditions, places of work and residence, and interact with integrated educational experiences that include assessment tests, discussions and practical exercises that help them understand, learn and achieve effective learning.

In spite of all these advantages and characteristics of e-learning, this type of education faces many challenges that may hinder its development and widespread spread. These challenges vary in different aspects; some of them are related to communication and social relations between students and teachers, which may affect human relations between them, in addition to other challenges such as educational challenges related to designing digital curricula and preparing and training teachers to teach and deal with them, and technical and economic challenges represented by weak infrastructure and the difficulty of providing e-learning requirements in some educational institutions due to the economic and spatial conditions present in them. There are other future challenges facing and will face e-learning, such as the digital gap and risks, artificial intelligence, etc., and throughout this chapter, these challenges will be presented in some detail. In addition to talking about the ways and methods of facing these challenges to make e-learning the ideal solution for implementing education in the future. However, before that, it is necessary to introduce the concept and importance of e-learning and its types in a brief manner as a kind of feedback to understand the nature of the challenges that e-learning has faced and will face in the future, and the proposed solutions and procedures to face these challenges.

2. The concept and importance of e-learning and its types

This section presents the concepts of e-learning and its importance in the educational process; in addition, it discusses the types of e-learning and compares them as follows:

2.1 The concept of e-learning

The term (e-learning) is one of the terms that appeared in the nineties of the twentieth century as a result of scientific and technological progress, and the information and communications revolution in the world, which made it possible to exchange information at a tremendous speed *via* the internet, and the possibility of accessing various educational sources around the clock and from anywhere through the extensive developments it has brought about in computers and their software and the spread of educational platforms. It is thus a term that describes the transformation and development in the field of education and reflects the impact of technology in transferring knowledge and exchanging information, and the possibility of learners at different educational levels accessing educational content from their geographical locations and at any time. This has brought about extensive transformations in various fields of education, and led to changes in the approach to education and developing educational curricula to keep pace with technological developments and distance education [1].

Smart technology has brought about tremendous developments in various areas of life, especially with smartphones and the emergence and spread of 4G and 5G technologies, high internet speeds, and others. As a result, people have become more technology-oriented day after day. The emergence of the World Wide Web has affected people's lifestyles and dealings, including what is known as online shopping, social networks, online food delivery, online money transactions, online learning, and the emergence of other modern applications based on the internet [2].

E-learning in its broad sense focuses on the use of technology in the teaching and learning process, whether in traditional classrooms or virtual distance learning. It includes a wide range of tools and technologies. Here, it should be noted that the concept of distance learning is a part of e-learning, which refers to the use of electronic media based on computers, smart devices and the internet in virtual distance learning classrooms, in which educational content is exchanged from the teacher to the learner remotely at any time and from anywhere without the need to be physically present at the same time and place, with the aim of expanding educational opportunities and overcome the geographical barriers that separate teachers and learners. The concept of e learning can be defined as follows:

Alawneh et al. [3] define e-learning as a self-learning process through mobile phones or computers, whether through an internet connection or CDs, as this process allows the learner to learn at anytime and anywhere, and there is another definition as education in which educational content is presented through electronic media such as the internet, intranet, satellites, laser disks, or audio/visual tapes [4]. Amer [5] defines e-learning as a process of teaching and learning using electronic media, including computers and their various software, networks, the internet, electronic libraries, etc., all of which are used to transfer and deliver information between the teacher and the learner, prepared according to specific and clear educational objectives.

Through the above, we can reach a definition of e-learning in general as a flexible educational system that uses modern technological means, such as the internet, computers and smart devices to provide educational content and achieve interaction between the teacher and learners, whether in traditional classrooms or in remote virtual classrooms.

2.2 The importance of e-learning

E-learning is considered a real revolution and a turning point in the field of education through its ability to provide tremendous opportunities to achieve continuous education and development and access to knowledge regardless of the circumstances of time and place, through various and advanced educational means that include interactive electronic materials, recorded video lectures, academic platforms, electronic tests and applications, electronic dialog, discussion platforms, forums and other diverse technological means, tools and applications to make learning more effective and attractive. To verify the impact of the experience of teaching based on e-learning and distance learning and its quality in the educational process and its reflections on students' performance and motivation toward learning, many recent studies have been conducted, such as study Almomani and Abu Musa [6]; Isroani et al. [1]; Almomani et al. [7]; the results of which showed that there are positive attitudes among students toward e-learning and distance learning, and that there is a statistically significant effect of using applications and e-learning tools on students' achievement and motivation toward learning. Based on the results of these studies and other studies [8, 9], the importance of e-learning can be explained as follows:

1. E-learning helps in achieving the educational process flexibly in a way that suits the characteristics and needs of learners and in an interesting and enjoyable way. E-learning helps in achieving educational goals with high efficiency and effectiveness, and the effective use of the learner's time and effort.

2. It contributes to changing the traditional education pattern in educational institutions by focusing on cooperative education and continuous training for teachers and learners in all educational and scientific fields.

3. It contributes to making the learning process more exciting and interesting, as it relies on the use of multiple forms, tools and techniques in presenting information and educational content such as videos, simulations, interactive interfaces... and others, to contribute to attracting students' attention and arousing their interests toward the educational material.

4. It encourages the learner to develop self-learning skills and self-reliance in acquiring information, knowledge and experiences, and to bear responsibility for his own learning, according to his capabilities and abilities, and at a time that suits him, and the ability to interact flexibly with the components of the electronic educational site.

5. It allows learners to control the learning process and receive immediate feedback to ensure their efficiency in implementing learning processes. It also creates an internal motivation that contributes to improving the effectiveness and efficiency of learning strategies and procedures, through their evaluation of the various programs in which they participate and choosing what suits their needs and abilities.

6. It encourages the learner to organize and manage his learning according to the method that suits him, as different learning styles are presented, such as reading, watching, listening, research, experimentation, and communication, and it enables the learner to choose the method that suits him.

7. E-learning provides diverse and information-rich resources and sources that are easy to access within a short period of time.

8. It improves the quality and continuity of education, expands the possibilities for education to reach multiple communities, and provides opportunities for continuous professional and career development throughout life.

9. It increases learners' motivation toward learning and keeping pace with scientific and technological development on an ongoing basis, and interacting with developments in various fields.

10. E-learning employs modern learning methods in a manner that suits the requirements of the current era, and prepares the future generation for the requirements of life.

11. E-learning meets the needs of students with disabilities or special circumstances by providing them with an educational opportunity supported by various media

such as videos and simulations that suit their individual needs and characteristics, where they can learn continuously and repeat their learning according to their needs at any time and from anywhere, which enhances their understanding and comprehension and increases their motivation toward learning.

12. E-learning contributes economically to reducing the cost of education compared to traditional education, which requires transportation and accommodation costs and expenses.

13. E-learning contributes to achieving environmental sustainability, as relying on it reduces the use of paper and printed materials, reliance on electronic archiving and the presence of digital curricula contributes to protecting the environment.

2.3 Types of e-learning

In order to meet the diverse needs of learners through e-learning and expand its spread, and achieve its benefits continuously, the forms of e-learning have diversified into three main types: (1-Synchronous education, 2-Asynchronous education and 3-Blended education), where these types can be explained and distinguished between them as follows [6, 8, 10, 11].

- *Synchronous e-learning*: It is a type of e-learning that requires the presence of the teacher and students together at the same time *via* the internet. This type of education is used to hold live lectures over the internet between the teacher and his students, allowing the teacher to display the educational content and share it with his students, and opening the way for students to ask the teacher questions, and interact with the content and with their colleagues simultaneously, remotely. As it was mentioned, this type of education requires the presence of the educational service provider and the service recipient at the same time in front of the computers, and requires a strong internet connection so that students can participate and interact in live sessions with teachers and their colleagues.

- *Asynchronous e-learning*: This type of e-learning does not require the presence of students and the teacher at the same time, as it allows students to learn and interact with the content at any time and from anywhere without the need for synchronization between the teacher and his students. This is done by displaying pre-recorded lessons and lectures, using email, or publishing educational content in the form of videos, texts, or exercises on educational platforms and giving students the ability to access it at any time, as well as opening the door to asynchronous dialog and discussion, or educational forums and blogs, for students to enable them to exchange information and knowledge between them and their teacher. This type of education allows flexibility in determining the time and place of learning according to what suits the students and their needs. Teachers can combine synchronous and asynchronous e-learning to achieve all the advantages resulting from their use and employment in the educational process. The choice of the type of learning depends on the needs of the learners, the technology available to them, and the goals that should be achieved through learning.

- *Blended learning*: This type of e-learning presents educational content in two ways at the same time: the traditional way and *via* the internet. The learner is given the flexibility to choose and move between them. It combines traditional and e-learning methods, through which e-learning tools and means are integrated with classroom learning, and employed in traditional classrooms in order to enrich the educational process and increase students' motivation to learn by using and employing them, and combining the advantages of the two types of e-learning and traditional learning.

3. Challenges facing e-learning

Based on the tremendous and rapid technological developments and the emergence of new technologies in the field of e-learning, which led to the expansion of the areas of use and employment of e-learning, such as artificial intelligence, augmented and virtual reality technologies, which have contributed and will contribute in the future to creating virtual educational environments that provide customized educational experiences that suit the needs of students and individual differences between them, in addition to contributing to the emergence of new technological innovations that enhance the efficiency of e-learning and make it more effective and attractive to learners. This expansion and development in e-learning and its various and multiple fields have led to the emergence of many challenges that have faced and will face e-learning, These challenges can be divided into five main axes: technical, educational, social, economic, and future challenges, as follows: [11–14].

3.1 Technical challenges

They refer to the obstacles or difficulties that hinder the use and employment of digital technologies, tools, and applications during e-learning. These obstacles affect the quality of the educational process and its access to learners. These challenges are related to the theory of technology and education, which examines how technology affects education and achieves positive outcomes through it in the educational process. These challenges are:

- The digital gap and the quality of internet connection; the digital gap challenge refers to the inequality in students' access to devices and the internet, due to the disparity and difference in students' geographical locations and their internet coverage, which affects the quality of internet connection, or it may be due to their economic and social circumstances. This challenge contradicts the theory of social justice, which focuses on the need to distribute materials and opportunities fairly in society, including educational opportunities to ensure that all students have equal opportunities to learn and achieve academic achievement regardless of their geographical locations, social, economic, gender, or ethnic backgrounds, and not to allow the influence of factors specific to students' circumstances on achieving learning and academic success.

- The difficulty of the availability and suitability of devices and software; this challenge refers to the different social and economic conditions of students that prevent the provision of advanced computer and technical equipment and devices for all students due to the circumstances of their families and their financial capabilities.

- Data security (cyber security): This challenge is represented by the difficulty of providing cyber security for all participants in e-learning, the difficulty of providing protection programs for their computers, and the possibility of students and teachers being exposed to electronic threats that affect their use, interaction and participation in e-learning.

- The existence of a technical infrastructure: One of the challenges facing e-learning is the difficulty of providing infrastructure in all schools and educational institutions due to weak capabilities and lack of financial resources, and thus the difficulty of providing sufficient and appropriate computer devices, laboratories, tools and technical software, in addition to the variation in the geographical locations of these institutions, which affects the quality of communication and the internet, which negatively affects the quality of e-learning and its outcomes.

- The lack of availability of integrated educational platforms, as many schools and educational institutions lack the availability of integrated educational platforms due to the weak capabilities and resources necessary for their availability, which reduces the effectiveness of e-learning and the motivation of teachers and students to interact through it.

3.2 Educational challenges

They refer to the obstacles or difficulties that directly affect the quality of the educational process, teaching methods and strategies, and the effectiveness of learning and interaction between the teacher and their students during e-learning. These challenges are related to the theory of instructional design, which provides a framework for designing effective educational experiences using technology, the theory of constructivist learning, which focuses on the importance of building knowledge through active interaction with content, the theory of social learning, which focuses on the importance of cooperation and interaction between the teacher and the learners and between the learners themselves, in addition to the theory of intrinsic motivation, which focuses on the importance of meeting students' needs for independence and self-efficacy. The most prominent of these educational challenges are:

- The weakness of teachers and students' possession of technical skills. This challenge is considered one of the most important challenges facing e-learning, as it makes it difficult for teachers to access information, use technical tools and devices, and design interactive and interesting lessons over the internet, and develop various educational materials as well as the difficulty of dealing with educational platforms and visual communication tools, which affects the quality of presentation and display of the material. In addition, the weakness of students' possession of technical skills will prevent them from being able to interact and participate in electronic discussions over the internet, and will lead to their feeling of frustration due to the difficulties they face while using and dealing with educational technologies, which reduces their motivation toward learning.

- The weakness of direct interaction between the teacher and students: Students suffer during e-learning from a lack of direct social interaction between them, their teacher and fellow students compared to traditional education, which reduces their enthusiasm, participation and motivation toward learning and weakens cooperative learning among them.

- The presence of effective digital content, as the use of e-learning requires the presence of flexible digital educational content of high quality that complies with standards and achieves the required educational goals, and it is appropriate for students' levels and takes into account individual differences between them. To achieve this, digital content must be prepared and designed by a specialized team and reviewed and evaluated. This requires high effort, time and cost by the educational institution.

- Difficulty in assessing student learning: Teachers face difficulty in assessing student learning in the e-learning environment, and students face difficulty in assessing their own learning and interaction in the e-learning environment, and their possession of the practical and applied skills necessary for learning, which reduces their motivation to continue self-learning.

- Training and preparing teachers (lack of competencies), as teachers need to acquire technical knowledge and skills that enable and qualify them to achieve effectiveness in e-learning. This requires designing and preparing various training programs for teachers and encouraging them to participate in these programs and the practical application of practices and activities related to them in educational situations during e-learning.

- Lack of availability of electronic activities and applications, because using these activities and electronic applications in their official version requires material capabilities, which is difficult to achieve for many users.

3.3 Social challenges

They refer to those difficulties that directly affect social relationships and interaction between teachers and students on the one hand, and between students themselves on the other hand, during e-learning. These social challenges of e-learning are linked to the social learning theory, which calls for the necessity of achieving learning through effective interaction with others by encouraging cooperative learning inside and outside the educational situation. Interaction outside educational situations is represented by distributing students into cooperative groups to implement and work on research projects and working papers. It is also linked to the social capital theory, which focuses on the importance of social relations in achieving success, and the impact of e-learning on the formation and distribution of social capital. The most prominent social challenges of e-learning are the following:

- Social isolation: The use of e-learning reduces direct interaction between students and teachers, and between students themselves, which may reduce their motivation to participate and learn.

- Difficulty in building social relationships in virtual learning environments: The distance between students and their lack of direct interaction as is the case in traditional environments reduces the possibility of building social relationships among them, which may make students feel isolated, self-reliant and lack of participation with others during e-learning.

- Changing the social roles of teachers and learners in e-learning environments: E-learning requires the teacher to develop new skills, manage online learning, display digital content and direct students toward distance learning, while the student's role is to follow-up on learning and rely on himself in the learning process, implement activities, and complete electronic assignments and tasks required by the teacher, which weakens their ability to interact with their teacher and other colleagues to gain direct experiences as in traditional education.

- Society's view of e-learning (beliefs about e-learning): Society views e-learning as a way to achieve learning and obtain academic degrees, but it is not of the same quality as traditional education, which requires direct interaction within direct educational situations in classroom settings. Therefore, we find that many countries and educational institutions still do not recognize certificates obtained through distance learning programs implemented through e-learning.

- Variation in readiness among members of society to deal with e-learning: The members of society vary in terms of the skills they possess to deal with e-learning, as this depends on the degree of their acceptance of e-learning and their desire to attend training programs that qualify them to interact and participate in e-learning, and keep pace with scientific and technological progress. This is what appears to us in the field: individuals who are qualified and enthusiastic about learning through e-learning, in addition to others who are not qualified and do not have the motivation to learn through e-learning and over the internet.

3.4 Economic challenges

This refers to the financial obstacles or difficulties that educational institutions and individuals in general face when using and applying e-learning in the educational process, and it affects the accessibility, quality and sustainability of e-learning. These challenges are related to the theory of academic economics, which aims to analyze the costs and benefits of investing in e-learning, and the theory of human capital, which focuses on the importance of investing in education to develop and enhance skills. The most prominent of these challenges are:

- The cost of technological infrastructure: The application of e-learning in educational institutions requires the provision of computers, tablets or smart phones and the internet network with definite specifications and high quality, which requires a high cost for educational institutions that will adopt it in their programs, and these institutions are often unable to cover these expenses, especially in developing countries, due to the lack of sufficient financial allocations to achieve this.

- Requirements for providing electronic applications: As the e-learning process requires most of the time the provision of electronic educational programs and applications, the provision of which by educational institutions requires a high cost.

- The cost of developing digital educational content: To achieve e-learning, it is necessary to provide interactive electronic educational content that is presented to students, and the design and preparation of this digital electronic content requires specific equipment and capabilities for this and the presence of a specialized team and a high financial cost, which hinders the spread of e-learning in many educational institutions due to their weak capabilities and inability to cover expenses.

- The cost of training and rehabilitation: The transition from traditional education to e-learning requires training faculty members on the use of technologies, their employment, and their use in developed curricula, and this requires financial allocations and a sufficient budget to cover these expenses.

- Providing qualified technical and teaching staff: As e-learning requires continuous support, and this requires the provision of qualified technical staff that can provide technical support to all users.

- Requirements related to time and effort: E-learning requires teachers to spend more time and effort planning, designing and implementing e-learning and it also requires students to allocate more time and effort compared to traditional education, and this may affect their productivity and motivation toward learning.

- The difference in the economic level of individuals, institutions and e-learning; as the use and employment of e-learning varies according to the income level of individuals and educational institutions, and therefore the use and employment of e-learning and the ability to bear the costs necessary to achieve this vary between segments of society according to their economic levels, for example, those with limited income find it difficult to deduct part of their income for e-learning, and this negatively affects achieving equality among members of society in educational opportunities.

- Additional costs and requirements for e-learning: In addition to the above, there are many other costs and requirements that constitute an economic challenge for e-learning. These requirements include the need to maintain the computers used in e-learning, provide anti-virus programs, and the need to pay attention to cyber security to protect the data and information of e-learning users.

4. Future challenges of e-learning

This refers to the set of obstacles or difficulties that e-learning may face in the future with the continued rapid technological development and the changing needs of learners. These challenges are not only related to technical aspects but also include various educational, social and economic issues. These future challenges are linked to the theory of innovation, which helps in understanding how to adopt new technology in education, and the theory of technological prediction, which helps in anticipating future technological developments and their impact on education. These challenges can be highlighted in three basic aspects, which are as follows:

4.1 Future challenges related to the development of technology

- Increased interest in artificial intelligence, expanded use, and increased reliance on it in the future; in light of the rapid developments, artificial intelligence has emerged and has begun to perform multiple tasks such as analyzing data related to students, such as their performance in tests and their learning patterns, and intelligently assessing the emotional states of learning by recognizing their feelings and adapting learning to their emotional state, providing interactive learning experiences and individual support to students. Despite the size of the positives of using and employing artificial intelligence in various areas of life, most notably in the field of education, there are many requirements and challenges that we will be faced in the future when relying on artificial intelligence in particular, and technology in general, most notably the loss of human interaction between students and teachers, which affects the social and emotional aspects of learning. Reliance on artificial intelligence also reduces students' opportunities to develop critical thinking skills and solve problems on their own, which will negatively affect the way students think in the future. In addition, reliance on artificial intelligence will affect issues related to privacy, given that it includes collecting sensitive information about users and the possibility of this data being hacked and misused. The use and development of artificial intelligence systems in the future will require a high cost, which reduces the possibility of relying on them in most educational institutions with limited resources. If adopted, it requires the institution educational develop new strategies to deal with the impact of artificial intelligence on education such as using it to personalize learning experiences and provide support to students, which will lead to changing the roles related to the teacher and the student, as the teacher's role will focus on guidance, counseling and developing students' skills, while the student's role will focus on self-learning and independence in learning. If students rely heavily on artificial intelligence, this will affect their mental abilities related to thinking and problem solving, and will lead to exposure to huge amounts of data that often contain biased opinions, errors, misleading information, or the spread of false news collected from multiple sources, due to the nature of artificial intelligence providing multiple sources of unreliable information that are difficult to verify their original sources, and artificial intelligence cannot evaluate the information it presents or think critically about it. Accordingly, reliance on artificial intelligence is considered a major challenge facing e-learning, and therefore, users must be made aware of the mechanisms for dealing with artificial intelligence and establishing laws and regulations that regulate dealing with it and ensure it is used responsibly.

- Employing virtual and augmented reality technologies in the educational process: This requires developing educational content appropriate for these technologies and using effective tools and equipment to display educational content and interact with it by learners.

- Increasing digital risks and threats with the development of technology: The spread of the internet of things in the future may lead to the provision of huge educational data that requires the development of mechanisms to protect the use of this data and the privacy of users. This indicates the increased exposure of the e-learning system to cyber-attacks and security threats, which will lead to the disruption of e-learning systems and digital protection systems (cyber security), and the loss of data related to users, including teachers and students, in some cases, or the exposure of this data to breaches and violations.

4.2 Future challenges related to social aspects

- The increasing changing needs of learners: With the increase in technological development in the future, the need to develop e-learning systems increases to be able to meet the individual needs of learners, and develop the skills they need in the changing labor market, such as critical thinking, problem solving and creative thinking skills, and work to provide continuous opportunities for learners to develop professionally and personally; this requires the following:

- The continuation of the digital gap: This challenge refers to the continuation of the disparity and variation in access to e-learning opportunities in the future between countries and regions according to their circumstances and terrain, as it is difficult to achieve justice and equality in providing e-learning requirements between these countries due to many reasons and variables, and this will make the digital gap continue over time in the future.

- The increasing social gap between teachers and students during e-learning: With the continued transformation of the world and its orientation toward distance e-learning, and the spread of educational platforms that provide interactive e-learning content to students in an asynchronous manner; it is expected that this will lead to a reduction in direct social interactions between students and their teachers as in traditional educational environments, which will result in a feeling of isolation, loneliness, weak social skills and relationships necessary to interact with others face to face.

4.3 Future challenges of e-learning related to educational and health aspects

- Difficulty in maintaining students' interaction and motivation in the e-learning environment, as their continued interaction with e-learning in the future will lead to a weakening of their motivation toward learning due to their feeling of isolation and boredom, which will reduce their focus and ability to absorb information and participate effectively, which will negatively affect their performance and academic achievement.

- Difficulty in designing educational systems that meet the needs of students with special needs; this is because this category of students includes a wide range of special needs, such as learning difficulties, physical disabilities, sensory disabilities, developmental disorders, etc., and each type of these needs requires a special design. It is also difficult for most of these students to access the assistive technologies they need, such as screen readers, hearing devices, and motor tools. There may be a lack of educational content designed specifically for this category, which makes it difficult for them to learn effectively. Teachers for these students also need specialized training in how to use assistive technologies and design computerized educational systems.

- Increasing health problems in the future for e-learning users due to excessive use of technology; these health problems include vision problems as a result of the eye being exposed to the computer screen for long periods, which will lead to vision problems, a feeling of fatigue and constant headaches, in addition to physical problems such as back and neck pain and obesity due to spending long periods sitting in front of computer screens. There are other psychological problems, such as feeling stressed, anxious, and socially isolated due to excessive use of the internet.

5. Solution to the challenges of e-learning

Addressing the challenges facing e-learning at present and in the future is of utmost importance and requires combined efforts of governments and educational institutions in the public and private sectors to ensure fair access to technology and the internet for all learners regardless of their geographical location or social and economic backgrounds, improve the quality of e-learning and increase the efficiency of the educational process through which it is conducted, develop the skills of teachers and students necessary to achieve it effectively, improve its quality and provide them with the necessary technical support, and increase the motivation of learners and society in general to accept this type of education and adopt it officially in all educational institutions, whether schools, universities or educational colleges, and review the algorithms used in e-learning systems to ensure that there are no societal biases in them. The most prominent solutions to address the challenges facing e-learning can be classified according to the type of challenges mentioned above as follows: [2, 15–17].

5.1 Solutions related to technical challenges

To overcome the technical challenges of e-learning, many solutions must be adopted, the most prominent of which are:

- Developing the technical infrastructure: This is done by investing by governments and relevant authorities in countries in improving and expanding internet networks to include all remote and nearby areas, to enable individuals to obtain equal educational opportunities, creating electronic educational platforms for e-learning, providing tablets or laptops for needy students, providing technical support for students and teachers, providing laboratories equipped with computers, software, equipment and necessary electronic applications, and working on continuously updating these devices and their programs to be able to run the latest educational applications and programs. In addition, there is a need to provide qualified technical support teams to help teachers and students solve the technical problems they face during e-learning, and to provide instructional guides and educational videos to help them use educational devices and programs and deal with them easily. This is consistent with the theory of technological development, which focuses on the importance of providing the technological infrastructure necessary for development in its various educational, economic and social fields.

- Reducing the digital gap, it is necessary to work on providing all the requirements of e-learning and establishing community centers that provide access to the internet and devices in different countries and regions in similar ways in order to ensure the achievement of equality in e-learning opportunities for all members of society, regardless of their circumstances and locations. This is consistent with the theory of human justice, which aims to provide equal opportunities for all to obtain education.

- Work to enhance cyber security requirements: This is done by implementing modern protection systems and applications in order to protect user data, encrypt all sensitive data such as student data and test results to protect them from unauthorized access, protect electronic processes and tests that take place during e-learning from hacking, facilitate the process of accessing them safely by users (students, teachers and other members of society), and work to educate teachers and students about the dangers of cyber security such as phishing and malware, and how to protect themselves and their data from them.

- To address security and privacy issues: Tt is necessary to use safe and reliable educational platforms, educate students and teachers about the dangers of the internet and how to protect their personal data, and implement strict policies to protect student privacy.

5.2 Solutions related to educational challenges

To overcome the educational challenges of e-learning, it is necessary to adopt many solutions that are based on constructivist and cognitive learning theories, which focus on the importance of achieving effective student participation by providing attractive and effective electronic experiences, technologies and content, exchanging experiences to build knowledge, and focusing on continuous training and development for them to develop their skills, in addition to the theory of educational measurement and evaluation, which focuses on the importance of using various assessment tools and techniques to measure learning outcomes comprehensively. These solutions are as follows:

- Keeping pace with the requirements of the digital age, developing educational curricula and teaching methods, and benefiting from modern technology.

- Not relying entirely on e-learning to implement the learning process; rather, the integrated (hybrid) type of e-learning must be adopted, which combines traditional and virtual classes, as more spread of hybrid education is expected in the future, in which virtual classes gain their importance through systematic participation in traditional classrooms, to become more applicable and to meet future educational requirements.

- Providing distinguished educational experiences according to the needs and abilities of learners, and improving educational content with the help of teachers and experts specialized in designing and producing content.

- Designing flexible and attractive interactive e-learning content that encourages students to interact, participate, research, innovate, communicate and learn remotely to achieve the desired educational goals and reach qualitative educational outcomes. Examples of methods that can be used include the game-based and simulation-based learning methods, providing incentives for outstanding students to create competition among them, and providing personal support for students who face difficulties during their learning.

- Preparing and training teachers and students: This is done by focusing on holding training courses to familiarize teachers with the latest e-learning technologies and urging them to diversify their use, training them on using e-learning, its tools and applications, and diversifying workshops and training programs for teachers and those concerned with e-learning in various fields of professional development and digital transformation.

- Using more fun and effective interactive technologies such as electronic simulation programs, interactive videos, computerized tests and practical applications, opinion polls, discussion forums, encouraging students to cooperate in group projects *via* the internet, and providing opportunities for direct communication with teachers through virtual sessions or office hours.

- Using various evaluation methods: To address the challenges of assessing student learning in e-learning environments, a variety of assessment methods must be used to enable teachers to assess their students' learning and help students assess their own learning. Examples of these methods include online tests, projects, presentations, peer assessment and the use of analytical tools to track student progress and identify their weaknesses.

5.3 Solutions related to social challenges

There are many solutions to overcome the social challenges of e-learning, the most prominent of which are:

- Organizing awareness campaigns and preparing and distributing educational and media brochures in the community, to explain the benefits of e-learning and its use in the educational process, increasing their skills and experience in using its tools, and the importance of acquiring skills related to it to keep pace with scientific and technological progress.

- Educating users of artificial intelligence in e-learning about the limitations of artificial intelligence models and that it is not considered an alternative to critical thinking, which is only an auxiliary tool for the human mind and not a substitute for it, working to verify the information obtained through artificial intelligence models by referring to reliable sources, developing transparent and flexible models that are free of biases, and setting laws and regulations that regulate dealing with it and using it responsibly.

- Promoting lifelong learning to enable members of society to continue learning and develop their knowledge and skills; this is done by encouraging them to participate in open extracurricular activities *via* the internet, creating virtual groups and clubs that take into account the various interests and inclinations of learners and increase communication and cooperation between them, and working to appreciate the efforts and achievements of learners during the educational stages and honoring them by granting them certificates and awards that serve as evidence of their skills and knowledge that are referred to and included in their CVs and personal files, in addition to providing opportunities for promotion and development for them in their areas of excellence by providing scholarship programs and training opportunities and participating in scientific conferences and seminars, to encourage them to continue learning throughout life and achieve more achievements.

- Providing opportunities for social interaction *via* the internet; this This is to confront social isolation among students themselves and among their teachers due to the use and employment of e-learning for students; this can be achieved through discussion forums and virtual groups, and working to organize virtual social events.
- Providing flexible schedules for students to freely implement the learning process as they see fit, working to provide them with diverse options for self-learning, and taking into account the views of parents and their families regarding the use of e-learning in distance learning environments for students and the appropriate conditions for its effective implementation.
- Providing training programs for parents on how to support their children's learning *via* the internet, opening communication channels between teachers and parents to discuss their children's progress, and involving community members in providing lessons or lectures *via* the Internet.
- Providing psychological and social support for students; this is done by providing psychological and social counselors to provide support to students who have difficulties during learning, and creating guidance programs for new students to help them adapt to the e-learning environment.
- Setting strict policies to combat cyber bullying, working to educate students about the dangers of bullying and how to deal with it, setting specific mechanisms and procedures for reporting cases of bullying to confront and overcome them, and providing support to students who are subjected to bullying.

5.4 Solutions related to economic challenges

To overcome the economic challenges of e-learning, it was necessary to develop the essential solutions to confront these challenges, the most important of which are:

- The necessity of educational institutions possessing modern technologies and means of communication, and ensuring the possibility of using them in the educational process effectively.
- Providing financial support to develop and digitize curricula and related projects; this is done by improving and developing educational curricula and digitizing these curricula, developing educational portals, and preparing educational projects based on the use of information and communication technology.
- Supporting and developing evaluation and accreditation systems; to improve e-learning, it is necessary to evaluate the performance of all parties to the educational process, monitor quality, and continuously improve technical means and

digital platforms to provide appropriate educational content and achieve interaction between teachers and learners *via* the internet. This is done by using various evaluation tools that ensure the integrity of tests and evaluate students' different skills.

- Providing financial support to develop comprehensive standards for the e-learning process, providing diverse and purposeful training for teachers, students, and administrators on the use of e-learning tools, and raising their awareness of their importance in communication between teachers and students.

- Continuous improvement of the e-learning experience, through the development of modern tools and technologies to improve the learning experience and meet the diverse needs of students by developing flexible interactive e-learning content, working to continuously improve this content, and providing various additional sources to enrich the interactive educational content and encourage students to research and learn independently.

- Providing free or discounted internet service to needy students, and working on using data compression technology to reduce internet consumption, in addition to providing government support programs and scholarships for needy students, and using free or open-source electronic programs and applications.

5.5 Solutions related to the future challenges of e-learning

To overcome the future challenges of e-learning, it was necessary to develop appropriate solutions that would ensure that we face these challenges in the future. The most prominent of these solutions are the following:

- Strategic planning for e-learning, which is considered one of the most prominent solutions necessary to face the future challenges of e-learning, as it provides an organized and comprehensive framework for thinking about the future of e-learning and preparing for it, and continuing to provide high-quality education for all learners in the future. Strategic planning can be achieved through:

- Determining future trends: This is done by analyzing the external e-learning environment (technological, social, and educational), understanding the rapid developments in technology and changing learners' needs and modern educational trends, and anticipating potential challenges that may face the future of e-learning such as the development of artificial intelligence, changing the nature of the labor market, and the emergence of new technologies.

- Developing a clear vision for the future of e-learning, identifying realistic and measurable strategic goals that must be achieved through this vision, and working to determine priorities and allocate resources to achieve strategic goals.

- Developing innovative educational and teaching strategies that encourage students to acquire and practice creative and critical thinking skills, benefit from modern technologies, work on developing training programs for students to develop their skills necessary to adapt to future developments, and provide effective, high-quality and relevant educational opportunities for all learners in the future.

- The necessity of investing in research and development: Research and development in the field of e-learning must be invested in to explore new technologies by developing innovative educational platforms, developing high-quality digital educational content, developing new educational tools and technologies, conducting research and studies, and utilizing artificial intelligence to customize learning experiences and provide support to students while taking into account potential risks, in order to contribute to building a future generation capable of keeping pace with the challenges of the era.

- Preparing for change and adopting a culture of continuous learning: Educational institutions must be prepared to adapt to technological changes and the changing needs of learners, in order to be able to understand these needs and respond to them effectively, and adopt a culture of continuous learning to follow the latest developments in the field of e-learning and benefit from them to improve the learning experience. Readiness for change is the key to success in facing the future challenges of e-learning and is achieved by adopting a culture of readiness for change, investing in skills development, and cooperating with others by establishing partnerships and cooperation agreements with other institutions in different sectors such as universities, research centers and technology companies, in order to exchange experiences and knowledge and develop innovative solutions to future challenges.

- Focus on the learner as the focus of the educational process: When designing and implementing e-learning programs, attention must be focused on the learner and work to provide diverse activities, programs, and learning experiences that take into account individual differences among them and their inclinations and meet their needs, as educational content, teaching methods, and assessment activities can be customized to suit each student's learning style. Students can also be allowed to work on realistic educational projects related to their interests, in addition to focusing on e-learning on developing the basic skills that learners need in the changing labor market, such as critical thinking, problem solving, creativity, cooperation and communication.

- Designing flexible and adaptable e-learning systems to meet the different needs of students, working to integrate assistive technologies into e-learning systems to facilitate access to and interaction with content for students with special needs, developing specialized content for these students and taking into account their different needs and abilities, enabling them to access and participate in education fully, and developing their skills and abilities to the maximum extent. E-learning can help integrate students with special needs into the educational community and reduce their sense of isolation. To achieve this, specialized training must be provided for teachers on how to use assistive technologies and design appropriate educational systems for students with special needs, involving students and their families in designing these educational systems, and cooperating with experts in the field of special education and educational technology to design effective and appropriate educational systems.

- Addressing the future challenges of e-learning related to health aspects requires joint efforts between students, teachers, parents and educational institutions through awareness of the health risks of e-learning and proper planning for how to deal with them, in addition to providing a comfortable learning environment and appropriate lighting, encouraging them to practice physical activity, providing psychological support to students and teachers to help them deal with stress and anxiety, and educating them about the safe and moderate use of technology and avoiding its excessive use.

6. Conclusions

In spite of the many advantages that appeared and coincided with the emergence and spread of e-learning as a qualitative shift in the field of education in the late twentieth century and the beginning of the twenty-first century; these advantages and positives of e-learning were accompanied by the presence of many challenges and negatives that led to the weak dealing with e-learning at the beginning by many educational institutions. Among these challenges were: lack of direct interaction between teachers and their students, weak technical infrastructure, the need for high-quality interactive e-learning content, the difficulty of assessing student learning during the e-learning process, the possibility of data and information related to e-learning being hacked and security threats, as well as the difficulty of maintaining their motivation toward self-learning in the absence of direct follow-up and guidance from teachers. In light of these great and broad challenges, it was necessary to unite and cooperate between educational institutions and technology developers to work on developing solutions and procedural methods that reduce the continuity of the impact of these challenges on e-learning in the future, and to provide various means of support to those concerned in the development process to ensure the achievement of quality in the educational outcomes of e-learning. Perhaps the most prominent measures and solutions to address these challenges are: developing comprehensive standards for teaching and evaluating content *via* e-learning, improving the technical infrastructure to enable teachers to implement e-learning effectively, preparing and training teachers to deal with the use and employment of e-learning in teaching, and enhancing cyber security requirements to protect the data, accounts, businesses and tasks of e-learning users. Through this, we can overcome the challenges of e-learning and reduce their impact on the future of this type of education, which has become widespread in most countries of the world, and achieve the maximum possible benefit from this type of education in various areas of life. It should be noted here that we cannot rely on e-learning completely in the future, but rather we must work to adopt what is known as hybrid education in educational institutions, which makes virtual classrooms more applicable through systematic participation with traditional classrooms.

Acknowledgements

The submitted work is original and has not been published in a peer-reviewed publication.

Conflict of interest

I confirm there are no conflicts of interest.

Author details

Jehad Ali Tawfiq Almomani
Amman Arab University, Amman, Jordan

*Address all correspondence to: jmomani@aau.edu.jo

References

[1] Isroani F, Jaafar N, Muflihaini M. Effectiveness of e-learning learning to improve student learning outcomes at madrasah Aliyah. International Journal of Science Education and Cultural Studies. 2022;**1**(1):42-51. DOI: 10.58291/ijsecs.v1i1.26

[2] Sumallika T, Raju DPVM, Indira DDNVSLS, Lakshmi PR. An overview of E-learning and its challenges in India. International Journal of Mechanical Engineering. 2022;7:314-319

[3] Alawneh Y, Masouda D, Lubna J, Musa G, Mithqal K. E-Learning and its Contemporary Challenges. Amman: Al-Yazouri Scientific House for Publishing and Distribution; 2022

[4] Hudhaifa AM, Mazhar A-A. Interactive e-Learning. 1st ed. Amman: Academic Book Center; 2015

[5] Tariq A. E-Learning and Virtual Education (Contemporary Global Trends). 1st ed. Cairo: Arab Group for Training and Publishing; 2015

[6] Ali AJ, Mofeed AM. A comparative study of the effectiveness of using Padlet in distance learning: Viewpoint of postgraduate students. Journal of Education and e-Learning Research. 2022;**9**(2):95-102. DOI: 10.20448/jeelr.v9i2.3954

[7] Ali AJ, Moen A, Nusaibah A. Evaluating the distance university education experience after using the zoom application in Jordan from the students point of view. Universal Journal of Educational Research. 2020;**8**(11B):6239-6247. DOI: 10.13189/ujer.2020.082262

[8] Tangirov KE, Jomurodov DM, Murodkasimova SK. The importance of e-learning and e-learning resources in individualized learning. Asian Journal of Multidimensional Research (AJMR). 2021;**10**(3):464-469. DOI: 10.5958/2278-4853.2021.00176.2

[9] Babu GS, Sridevi K. Importance of E-learning in higher education: A study. International Journal of Research Culture Society. 2018;**2**(5):84-88

[10] Tawafak RM, AlSideir A, Alfarsi G, Al-Nuaimi MN, Malik SI, Jabbar J. E-learning vs. traditional learning for learners satisfaction. e-Learning. 2019;**29**(3):388-397

[11] Hussein AAA. Problems of using e-learning in teaching social subjects for the sixth grade from the point of view of teachers. Basic Education College Magazine For Educational and Humanities Sciences. 2022;**14**(57):1367-1381

[12] Osaily DRZ. The Challenges Facing Learners in Implementing E-Learning in Hebron Educational Region Al-Quds Open University/Palestine (Case Study). Palestinian Journal for Open Learning & e-learning; 2018:**4**(7):1-24

[13] Dumbiri DN, Nwadiani CO. Challenges facing application of E-learning facilities in vocational and technical education program in South Nigeria universities. Asian Journal of Vocational Education and Humanities. 2020;**1**(2):1-8. DOI: 10.53797/ajvah.v1i2.1.2020

[14] Eli-Chukwu NC, Igbokwe IC, Ifebude B, Nmadu D, Iguodala W, Uma U, et al. Challenges confronting e-learning in higher education institutions in Nigeria amid Covid-19. Journal of Applied Research in

Higher Education. 2023;**15**(1):238-253. DOI: 10.1108/JARHE-09-2021-0346

[15] Shahmoradi L, Changizi V, Mehraeen E, Bashiri A, Jannat B, Hosseini M. The challenges of E-learning system: Higher educational institutions perspective. Journal of Education and Health Promotion. 2018;**7**(1):116. DOI: 10.4103/jehp.jehp_39_18

[16] Azairok M, Fathurohman A. Development of E-learning based learning media assisted by Chamilo in learning physics to improve learning outcomes of high school students. Jurnal Penelitian Pendidikan IPA. 2023;**9**(10):7871-7878. DOI: 10.29303/jppipa.v9i10.4594

[17] Hakimi M, Katebzadah S, Fazil AW. Comprehensive insights into E-learning in contemporary education: Analyzing trends, challenges, and best practices. Journal of Education and Teaching Learning (JETL). 2024;**6**(1):86-105. DOI: 10.51178/jetl.v6i1.1720

Chapter 8

Learning in the Digital Age: COVID-19's Impact and the Rise of Education 4.0

Fortunate Tintswalo Silinda

Abstract

E-learning transitioned from being a supplementary educational tool to a critical global resource during the COVID-19 pandemic, reshaping the education landscape. This chapter explores its progression from enhancing engagement to promoting emotional resilience amid prolonged disruptions. As education transitions towards a post-pandemic era, hybrid models that integrate physical and digital spaces are becoming increasingly relevant, aligning with the adaptive and personalised learning focus of Education 4.0. This chapter draws on Transformative Learning Theory to explore how the disruption brought about by the COVID-19 pandemic altered educational practices and influenced institutional preparedness for Education 4.0. Particular attention is given to issues of inclusivity, educator readiness, and data privacy within digital learning environments. By adopting this lens, the chapter offers a fresh perspective on how systemic challenges and opportunities in education can be reconsidered through critical reflection and meaningful transformational change.

Keywords: E-learning, Education 4.0, digital transformation, equity, lifelong learning

1. Introduction

In an era marked by globalisation, cultural shifts and identity conflicts, today's teaching and learning pedagogy is increasingly shaped by the emergence of digital technologies. The traditional, classroom-based educational model has been challenged by the rise of online and hybrid learning environments, and e-learning has become a fundamental resource in this transformation. E-learning refers to the use of digital platforms and technology to facilitate education and learning, allowing students to engage with content, collaborate and receive instruction through the internet and electronic devices [1]. It can be implemented through on-campus or off-campus models.

E-learning enables universities and other educational institutions to offer innovative delivery methods that provide flexibility and accessibility [2]. As a result of e-learning, digital platforms allow learning to extend beyond physical boundaries, where students access course content and collaborate from different locations around the world using devices like smartphones, tablets and laptops [3, 4].

The model of integrating technology and the internet into education began in the early 2000s and has since allowed for the personalisation of learning experiences [1]. One of the benefits of the use of technology in education is that students can engage with materials at their own pace, enabling them to process information in ways that best suit their individual learning styles. Also, students are motivated and engaged in collaborating with their peers; have access to hands-on learning opportunities; are able to learn at all levels; are more confident and have improved technology skills [3, 5].

Since many schools and universities offered learning through face-to-face methods, they had not given much thought to incorporating technology or the internet into their teaching. However, the COVID-19 pandemic served as an unexpected accelerator for the widespread adoption of e-learning [5]. It prompted schools and universities to transition rapidly to online learning platforms in response to physical distancing measures [6]. What began as a supplementary option became the primary mode of instruction for millions of students worldwide. Initiatives like "Classes Suspended but Learning Continues" ensured that education could continue despite the closure of educational institutions. During this time, e-learning helped bridge the gap caused by physical classroom closures, but it also raised new challenges, particularly around maintaining student engagement and fostering emotional resilience amidst prolonged periods of isolation and uncertainty.

As the pandemic gradually subsides and physical learning spaces reopen, it is crucial to rethink the role of e-learning within the educational ecosystem and explore hybrid models that combine the strengths of traditional and digital learning. Hybrid models, also known as blended learning models, combine both physical and digital learning environments and are becoming increasingly relevant. A hybrid model of education integrates traditional face-to-face classroom experiences with digital tools and online learning platforms. This model allows students the flexibility to participate in education in a way that combines the benefits of both in-person and remote learning [7]. The hybrid model is particularly important in a post-pandemic world, where digital and physical learning will coexist to offer more inclusive, personalised and flexible education.

The shift to hybrid learning aligns with the principles of Education 4.0, a framework driven by the technological advancements of the Fourth Industrial Revolution (4IR). Education 4.0 refers to a transformation in education that seeks to integrate emerging technologies – such as artificial intelligence (AI), the Internet of Things (IoT), blockchain, and big data analytics – into learning environments [8, 9]. This approach places emphasis on flexibility, student-centred learning, the development of critical skills, and the integration of digital technologies to prepare students for the challenges of a rapidly changing, tech-driven world.

The global outbreak of COVID-19 brought about more than a temporary interruption to education – it compelled institutions, educators and learners to reconsider the very foundations of how learning is structured and delivered. What initially began as an emergency shift to online learning has, over time, revealed broader possibilities and long-term shifts in educational thinking and practice.

Out of this disruption has emerged a more digitally integrated approach to education, increasingly referred to as Education 4.0. Here, technology is no longer viewed as an add-on but as an essential part of the learning process. Education 4.0 promotes adaptive, learner-centred environments driven by digital tools and aligned with the demands of the Fourth Industrial Revolution (4IR). It also supports one of the key objectives of the United Nations' 2030 Agenda for Sustainable Development – to ensure inclusive, equitable and quality education for all.

This chapter explores how the pandemic has influenced the development and use of e-learning and considers how these shifts might support or hinder progress towards the goals of Education 4.0. Drawing on Transformative Learning Theory, it seeks to understand not just what changed but also how individuals and institutions experienced and responded to these changes on a deeper level.

The chapter begins by offering a historical overview of e-learning, followed by a reflection on how learning practices evolved during the pandemic—from basic digital engagement to the development of more resilient and reflective approaches. It then examines emerging challenges and insights in the post-pandemic context, with particular attention to issues such as equity and access, educator readiness, pedagogical innovation, and data privacy.

Finally, the chapter looks ahead to the future of e-learning, identifying opportunities for continued growth and improvement. It reflects on how education systems can build on the lessons of the pandemic to create more responsive, inclusive and sustainable digital learning environments that are well-aligned with the evolving needs of society and the world of work.

2. Historical context of E-learning

The roots of e-learning can be traced back to the early 1990s when educational institutions began exploring the potential of distance learning technologies. With the advent of the internet and email, students in geographically remote areas were able to access course materials and interact with their instructors without being physically present on campus. This laid the foundation for what we now understand as online learning.

Though often treated as a modern phenomenon, the origins of e-learning can be linked to the early twentieth century with correspondence education. By the late 1990s, as the internet became more accessible, digital learning environments began to take shape. Virtual learning environments, such as Moodle and Blackboard, gradually became fixtures in higher education, although their use remained largely supplemental rather than systemic. It wasn't until the pandemic that digital learning was positioned as central to the continuity of education, revealing both its potential and its limits.

In the early stages of e-learning, much of the focus was on providing information via static web pages, CDs and email [9]. However, as the internet evolved, so did the tools and methods for online education. Multimedia content, including videos, animations and interactive quizzes, became increasingly common, allowing for richer, more engaging learning experiences. The use of learning management systems (LMS) such as Moodle and Blackboard also facilitated the centralisation of course materials and administrative functions, making it easier for both students and educators to manage coursework and assignments [10, 11].

By the early 2000s, e-learning had become increasingly integrated into mainstream education, and its benefits were evident [10, 11]. It was seen as an effective way to increase student engagement, personalise learning, and reduce the barriers imposed by traditional classroom settings. Not only could students access materials at their convenience, but they could also work at their own pace, allowing for a more flexible and tailored learning experience.

One of the key advantages of e-learning is its ability to reduce the logistical burden on students. For instance, students no longer need to commute long distances to attend lectures, saving both time and money. Furthermore, the internet has enabled access to a wide variety of resources, including readings, tutorials and discussion forums, all of which can be accessed at any time. E-learning has also proven advantageous for students who face challenges related to geographical location, physical disabilities or work commitments, as it allows them to engage with educational content from anywhere.

The rapid shift to online learning due to the COVID-19 pandemic highlighted both the strengths and weaknesses of the e-learning system. On the one hand, e-learning facilitated continuity of education when physical classrooms were no longer an option. On the other hand, the pandemic also exposed the significant digital divide that exists globally, with many students lacking access to devices or reliable internet connections [12]. The sudden shift also revealed the need for educator training in new digital tools and techniques, as many educators were not prepared to deliver lessons in an entirely online environment [13].

As we move forward, it is crucial to build on the lessons learned during the pandemic. E-learning must be integrated into the broader educational ecosystem, combining the benefits of online and face-to-face learning. Hybrid models, which blend traditional classroom learning with digital tools, will play a key role in this future. The pandemic has underscored the need for equity in access to digital resources and for the ongoing professional development of educators to ensure that they are prepared to meet the needs of students in a post-pandemic world.

Before the pandemic, e-learning was primarily supplementary, with many institutions reluctant to shift away from face-to-face models. In much of the Global South, including South Africa, digital learning was viewed as a distant goal due to infrastructure challenges, unequal access and limited training for educators. Transformative Learning Theory helps us reflect on why this inertia existed – many educators had not yet encountered a disorienting dilemma strong enough to question and shift entrenched teaching methods.

3. The evolution of E-learning: From engagement to resilience during the COVID-19 pandemic

The evolution of e-learning has been characterised by continuous innovation and adaptation. Over the years, educational technology has progressed from simple email-based correspondence courses to sophisticated, interactive digital environments that facilitate collaboration and engagement [14]. The ability to create dynamic, multimedia-rich educational experiences has been a game-changer for e-learning, making it more engaging and effective for students [15].

Initially, much of the focus of e-learning research centred on its ability to increase student engagement and make education more accessible to learners facing geographical, financial or physical barriers. Organisations like Khan Academy, founded in 2008, were at the forefront of this movement, offering free, interactive educational resources to communities that otherwise had limited access to educational materials [15, 16]. Similarly, institutions like the Open University in the UK used multimedia platforms to deliver high-quality, accessible learning materials to students in remote areas.

As e-learning became more widely adopted, new pedagogical strategies began to emerge. The traditional, lecture-based model was challenged by the opportunities for active, student-centred learning that digital technologies afforded. Instead of merely passively receiving information, students were encouraged to interact with course content, collaborate with peers, and apply their knowledge in real-world contexts [3]. This shift towards more participatory learning models has been shown to improve student outcomes by fostering deeper engagement and critical thinking [3].

The onset of COVID-19 served as that disorienting dilemma. Institutions and educators had to swiftly re-evaluate traditional delivery methods and move into fully digital environments. This transformation was not merely logistical but conceptual—prompting deeper reflection on pedagogy, access and student engagement.

3.1 Regional innovations: South Africa and beyond

The COVID-19 pandemic affected countries worldwide, including those in Africa, where e-learning adoption had previously been slower due to infrastructure challenges. However, the necessity of continuing education in the face of lockdowns prompted significant innovation in regions like South Africa and Kenya.

In South Africa, where many students in underprivileged communities have limited access to devices and stable internet connections, educators adapted by using WhatsApp for asynchronous learning [17]. This simple, low-cost tool enabled educators to share study materials, facilitate discussions and provide guidance to students remotely. The University of South Africa (UNISA) took additional steps by launching mobile learning strategies that allowed students to access lecture recordings and course materials through mobile-friendly portals. By partnering with telecom companies, UNISA also made these resources available to students without the added financial burden of data costs. These efforts helped bridge the digital divide and ensure that education continued despite the crisis.

In Kenya, Ethiopia, Democratic Republic of Congo, Rwanda, Ghana, Morocco, Mali and South Africa where internet access was even more limited in some regions, the government and educational institutions turned to alternative methods of deliver educational content [18, 19]. For example, radio and television broadcasts were used to distribute lessons to students in remote areas, ensuring that learning could continue even without internet access. These low-tech, scalable solutions provided an effective means of overcoming the challenges posed by the pandemic and demonstrated the importance of context-sensitive, adaptable solutions to educational disruptions.

Across many African countries, responses to the disruption of education during the pandemic were shaped by local realities and available resources. Zero-rated educational websites, lessons broadcast over radio and television and mobile-accessible platforms became practical tools for reaching students who had limited or no access to the Internet. While these measures had their shortcomings, they helped keep learning going in uncertain times. Institutions and governments in places like South Africa, Kenya, Ghana and Ethiopia worked with what they had, showing that flexible and context-aware solutions can make a real difference. The pandemic highlighted the need for education systems that are not only inclusive but also better prepared for future challenges.

3.2 Lessons in resilience and adaptation

The rapid adoption of e-learning during the pandemic emphasised the importance of resilience and adaptability in education. Educational systems had to adjust quickly to the changing circumstances, and both educators and students demonstrated remarkable flexibility in responding to new challenges.

For instance, Finland and Korea implemented digital well-being initiatives aimed at supporting students' mental health. In Finland, it was revealed that the shift to remote learning was generally viewed positively by students, educators and parents or guardians [20–22]. According to UNESCO, these groups felt that communication during the transition was adequate, though many expressed a desire for more structured lessons, particularly ones delivered via video [20].

However, it remains difficult to determine whether having a more relaxed timetable is entirely beneficial, especially as some students reported feelings of isolation and a lack of social interaction. Other perceived benefits cited by learners included increased access to digital devices like phones and computers, a decrease in bullying, which improved concentration, and receiving more personalised assistance from teachers.

Most educators maintained daily contact with their students through digital platforms using written messages, phone calls, or video sessions [23]. Some educators even highlighted that chat groups, video conferencing, voting tools and document sharing spaces made it more effective and efficient for them to reach out to students, underscoring that they will continue to adopt the online model in the post-pandemic era [24]. Notably, providing individual feedback became a major focus, consuming significant time and energy and adding pressure to teachers' workloads [25].

Despite its many benefits, the shift to e-learning also revealed several challenges. These included screen fatigue, the lack of social interaction and unequal access to devices and reliable internet, which disproportionately affected students from low-income households [26]. Moreover, the rapid shift to online education often left educators with little time to adapt their teaching methods, resulting in inconsistent learning experiences for students.

Nevertheless, the pandemic acted as a catalyst for change, accelerating the shift towards more flexible, technology-driven approaches to teaching and learning. As educational institutions move forward, the lessons learned during this time can be used to shape a more inclusive, equitable and resilient future for education.

Educators who had never used digital tools began to adapt rapidly –evidence of transformative learning through experience, reflection and action. This period saw the emergence of resilience among both students and lecturers, not just in managing digital platforms but also in rethinking what meaningful engagement looks like in virtual settings [3, 27].

4. COVID-19's impact and the rise of Education 4.0: A transformative learning perspective

The unprecedented disruption brought about by the COVID-19 pandemic prompted an urgent re-evaluation of educational structures worldwide. What began as an emergency shift to remote learning has evolved into a sustained transformation of how education is delivered, experienced and conceptualised. To make sense of this shift – and to understand the enduring changes in teaching practices, institutional frameworks and learner experiences – it is vital to engage with a theoretical model that accounts not only for adaptation but also for deep, reflective change. One such framework is Transformative Learning Theory, developed by Jack Mezirow, which offers critical insight into how individuals and systems recalibrate in response to disruption.

Transformative Learning Theory, first articulated by Mezirow in 1978, posits that adults learn most profoundly when they are compelled to critically examine their assumptions, values and habitual ways of thinking. This process is often initiated by what Mezirow termed a "disorienting dilemma" – an event or experience that challenges existing worldviews and compels a reconsideration of previously held beliefs.

Unlike surface-level learning, which may involve acquiring new skills or information, transformative learning involves a restructuring of the learner's frame of reference. It requires critical reflection, rational discourse and the capacity to act upon newly formed insights. While this process often begins at the individual level, it can extend into organisational, cultural and systemic spheres, fostering collective transformation in response to shifting circumstances.

4.1 The pandemic as catalyst for transformative learning

The global education sector experienced a disorienting dilemma during the pandemic. The sudden closure of schools and universities, the loss of physical learning environments and the urgent need to deliver instruction through digital means forced educators, learners and policymakers into a process of rapid reflection and adaptation [28].

Educators who had long relied on in-person pedagogy were compelled to experiment with online platforms, redesign assessment strategies and manage virtual engagement – all while grappling with their own uncertainty and personal challenges. For learners, the transition demanded heightened independence, digital literacy and emotional resilience. Institutions, meanwhile, were required to rethink infrastructure, reallocate resources and devise new policies for inclusion and access.

In Mezirow's terms, this period marked the initiation of a transformative learning process on a global scale – a rethinking not merely of methods but also of meanings. The core questions extended beyond "how can we teach online?" to "what is the purpose of education in this context?", "who is being left behind?", and "how must our systems evolve to remain relevant and equitable?"

5. Emerging insights and challenges in the post-pandemic era

As we enter the post-pandemic era, educational systems are faced with the challenge of reimagining the role of e-learning within a hybrid model of instruction. While physical classrooms are reopening, it is clear that the lessons learned from the pandemic can help shape more inclusive and engaging learning experiences moving forward. Hybrid models, which blend online and in-person learning, offer the potential for more flexible and personalised education.

However, there are several challenges to overcome to fully realise the potential of e-learning in the post-pandemic world. Key issues include ensuring equitable access to digital tools and infrastructure, training educators to effectively use digital platforms and safeguarding student data privacy [29].

Digital learning has the potential to democratise education, but persistent inequalities in connectivity, device access and digital literacy remain. The experience of the pandemic invites a transformative rethinking of equity – not simply as access to technology, but as access to meaningful, supported and context-sensitive learning experiences.

5.1 Equity and access

The COVID-19 pandemic exposed the stark disparities in access to digital tools, broadband internet and technology between different demographic groups, particularly between urban and rural areas and in low-income communities. In many parts of the world, including Sub-Saharan Africa [30] and parts of Asia [31] and the USA [30], a significant number of students faced obstacles that made e-learning and hybrid education models difficult to implement. For example, many students lacked reliable internet connections, access to personal devices or even electricity in some remote regions. This digital divide has led to unequal learning opportunities, further exacerbating existing inequalities in education [29].

During the pandemic, governments and institutions made attempts to bridge this gap, such as providing students with free data or subsidising internet access. In countries like Kenya and Nigeria, radio and television broadcasts were used to reach students in rural areas. While these solutions helped to mitigate the immediate challenges, they were not long-term solutions. The key to overcoming the digital divide lies in sustained investment in digital infrastructure, including reliable and affordable broadband access in rural and underserved areas.

In addition to infrastructure, there needs to be a focus on ensuring that devices are made available to students who cannot afford them. Public-private partnerships can be instrumental in providing low-cost devices to students, as seen in some initiatives in Africa where telecom companies and governments collaborated to offer subsidised smartphones and laptops for educational purposes.

Moreover, the digital divide goes beyond access to technology. The skills needed to use these tools effectively also vary greatly among students and educators [4]. As a result, digital literacy must become an integral part of the curriculum, ensuring that both students and educators are equipped to navigate the digital environment effectively.

Educators were pushed to redesign curricula in ways that prioritised learner autonomy, digital collaboration and problem-based learning. These shifts represent a move away from rote learning towards critical and reflective thinking, aligning with Mezirow's emphasis on learning that transforms worldviews.

5.2 Pedagogical innovation

The integration of e-learning into the educational ecosystem requires a shift in teaching methods and strategies. While traditional, lecture-based teaching remains the norm in many educational institutions, the growing presence of e-learning demands the adoption of more interactive, student-centred pedagogical models. The key to a successful hybrid model is ensuring that online and offline learning are seamlessly integrated to foster deeper engagement, critical thinking and collaboration.

The flipped classroom model, which encourages students to engage with content before attending class and using in-person time for application, discussion and problem-solving, is one of the most effective pedagogical innovations made possible by e-learning. This model shifts the role of the educator from a "lecturer" to a facilitator of learning. Educators guide students through complex concepts, encourage collaborative learning and provide feedback in real-time, rather than simply delivering content. Research has shown that the flipped classroom model can significantly improve students' engagement and mastery of the material, as it promotes active learning and deepens understanding [32].

Moreover, gamification – the integration of game-like elements such as points, badges and leaderboards into educational environments – has been shown to increase motivation and engagement [33]. By making learning interactive and rewarding, gamification can foster a sense of achievement and encourage students to stay motivated and committed to their educational journey [34, 35].

The use of virtual simulations and project-based learning also plays an essential role in the hybrid model. Platforms like Labster, which provides virtual laboratories for STEM students, allow students to conduct experiments and interact with complex concepts that would otherwise be inaccessible in a traditional classroom environment. These technologies not only enhance understanding but also allow students to learn by doing, which improves their problem-solving and critical thinking skills [35].

A key outcome of the crisis has been the need for sustained investment in digital capacity-building. Preparedness is no longer a question of platform familiarity but of pedagogical agility – the ability to respond creatively and reflectively to changing learning environments.

5.3 Educator preparedness

One of the most significant challenges in adopting e-learning and hybrid models is the preparedness of educators. As the shift to online and hybrid learning accelerated during the pandemic, many educators faced challenges in adapting to new digital platforms and technologies [24, 36]. The sudden transition left many educators without the necessary training to effectively use learning management systems, engage students online or assess learning in a virtual environment [36].

To ensure the success of e-learning in the post-pandemic era, ongoing professional development for educators is essential. Educators' preparedness involves not just technical proficiency but also the ability to adapt pedagogical strategies for digital environments [25, 36]. Professional development programmes should focus on enhancing digital literacy, exploring innovative teaching techniques for online environments and integrating e-learning tools effectively into the curriculum.

During the COVID-19 pandemic, Japan's Ministry of Education, Culture, Sports, Science and Technology (MEXT) launched the "Suspending Classes Without Stopping Learning" initiative, placing strong emphasis on teacher preparedness to ensure continuity in education [37]. Central to this approach was the fast-tracked GIGA School Programme, which provided digital devices and internet access to all public school students, enabling teachers to adapt to hybrid teaching environments. MEXT supported educators through targeted professional development, enhanced ICT infrastructure and the provision of teaching resources to facilitate online and blended learning [37]. Additional measures included flexible staffing arrangements, recruitment of retired teachers and support personnel and ongoing mental health support [37]. These initiatives helped teachers not only to sustain learning during school closures but also to build capacity for more resilient, inclusive and digitally integrated teaching practices. Such programmes help educators build the skills needed to navigate the complexities of digital education and ensure that they are well-prepared for the future of teaching and learning.

5.4 Reclaiming student agency and the responsible use of AI

As we move through the post-pandemic educational landscape, institutions are being challenged to reconceptualise the place of e-learning within hybrid learning frameworks. Although face-to-face teaching has largely resumed, the pedagogical shifts introduced during the pandemic continue to shape how teaching and learning are approached. Hybrid learning, characterised by the intentional integration of digital and in-person modes, offers opportunities for increased flexibility, accessibility, and personalisation [37, 38]. However, for this potential to be realised, a fundamental shift in educational culture is required, particularly in how students understand and interact with digital learning spaces.

E-learning should no longer be regarded as a stopgap or secondary to traditional classroom instruction [38]. Rather, it must be recognised as a legitimate, dynamic component of a contemporary academic experience. Students need to engage with online platforms as spaces for meaningful learning, where collaboration, critical thinking and active participation are fostered [38]. This involves moving beyond passive content consumption and embracing the possibilities of asynchronous discussions, digital peer learning and reflective self-paced study.

At the same time, students must resist the temptation to view e-learning as a one-size-fits-all solution. The hybrid model demands a higher level of self-awareness and adaptability that includes identifying when support is needed, whether technological, academic, or emotional, and advocating for inclusive, responsive learning environments. Understanding and addressing digital inequalities is key. Students should not only recognise the challenges faced by peers with limited connectivity or access to devices but also participate in conversations around educational equity and digital justice.

The pandemic highlighted that true inclusion extends beyond mere access. It involves designing learning experiences that are responsive to students' contexts and lived experiences [39]. As we build forward, students must be encouraged to think critically about the educational systems they are part of and contribute to shaping learning environments that are not only technologically innovative but also ethically grounded, socially just and collaboratively developed.

In my role as Chair of the Department of Psychology, I have observed a growing concern: the increasing reliance on AI is gradually displacing students' own creative and intellectual efforts. It is becoming apparent that some assignments reflect the generic tone of algorithm-generated content, with diminished depth and originality affecting students' critical cognitive capabilities, including decision-making, critical thinking and analytical reasoning [40]. While AI tools can be valuable for research support, drafting assistance or grammar refinement, they should serve as aids to, not replacements for, human thought. Students should consider AI as a supplementary tool, much like a mentor or research assistant: valuable for guidance and inspiration, but never a substitute for critical engagement, personal insight and academic integrity. In this new educational era, success will lie not in outsourcing thought but in mastering the balance between human creativity and responsible use of technology.

5.5 Data privacy and security

With the rise of e-learning and the widespread use of digital platforms in education, data privacy and security have become major concerns. As e-learning platforms collect large amounts of data on student behaviours, academic progress and personal information, safeguarding this data is paramount to protect students from potential breaches of privacy and misuse.

Regulatory frameworks such as the European Union's General Data Protection Regulation (GDPR) and India's Personal Data Protection Bill are important steps in addressing these issues [41]. These regulations set standards for how institutions should collect, store and share personal data while ensuring transparency and consent. However, global standardisation of data privacy regulations remains a challenge, and enforcement varies across regions.

To mitigate risks, educational institutions must adopt robust data governance policies that prioritise transparency, informed consent and security. Moreover, e-learning providers should work closely with educational institutions to implement advanced encryption, secure cloud storage and regular audits to ensure compliance with data protection laws [42]. It is crucial that both educators and students are made aware of their rights and responsibilities regarding data security and that institutions invest in the necessary infrastructure to maintain a safe digital learning environment.

The rapid adoption of digital platforms also raised concerns around the protection of personal data. Ethical considerations, often overlooked during the emergency response, now demand sustained attention. This ethical dimension, too, forms part of a transformative learning journey – questioning assumptions and acting in more responsible ways.

5.6 The role of E-learning in Education 4.0

Education 4.0 is a concept that aligns educational practices with the principles and technologies of the 4IR. At the heart of this transformation are technologies such as AI, big data analytics, IoT, robotics, blockchain and virtual reality (VR), all of which are reshaping industries and driving societal change [43]. Education 4.0 seeks to integrate these technologies into teaching and learning environments to create personalised, flexible and adaptive learning experiences that cater to the needs of every learner.

E-learning, as a central component of this paradigm, plays a pivotal role in facilitating the goals of Education 4.0. The transition from traditional education models to more dynamic, technology-driven educational systems has been accelerated by the COVID-19 pandemic, and e-learning has emerged as a fundamental tool for achieving the vision of Education 4.0. Here, e-learning is not just about digitising traditional content but about fostering deeper engagement, critical thinking and problem-solving skills that will prepare students for the complexities of the 4IR.

5.6.1 Personalisation through technology

One of the core principles of Education 4.0 is the personalisation of learning. E-learning enables personalised education by offering students the opportunity to learn at their own pace, according to their individual needs, preferences and learning styles. Unlike traditional educational models, where every student follows a one-size-fits-all approach, e-learning platforms use data analytics and AI to tailor content and recommendations to suit each learner's progress and proficiency levels [4].

For example, adaptive learning platforms such as DreamBox and Knewton utilise AI algorithms to analyse a student's interaction with the content, assess their learning progress and then adjust the difficulty and type of content delivered. This ensures that each student receives targeted support and challenges, helping them to progress efficiently. Such platforms make learning more student-centred, where the learner is actively engaged in managing their educational path.

Another notable example of personalised learning through e-learning is Duolingo, a language-learning platform that uses gamification techniques alongside adaptive algorithms to adjust lesson difficulty based on the learner's performance. This system maximises engagement and retention while ensuring that lessons are always appropriately challenging.

Personalisation not only enhances student engagement but also contributes to the development of lifelong learning [29], a key pillar of Education 4.0. By allowing learners to engage with content at their own pace and in ways that align with their learning styles, e-learning fosters a more flexible and accessible educational experience that prepares individuals for the demands of the digital economy, where continuous upskilling and reskilling are essential.

5.6.2 Bridging the gap between theory and practice

Another central feature of Education 4.0 is the emphasis on practical, real-world learning experiences that prepare students for the complexities of modern workplaces. E-learning supports this shift by providing opportunities for experiential learning and applied knowledge. Digital platforms enable students to engage in simulations, virtual labs and interactive case studies that help bridge the gap between theoretical knowledge and practical application [4].

Virtual labs and simulations, for example, have revolutionised education in fields like science, engineering and healthcare. Platforms such as Labster provide fully immersive virtual labs where students can conduct scientific experiments without the need for physical lab facilities. These tools enable students to engage in hands-on learning in a risk-free environment, allowing them to explore complex topics at their own pace. This is especially valuable in areas like chemistry or biology, where access to physical labs may be limited or costly.

Similarly, VR and augmented reality (AR) offer opportunities for students to immerse themselves in simulated environments where they can practice complex procedures or explore real-world scenarios. VR tools like zSpace in healthcare allow medical students to practice surgical procedures in a controlled, virtual space, helping them to build confidence and skills before performing on real patients. In engineering, Autodesk Fusion 360 provides a platform for students to design and test prototypes virtually, without the need for physical resources or materials. These immersive tools bring abstract concepts to life, making learning more interactive and relevant.

Moreover, project-based learning (PBL), facilitated through e-learning platforms, allows students to collaborate on interdisciplinary projects that reflect real-world challenges [44]. For instance, students in a business school might collaborate with engineering students to develop a sustainable energy solution. By working in teams to solve real-world problems, students not only gain knowledge but also develop critical skills like teamwork, communication and problem-solving, which are highly valued in today's workforce.

5.6.3 Collaborative learning and real-world projects

E-learning in the context of Education 4.0 also fosters collaboration, another key component of twenty-first-century skills development. With the rise of digital technologies, learning is no longer confined to the classroom [4]. Online platforms enable students to connect with peers, experts and mentors from all over the world, facilitating global collaboration and creating a more inclusive and diverse learning environment [29].

Tools such as Google Workspace for Education and Microsoft Teams provide students with digital workspaces where they can collaborate on projects, share documents and communicate in real time. These platforms mimic professional environments, allowing students to experience the dynamics of teamwork and collaboration in the digital world. This prepares them for the collaborative nature of the modern workforce, where cross-disciplinary and cross-cultural collaboration is the norm.

Moreover, e-learning platforms support interdisciplinary projects, where students from different fields work together to solve complex problems. For example, a project involving engineering students designing a sustainable energy solution can include business students who develop the financial model for its implementation. These types of real-world projects mirror the collaborative, multidisciplinary nature of industries such as technology, healthcare and engineering.

As Education 4.0 continues to emphasise collaboration and problem-solving, e-learning offers a powerful tool to facilitate these skills, preparing students for the collaborative and dynamic nature of today's global economy.

5.6.4 Gamification and real-time feedback

Gamification has emerged as a highly effective strategy in e-learning to increase student engagement and motivation. By integrating game-like elements, such as badges, points, leaderboards, and rewards, into educational platforms, e-learning makes the learning process more interactive and enjoyable. Gamified platforms like Kahoot! and Quizizz provide opportunities for students to engage in competitive, yet supportive, learning experiences. These platforms increase motivation by offering immediate feedback and incentivising students to continue learning.

Real-time feedback is another crucial aspect of e-learning in Education 4.0. Unlike traditional education, where feedback may be delayed, e-learning platforms powered by AI and data analytics can offer instant feedback on assignments, quizzes and activities [17]. Platforms like Smart Sparrow use data-driven algorithms to track students' progress and provide immediate, personalised feedback, helping them understand their strengths and areas for improvement. This iterative feedback loop mirrors real-world problem-solving processes, where individuals continuously refine their approaches based on outcomes.

Instant feedback is vital for fostering a growth mindset, where students are encouraged to view challenges and mistakes as opportunities to learn and improve [17]. This aligns with the goals of Education 4.0, which emphasises continuous learning, adaptability and resilience and revisits challenging concepts.

5.6.5 Case study: E-learning in STEM education

The impact of e-learning on Science, Technology, Engineering, and Mathematics (STEM) education is profound, as these fields often rely on hands-on, practical learning experiences [45]. E-learning provides a solution to the logistical and resource-based limitations of traditional STEM education, making complex experiments and simulations more accessible to students globally. During the COVID-19 pandemic, many educational institutions pivoted to online platforms, and STEM courses were among the most impacted due to the practical, hands-on nature of the subjects.

One of the most notable advancements in e-learning for STEM education is the rise of virtual laboratories. These platforms offer students the ability to conduct experiments in a safe, interactive and cost-effective virtual environment. Labster, for example, provides immersive, interactive virtual labs in subjects like biology, chemistry and physics. Students can manipulate variables, conduct experiments and even visualise complex scientific processes, which would have been impossible in many traditional classrooms due to limitations in equipment, time or safety.

Labster uses 3D simulations to create realistic, fully interactive virtual environments where students can practice experiments like DNA analysis or chemical reactions. The platform not only replicates the hands-on lab experience but also allows students to repeat experiments multiple times, which is not possible in a traditional setting where resources are limited. These simulations provide immediate feedback and allow for deeper engagement, helping students grasp difficult concepts in a dynamic and supportive learning environment.

Moreover, e-learning in STEM education has leveraged interactive tools such as Simulations Plus for the study of mathematics and engineering design. Through platforms like these, students can apply mathematical formulas and test engineering designs in real-time, helping them understand how theoretical knowledge translates into practical solutions. The use of gamification in platforms like Minecraft Education Edition has also seen success in introducing students to programming, physics and geometry, enhancing problem-solving and creative thinking skills.

The effectiveness of these tools is evident in their ability to democratise access to STEM education, enabling students from different regions or those with limited access to physical lab spaces to engage in high-quality, interactive learning [29]. Moreover, virtual labs and simulations are scalable, making it easier for educational institutions to cater to large numbers of students without compromising the quality of their learning experiences.

Thus, the integration of e-learning tools into STEM education has made education more accessible, flexible and engaging while allowing students to develop practical skills in a virtual environment that prepares them for real-world challenges [29].

The pandemic highlighted the urgency of digital innovation in science and technology fields. Virtual laboratories and collaborative coding platforms emerged as viable alternatives, offering access to practical experience when physical labs were unavailable.

5.6.6 Continuous learning opportunities

One of the most significant advantages of e-learning is its ability to support continuous learning. In the rapidly changing global economy, where new technologies, industries and skill sets emerge regularly, continuous learning is essential for personal and professional development. E-learning provides the flexibility and accessibility needed for individuals to engage in lifelong learning, ensuring that they remain competitive and adaptable in the face of new challenges [44].

E-learning platforms such as LinkedIn Learning, Coursera, Udemy, and edX have played a pivotal role in fostering continuous learning opportunities. These platforms offer on-demand courses in a wide variety of fields, allowing learners to upskill and reskill at their own pace. For instance, someone working in the marketing industry might take a course in data analytics or digital marketing to stay up to date with the latest trends, while a software engineer might learn about blockchain or machine learning to remain relevant in an increasingly tech-driven landscape.

These platforms not only offer courses but also offer certifications and micro-credentials that enhance learners' professional portfolios. These credentials are increasingly recognised by employers as proof of expertise in specific areas, which is valuable for career advancement. In this way, e-learning contributes to building a flexible, dynamic workforce that is constantly evolving to meet new demands.

Moreover, the accessibility of e-learning plays a significant role in fostering lifelong learning [29]. Individuals from all backgrounds can access learning materials and courses without the constraints of time, location or financial resources. Open educational resources (OERs) and massive open online courses (MOOCs), for example, have made high-quality learning content available to anyone with an internet connection. These resources provide an opportunity for anyone, regardless of socio-economic status, to acquire new knowledge and skills.

Through e-learning, continuous learning becomes a seamless part of an individual's life. As the demand for new skills rises, individuals can access relevant training materials and professional development courses, facilitating a more agile and adaptive workforce.

5.6.6.1 *The role of E-learning in lifelong learning*

Lifelong learning refers to the concept of acquiring knowledge and skills throughout one's life, with the aim of personal development, career advancement and maintaining adaptability in a rapidly changing world. E-learning is a powerful tool in this process, providing an accessible and flexible method for individuals to engage in learning at all stages of life.

In the context of Education 4.0, where rapid technological advancements demand that individuals continually update their skills, e-learning has become essential in providing lifelong access to learning opportunities [29]. The availability of on-demand courses means that people can learn whenever and wherever it is convenient for them. This flexibility is particularly important for adults balancing careers, family and other responsibilities, as it allows them to engage with education without having to commit to a traditional classroom setting.

Moreover, e-learning fosters self-directed learning, allowing individuals to take control of their learning journeys. Unlike traditional education, where the pace and structure are often set by the institution, e-learning enables learners to choose topics that interest them and set their own learning schedules. This encourages intrinsic motivation and lifelong curiosity, which are critical components of personal growth and development.

For example, platforms like Khan Academy and FutureLearn offer a wide range of educational content that supports lifelong learning [16]. Whether individuals are looking to learn a new language, gain a professional certification or explore a new hobby, e-learning offers opportunities to cater to diverse learning needs and interests.

Moreover, as the global economy increasingly relies on remote work, lifelong learning ensures that individuals can continually upskill to remain competitive. Skills such as digital literacy, communication, project management and problem-solving are becoming more important, and e-learning provides a flexible way to acquire these competencies.

Thus, e-learning serves as a crucial enabler of lifelong learning, offering opportunities for people to stay relevant in their careers, contribute meaningfully to their communities and enhance their overall quality of life.

5.6.6.2 Lifelong learning and the future of work

As industries evolve and new technologies emerge, the future of work is becoming increasingly reliant on individuals who can continuously adapt to changes in the workplace. Lifelong learning is essential for individuals to remain employable and competitive in the global job market. The rapid pace of technological advancement means that skills that were once in demand may quickly become obsolete, while new skill sets will be required to fill emerging roles [45].

The 4IR, driven by technologies such as AI, machine learning, automation, and robotics, has already begun to reshape industries ranging from manufacturing to healthcare, finance, and beyond. As the job market adapts to these changes, the demand for workers who possess advanced technological skills, alongside traditional skills like creativity, problem-solving and communication, will increase.

E-learning plays a vital role in preparing workers for these shifts. By offering courses and training in emerging fields such as data science, cybersecurity, AI and digital marketing, e-learning provides workers with the opportunity to acquire new skills that are crucial for the future job market. Moreover, micro-credentials and badges can be used to validate specific skills and competencies, allowing individuals to showcase their expertise and stand out to employers.

Furthermore, e-learning supports reskilling and upskilling efforts. As industries evolve, workers can continually update their skill sets to meet new demands, ensuring that they remain relevant in an ever-changing work environment [45]. For instance, an individual working in a traditional office setting might transition to a career in digital marketing or data analysis by taking relevant e-learning courses.

Thus, e-learning facilitates a more adaptable workforce by enabling lifelong learning that supports both career advancement and personal growth, ultimately contributing to the development of a more resilient, future-ready workforce.

As industries evolve, so too must education. E-learning enables continuous upskilling and reskilling, helping individuals stay relevant in a changing economy – another instance of transformative learning as individuals reconstruct their professional identities.

5.6.6.3 Global impact and inclusion

One of the most significant impacts of e-learning is its ability to promote global inclusion and break down barriers to education [29]. Historically, access to quality education has been limited by geographic location, economic factors and social inequality. However, e-learning has the potential to democratise education by providing anyone with an internet connection the opportunity to access high-quality learning materials.

This is particularly impactful in developing countries, where educational infrastructure may be limited, or in remote areas where students may have no access to physical schools or instructors [29]. Platforms such as edX, Coursera, and Udemy offer free or low-cost courses from prestigious institutions, making world-class education available to anyone with an internet connection. This opens doors to education for people who otherwise might not have had the opportunity to pursue higher education or career-specific training.

Moreover, e-learning helps address the gender gap in education, particularly in regions where cultural or social factors may prevent women and girls from attending school. By offering flexible learning options that can be accessed from home, e-learning gives women and girls the chance to learn without the constraints of traditional classroom environments. It also enables working adults, particularly women, to pursue education while balancing family and career responsibilities.

In addition to increasing access to education, e-learning fosters global collaboration [40]. Learners from different cultural and linguistic backgrounds can interact with one another in online forums, discussion groups, and collaborative projects. This exposure to diverse perspectives enhances cross-cultural understanding and prepares students for working in a globalised economy.

Ultimately, the global impact of e-learning lies in its ability to create equal opportunities for education, irrespective of socio-economic background, geography or gender [3, 44]. It empowers individuals around the world to take control of their learning journey and contributes to the development of a more inclusive, diverse and equitable global society.

6. Contribution and significance

This chapter provides a timely and reflective analysis of the shifts in higher education brought about by the COVID-19 pandemic, focusing on the rise of digitally enabled learning under the broader umbrella of Education 4.0. Drawing on global and local experiences, it examines how institutions were forced to adapt to remote learning environments almost overnight and how these emergency measures have given rise to more permanent changes in how we think about teaching, learning and student engagement.

A key contribution of the chapter lies in its examination of how digital tools and platforms have shaped not only the delivery of content but also the broader culture and structure of learning. It reflects on how educators were required to adopt more flexible, learner-centred approaches in response to the demands of online education, often while managing challenges around access, infrastructure and digital literacy, particularly in less-resourced settings. Beyond the shift to remote delivery, the chapter explores how the learning experience itself was transformed, altering the roles of educators, the expectations placed on students and the nature of academic support. It also engages with the core principles of Education 4.0, such as personalised learning, the use of data to inform teaching decisions and the integration of technologies like artificial intelligence and learning analytics to support both learners and institutions.

These shifts had a direct impact on the student experience. For many students, the transition to digital platforms required not only new technical skills but also greater self-discipline and adaptability. While some students thrived in more flexible, self-directed environments, others struggled with limited access to devices, unreliable internet connectivity or a lack of academic support at home. The chapter acknowledges these disparities and considers how institutions responded, in some cases by introducing additional support mechanisms, and in others by rethinking assessment and feedback practices to better suit an online learning context. Importantly, the chapter emphasises that digital transformation must go hand in hand with inclusive planning and capacity-building to ensure that all students are able to participate fully and benefit from the opportunities that Education 4.0 offers.

The chapter also contributes to critical discourse on digital equity. It highlights how the pandemic exposed long-standing disparities in access to technology, connectivity and digital literacy. By drawing attention to these gaps, the chapter offers insight into the risks of further marginalising already vulnerable student populations and stresses the importance of inclusive digital strategies moving forward.

Importantly, the work brings together practical and theoretical perspectives. It reflects on institutional responses – both successful and problematic – and offers guidance on how higher education can prepare for a future in which digital transformation is no longer optional but integral to academic resilience and innovation.

In terms of significance, the chapter serves as a historical and analytical record of how a global crisis catalysed a rethinking of educational practice. It is valuable to educators, institutional leaders, policymakers and researchers who are shaping the future of higher education in a post-pandemic world. The insights offered support efforts to build more agile, student-centred and sustainable education systems that are better equipped to respond to future disruptions.

7. Recommendations and future directions

As we look to the future of education, it is increasingly clear that e-learning and hybrid models are not short-term solutions but permanent features of the educational landscape. However, for these approaches to realise their full potential, a number of critical areas must be addressed. The pandemic has exposed the urgency of bridging the digital divide, strengthening pedagogical practice, equipping educators for the demands of new learning environments and ensuring the protection of student data. The recommendations outlined here aim to support the continued development and meaningful integration of e-learning within education systems.

The adoption of hybrid learning models, which combine synchronous and asynchronous methods, should be given priority. These approaches provide flexibility while maintaining the benefits of structured engagement. When thoughtfully implemented, hybrid models can meet a wide range of learning needs, offering students more autonomy over their learning while maintaining valuable interaction. Tools such as the flipped classroom, gamification and virtual simulations should be included to increase motivation, promote deeper engagement and enhance understanding.

To support the effective roll-out of hybrid education, institutions should establish clear policies and implementation guidelines. This will ensure that both digital and in-person components are well aligned and that the shift between them is seamless. Curriculum design, assessment strategies, and educator roles must be carefully considered as part of this planning.

The digital divide remains one of the most pressing challenges. Equal access to education cannot be achieved unless all students are able to participate fully in online learning. Governments, the private sector and educational institutions must collaborate to invest in digital infrastructure, provide affordable and reliable internet and ensure access to devices for learners. Special attention should be given to underrepresented and marginalised groups, including learners in rural areas, students with disabilities and those from low-income households. These efforts should go beyond access, by including digital literacy training and additional academic support to ensure students can make the most of the tools available to them.

Alongside these efforts, it is essential to strengthen educator training and development. While digital fluency is important, professional development must also focus on effective teaching methods for online and hybrid environments. Educators need to be equipped not only with practical skills but also with the confidence and creativity to design engaging, inclusive and flexible learning experiences. Training should include modules on digital pedagogy, innovative teaching techniques and the use of educational technologies. In addition, particular attention should be given to emotional intelligence and mental health awareness, so that educators are better prepared to support learners' well-being – an increasingly important concern in digital and hybrid settings.

The growth of e-learning has also made it necessary to pay close attention to data protection and ethical digital practice. Institutions must establish strong governance structures to safeguard personal information and comply with relevant data protection laws. This includes the use of encryption, regular security audits and clear policies around data collection and use. Ensuring the integrity and safety of digital education systems is essential for building trust among learners, educators and broader society.

Looking ahead, investment in emerging technologies will play a key role in shaping the future of e-learning. Technologies such as AR, VR and blockchain offer exciting possibilities – from immersive learning experiences to secure and verifiable academic credentials. Institutions are encouraged to explore pilot programmes to test the feasibility and effectiveness of these innovations before scaling them more broadly.

Furthermore, broader actions must be taken to embed transformative learning approaches in both policy and practice. The pandemic has shown the value of reflection, critical thinking and adaptability. Education systems should actively support environments where learners and educators can reflect on their experiences, challenge assumptions and grow. This means designing learning opportunities that go beyond knowledge transmission and instead foster meaningful change, both in thinking and in behaviour.

Cross-sector collaboration will also be essential. Partnerships between higher education institutions, industry, government bodies and civil society can lead to innovative solutions tailored to different contexts. Such partnerships can support resource sharing, help scale effective interventions and create stronger networks of support for both learners and educators.

Finally, as e-learning becomes more deeply embedded, institutions must commit to ongoing monitoring and evaluation. Educational strategies should be continuously assessed, informed by feedback from staff and students, and adjusted in response to changing needs. Only through this kind of reflective practice can education remain responsive, relevant and inclusive.

Taken together, these recommendations provide a roadmap for a more resilient, equitable and future-oriented education system. They call for a shift not just in tools and technologies, but in thinking, practice and culture, ensuring that digital learning contributes meaningfully to inclusive, high-quality education for all.

8. Conclusion: E-learning evolution and the road ahead

The COVID-19 pandemic, though highly disruptive, marked a significant turning point for education systems across the globe. What initially began as a rapid, and often improvised, shift to online learning soon developed into a broader reconsideration of how teaching and learning take place, and how education is structured and delivered. This chapter has followed that path – from the initial hesitation surrounding e-learning, through the urgent innovations prompted by the crisis, to the longer-term transformations now unfolding under the principles of Education 4.0.

By drawing on Transformative Learning Theory, we gain insight into how both individuals and institutions responded during this period of upheaval. The crisis forced reflection, and through that reflection, meaningful change began to take root. Teachers, students and policymakers alike were challenged to adapt swiftly and to rethink their roles within a shifting educational landscape.

Looking ahead, e-learning should no longer be viewed as a temporary fix or an optional extra. Instead, it ought to be recognised as a key element of a more resilient, inclusive education system. The task now is to build on the momentum gained – by improving digital infrastructure, addressing persistent inequalities and investing in the professional growth of educators.

Crucial areas such as data protection, creative approaches to teaching and support for lifelong learning must remain central. Technology alone will not lead to better education – it needs to be used in ways that are thoughtful, ethical and centred on the learner. The future of education lies in maintaining a careful balance: between technological innovation and human connection, between access and quality and between individual opportunity and collective advancement.

As we look to the future, the progress made during the pandemic must not be lost. Rather than reverting to old ways, this is a chance to shape a stronger, fairer system – one that is more flexible, inclusive and responsive to the evolving needs of learners in an ever-changing world.

Author details

Fortunate Tintswalo Silinda
University of South Africa, Pretoria, South Africa

*Address all correspondence to: silinft@unisa.ac.za

References

[1] Kumar Basak S, Wotto M, Bélanger P. E-learning, M-learning and D-learning: Conceptual definition and comparative analysis. E-learning and Digital Media. 2018;**15**(4):191-216

[2] Elumalai KV, Sankar JP, Kalaichelvi R, John JA, Menon N, Alqahtani MSM, et al. Factors affecting the quality of e-learning during the COVID-19 pandemic from the perspective of higher education students. COVID-19 and Education: Learning and Teaching in a Pandemic-Constrained Environment. 2021;**189**(3):169

[3] Haleem A, Javaid M, Qadri MA, Suman R. Understanding the role of digital technologies in education: A review. Sustainable Operations and Computers. 2022;**3**:275-285

[4] UNESCO. Global Education Monitoring Report, 2023: Technology in Education: A Tool on Whose Terms. [Internet]. 2023. Available from: https://www.unesco.org/gem-report/en/technology [Accessed: December 04, 2024]

[5] Gopika JS, Rekha RV. Awareness and use of digital learning before and during COVID-19. International Journal of Educational Reform. 2023;**34**(4):754-766. DOI: 10.1177/10567879231173389

[6] Aristovnik A, Karampelas K, Umek L, Ravšelj D. Impact of the COVID-19 pandemic on online learning in higher education: A bibliometric analysis. In Frontiers in Education. 2023;**8**:1-13. DOI: 10.3389/feduc.2023.1225834

[7] Kumar A, Krishnamurthi R, Bhatia S, Kaushik K, Ahuja NJ, Nayyar A, et al. Blended learning tools and practices: A comprehensive analysis. IEEE Access. 2021;**2021**(9):85151-85197. DOI: 10.1109/ACCESS.2021.3085844

[8] EL-Nwasany RI, Bakr AF, Fathi AA. A sustainable vision for technical education 4.0 of post COVID-19. Sustainability. 2024;**16**(21):1-29. DOI: 10.3390/su16219355

[9] Oke A, Fernandes FAP. Innovations in teaching and learning: Exploring the perceptions of the education sector on the 4th industrial revolution (4IR). Journal of Open Innovation: Technology, Market, and Complexity. 2020;**6**:31

[10] Bezovski Z, Poorani S. The evolution of e-learning and new trends. In Information and Knowledge Management. 2016;**6**(3):50-57

[11] Li KC. The evolution of open learning: A review of the transition from pre-e-learning to the era of e-learning. Knowledge Management and E-Learning. 2018;**10**(4):408-425

[12] Selvaraj A, Radhin V, Nithin KA, Benson N, Mathew AJ. Effect of pandemic based online education on teaching and learning system. International Journal of Educational Development. 2021;**85**:1-11. DOI: 10.1016/j.ijedudev.2021.102444

[13] Osman Abdelmola A, Makeen A, Makki Hanafi H, Ageeli E. E-learning during COVID-19 pandemic, faculty perceptions, challenges, and recommendations. MedEdPublish. 2021;**10**(112):1-15. DOI: 10.15694/mep.2021.000112.1

[14] Niaz S, Memon S, Khokhar S. Development of E-learning: A historical review with global perspective. International Research Journal of

Arts and Humanities (IRJAH). 2021;**49**(49):135-149

[15] Costley KC. The Positive Effects of Technology on Teaching and Student Learning [Internet]. 2014. Available from: https://files.eric.ed.gov/fulltext/ED554557.pdf [Accessed: December 04, 2024]

[16] Light D, Pierson E. Increasing student engagement in math: The use of khan academy in Chilean classrooms. International Journal of Education and Development using ICT. 2014;**10**(2):103-119

[17] Nkambule BI. WhatsApp messenger as a supplementary tool for school curriculum knowledge transfer and acquisition during COVID-19 stricter lockdown: Educators' perceptions. Research in Social Sciences and Technology. 2023;**8**(2):37-55

[18] Yorke L, Rose P, Hagos B, Woldehanna T. The Effects of COVID-19 on Primary Education in Ethiopia: Perspectives of School Principals and Teachers Research and Policy Paper No. 20/10. Cambridge, UK: Faculty of Education University of Cambridge; 2020

[19] Association for the Development of Education in Africa (ADEA). COVID19 Impact on Education in African Countries [Internet]. 2020. Available from: https://www.adeanet.org/sites/default/files/report_summary_covid-19_impact.pdf [Accessed: January 02, 2025]

[20] National Distance Learning Programmes in Response to the COVID-19 Education Disruption: Case Study of Finland. UNESCO. 2022. Available from: https://unesdoc.unesco.org/ark:/48223/pf0000382447 [Accessed: June 10, 2025]

[21] National Distance Learning Programmes in Response to the COVID-19 Education Disruption: Case Study of the Republic of Korea. UNESCO. 2021. Available from: https://unesdoc.unesco.org/ark:/48223/pf0000382826?posInSet=3&queryId=7e3b60d6-4a17-48e9-8588-25753da36be3 [Accessed: June 10, 2025]

[22] Kang B, Hong M. Digital interventions for reducing loneliness and depression in Korean college students: Mixed methods evaluation. JMIR Formative Research. 2024;**8**:e58791. DOI: 10.2196/58791

[23] Byun S, Slavin RE. Educational responses to the COVID-19 outbreak in South Korea. Best Evidence in Chinese Education. 2020;5(2):665-680. DOI: 10.15354/bece.20.or030

[24] Li D. The shift to online classes during the COVID-19 pandemic: Benefits, challenges, and required improvements from the students' perspective. Electronic Journal of E-Learning. 2022;**20**(1):1-18

[25] Korhonen T, Juurola L, Salo L, Airaksinen J. Digitisation or digitalisation: Diverse practices of the distance education period in Finland. CEPS Journal. 2021;**11**(Sp. Issue (2021): Education in the Covid-19 Era:165-193

[26] Reddy Moonasamy A, Naidoo GM. (2022). Digital learning: Challenges experienced by south African university students' during the COVID-19 pandemic. The Independent Journal of Teaching and Learning. 2022;**17**(2):76-90

[27] Suphasri P, Chinokul S. Reflective practice in teacher education: Issues, challenges, and considerations. Pasaa. 2021;**62**(1):236-264

[28] Mhlongo S, Mbatha K, Ramatsetse B, Dlamini R. Challenges, opportunities,

and prospects of adopting and using smart digital technologies in learning environments: An iterative review. Heliyon. 2023;**9**(6):1-20. DOI: 10.1016/j.heliyon.2023.e16348

[29] Saldívar-Almorejo MM, Flores-Herrera LA, Rivera-Blas R, Niño-Suárez PA, Rivera-Blas EZ, Rodríguez-Contreras N. E-learning challenges in STEM education. Education in Science. 2024;**14**(12):1370. DOI: 10.3390/educsci14121370

[30] Lai J, Widmar NO. Revisiting the digital divide in the COVID-19 era. Applied Economic Perspectives and Policy. 2021;**43**(1):458-464. DOI: 10.1002/aepp.13104

[31] Faturoti B. Online learning during COVID19 and beyond: A human right based approach to internet access in Africa. International Review of Law, Computers and Technology. 2022;**36**(1):68-90. DOI: 10.1080/13600869.2022.2030027

[32] Strelan P, Osborn A, Palmer E. The flipped classroom: A meta-analysis of effects on student performance across disciplines and education levels. Educational Research Review. 2020;**30**:100314

[33] Smiderle R, Rigo SJ, Marques LB, de Miranda P, Coelho JA, Jaques PA. The impact of gamification on students' learning, engagement and behavior based on their personality traits. Smart Learning Environments. 2020;**7**(1):1-11. DOI: 10.1186/s40561-019-0098-x

[34] Hellín CJ, Calles-Esteban F, Valledor A, Gómez J, Otón-Tortosa S, Tayebi A. Enhancing student motivation and engagement through a gamified learning environment. Sustainability. 2023;**15**(19):14119. DOI: 10.3390/su151914119

[35] Sellberg C, Nazari Z, Solberg M. Virtual laboratories in STEM higher education: A scoping review. Nordic Journal of Systematic Reviews in Education. 2024;**2**:58-75. DOI: 10.23865/njsre.v2.5766

[36] Maphalala MC, Khumalo NP, Khumalo N. Student teachers' experiences of the emergency transition to online learning during the Covid-19 lockdown at a south African university. Perspectives in Education. 2021;**39**(3):30-43

[37] Yu P, Anezaki K. "Suspending classes without stopping learning": An initiative to ensure learning in Japan during the pandemic. ECNU Review of Education. 2024;7(1):195-206

[38] Al Rawashdeh AZ, Mohammed EY, Al Arab AR, Alara M, Al-Rawashdeh B. Advantages and disadvantages of using e-learning in university education: Analyzing students' perspectives. Electronic Journal of E-learning. 2021;**19**(3):107-117. DOI: 10.34190/ejel.19.3.2168

[39] Haywood BK, Boyd DE, McArthur JA. Purpose, place, and people: How the pandemic helped foster open and inclusive course design. To Improve the Academy: A Journal of Educational Development. 2023;**42**(1):5. DOI: 10.3998/tia.1680

[40] Bayly-Castaneda K, Ramirez-Montoya MS, Morita-Alexander A. Crafting personalized learning paths with AI for lifelong learning: A systematic literature review. Frontiers in Education. 2024;**9**:1-12. DOI: 10.3389/feduc.2024.1424386

[41] Sinha S. Harmonizing data privacy Laws: A comparative study of approaches in the EU, US and India. Legal Spectrum Journal. 2024;**4**(1):1-59

[42] Mahmood HS, Abdulqader DM, Abdullah RM, Rasheed H, Ismael ZNR, Sami TMG. Conducting In-depth analysis of AI, IoT, web technology, cloud computing, and Enterprise systems integration for enhancing data security and governance to promote sustainable business practices. Journal of Information Technology and Informatics. 2024;**3**(2):297-322

[43] Rampersad R, do Lago MM, Fernandes E. Education 4.0 (ED4. 0): A global higher educational paradigm for BRICS countries. African Journal of Inter/Multidisciplinary Studies. 2024;**6**(1):1-10. DOI: 10.51415/ajims.v6i1.1460

[44] Zhai C, Wibowo S, Li LD. The effects of over-reliance on AI dialogue systems on students' cognitive abilities: A systematic review. Smart Learning Environments. 2024;**11**(1):28

[45] Ra S, Shrestha U, Khatiwada S, Yoon SW, Kwon K. The rise of technology and impact on skills. International Journal of Training Research. 2019;**17**(1):26-40. DOI: 10.1080/14480220.2019.1629727